HONG KONG IN 100 PHOTOS

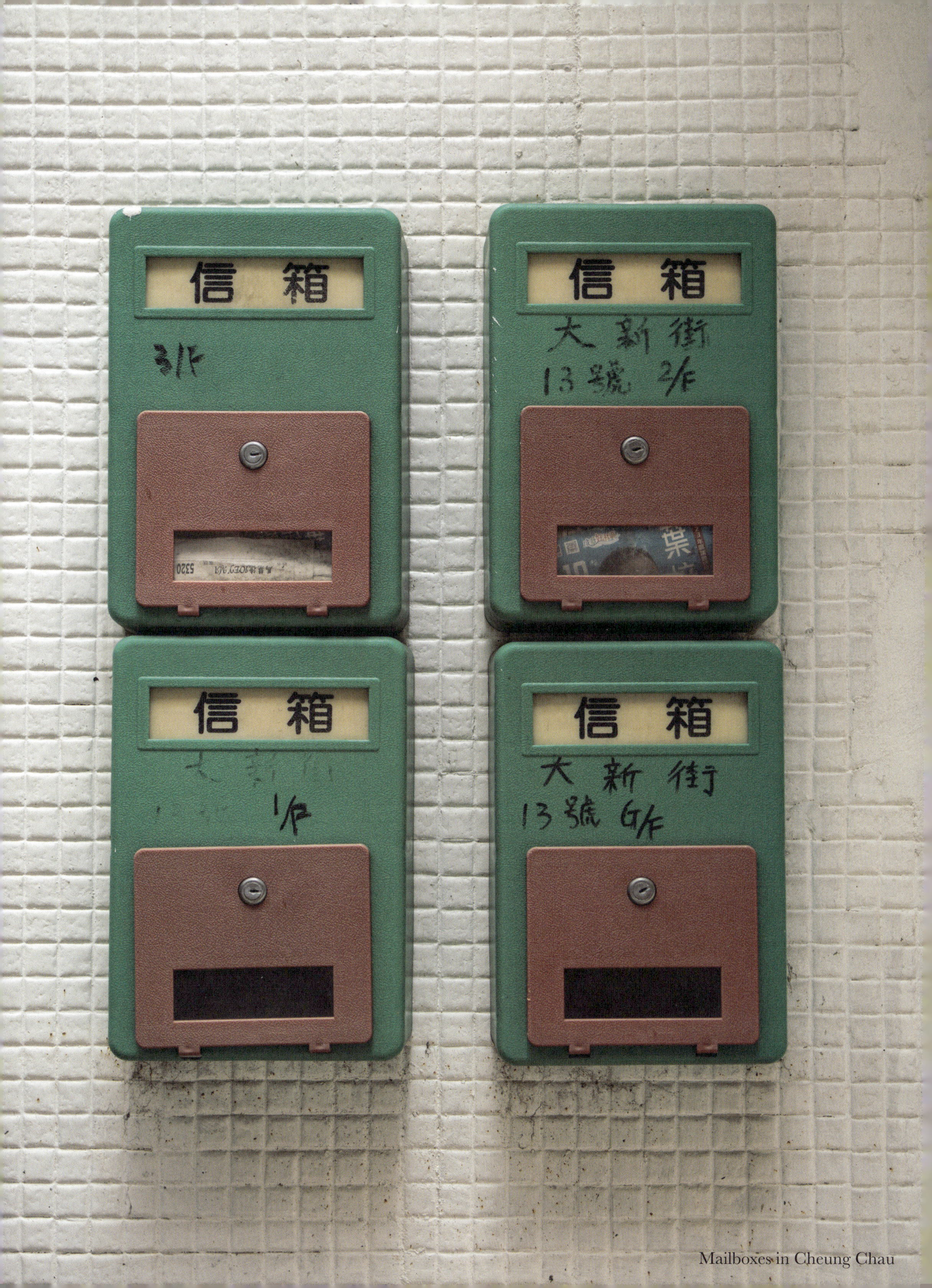

Mailboxes in Cheung Chau

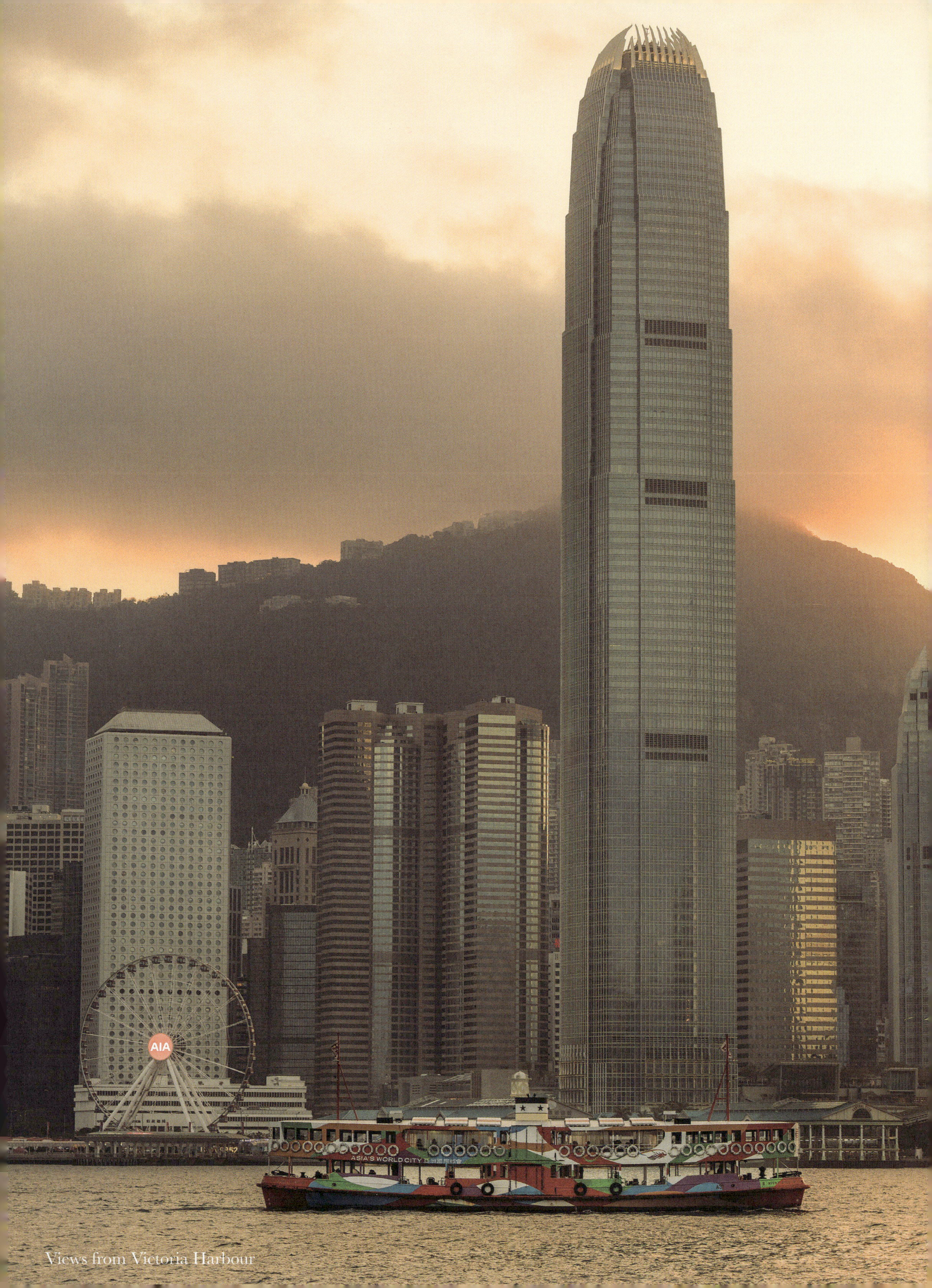

Views from Victoria Harbour

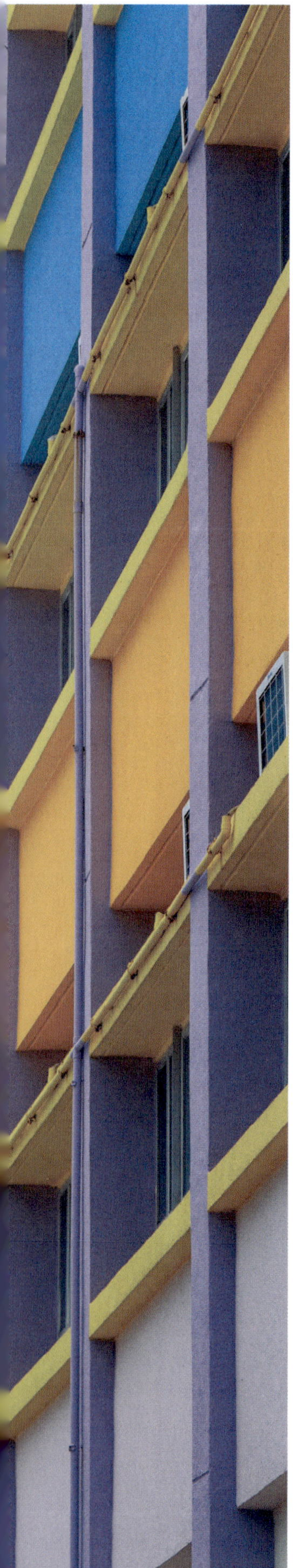

DEAR READER

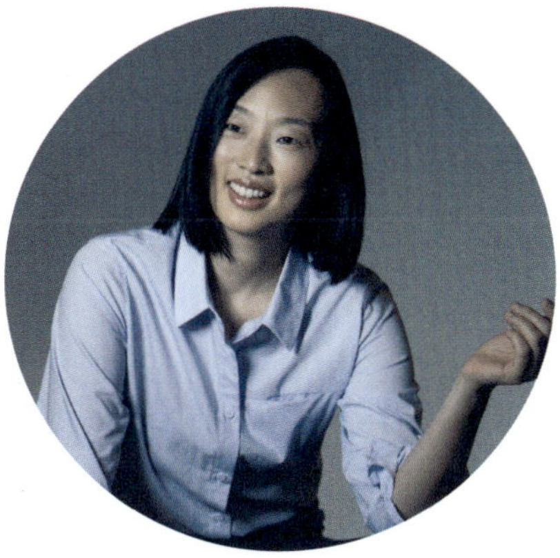

Hi, I'm Joyce. I'm a photographer based in Hong Kong.

I have always loved taking photos, for as long as I can remember — although I didn't really think that this passion was going to turn into a professional career.

When I was young, my parents loved to travel and always made it a point to take at least one family trip per year. I remember my dad would be taking photos of all of us during these trips, and I would be intrigued by his technical maneuvers. The seeds were planted.

But I wouldn't get into serious photography until my late 20s. Before that, I studied engineering at Cornell University in the US, and went into a very traditional corporate career in credit risk management at an American financial institution straight afterwards. My job brought me back to Hong Kong, and gave me an opportunity to be closer to my family after being away for 12 years. It also allowed me to experience Hong Kong as an adult, along with my husband.

Over the years, I've lived in different countries, including Thailand, England, and the US. I've had the opportunity to observe and adapt to different cultures. I pride myself in being able to see things in a different light. Coming back to the city as an adult, I had the unique opportunity to experience Hong Kong both as a local and as an outsider. This book is my love letter to the city.

I have always had the goal of eventually making a book out of my photographs. Now, 15 years after becoming a photographer, this project is a dream come true. It combines my love of photography with the desire to show my beloved city through a lens that has been enlightened by all my lived experiences.

This book is a collection of my photos, but it's also a lot more than that — it's a journey through the city from the eyes of someone who knows it and loves it.

I want to dedicate this book to my family, who has always been so supportive.
A huge thank you to Derek, Jacob, my parents, the Yungs and the Tings.

Love,

Joyce Yung

HOW TO READ THIS BOOK

Consider this tome a very personal and intimate visual destination guide to Hong Kong. In exactly 100 photos.

The photos themselves are divided into four thematic sections, each capturing a distinct aspect of the city. There is no chronological or hierarchical order to the photos or sections, apart from a thematic flow that aims to make sense of the multiple perspectives of Hong Kong.

1

DAILY LIVING

Documents the day-to-day wonders of the city and the people in it.

2

URBAN RHYTHMS

Provides a snapshot of the infrastructure that makes the city tick.

3

CULTURE & HERITAGE

Looks at the traditions and practices that make the city so colorful and vibrant.

4

NATURAL PERSPECTIVES

Offers a macro view of the very land that the city is built on.

In many ways, Hong Kong is a city that has it all. It's got the conveniences of a major urban center, with everything available at one's fingertips. Its skyline is iconic, packed with skyscrapers that shimmer along both sides of Victoria Harbour.

At the same time, it is also covered in country parks and glorious mountains, blessed with amazing coastlines, and dotted with outlying islands. The hiking trails and beaches are just as accessible as the shopping plazas and restaurants.

You'll be able to see all these different sides of Hong Kong when you browse through the photos of this book.

Please enjoy the journey.

DAILY LIVING

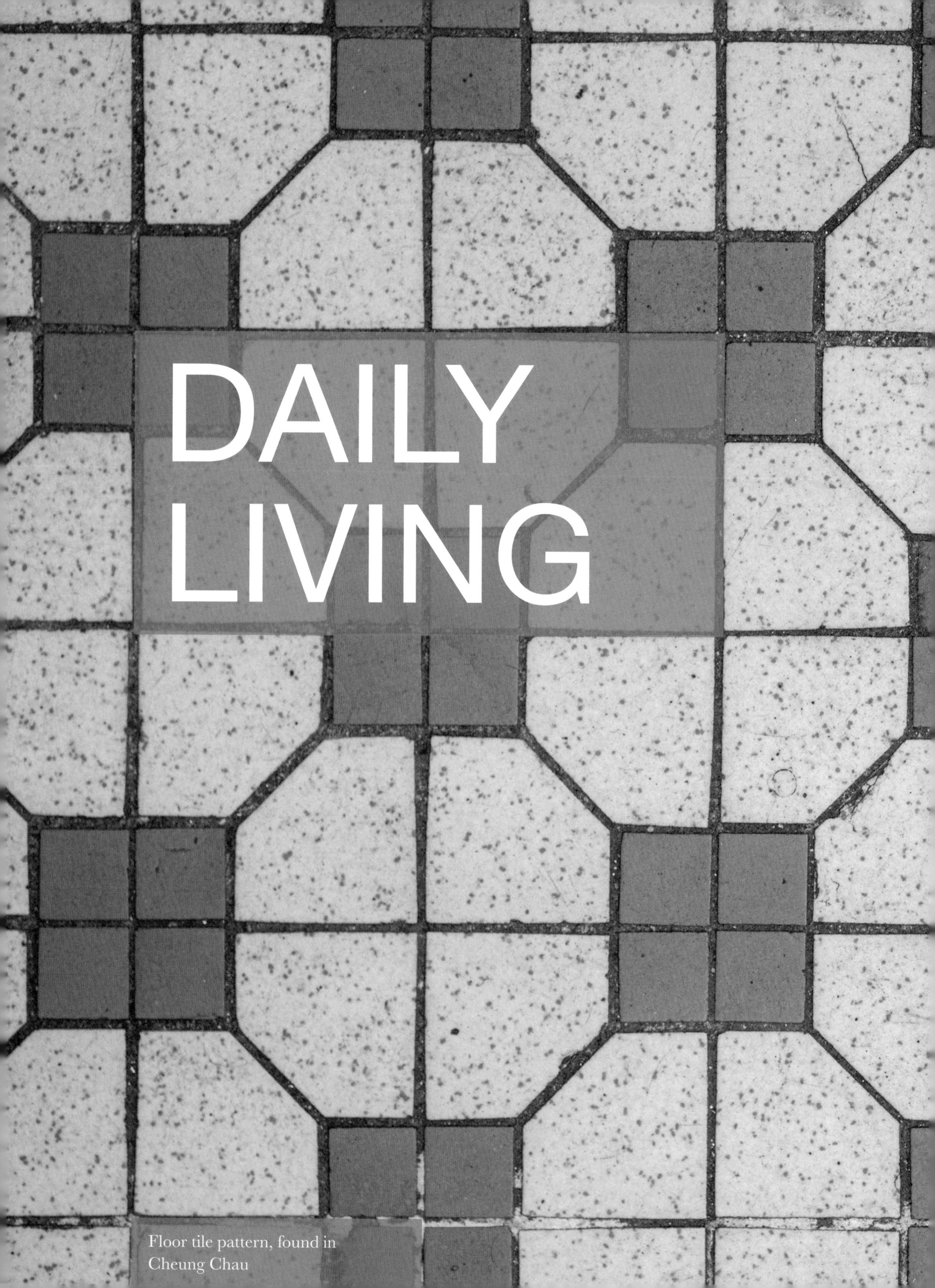

Floor tile pattern, found in Cheung Chau

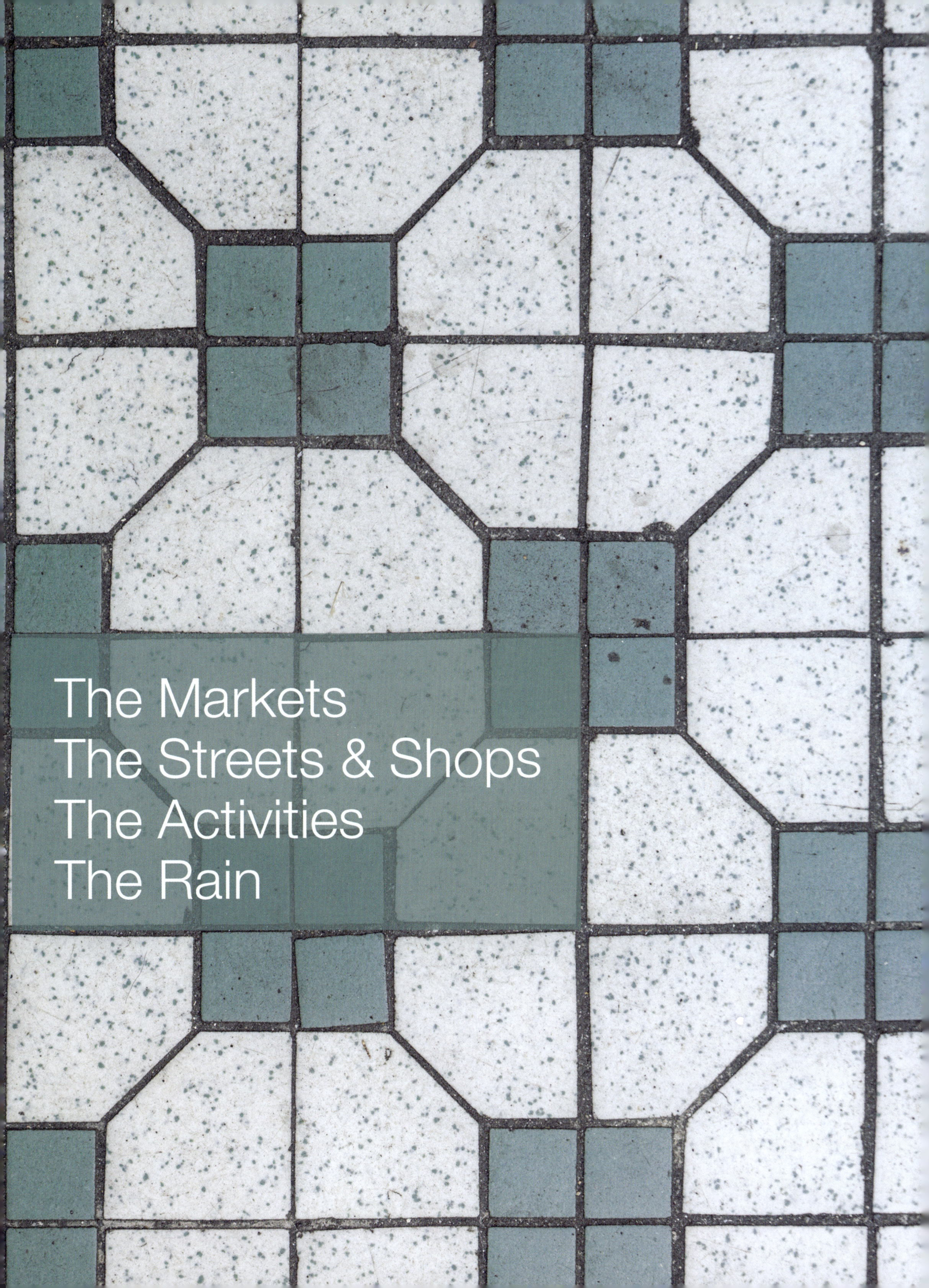

The Markets
The Streets & Shops
The Activities
The Rain

DAILY LIVING

THE MARKETS

I remember going to the wet markets with my mom, as a kid.
I can still recall the strong scents coming from the stalls,
which remind me of the great meals my mom has created out of them.
I especially like getting the seafood from the wet markets, as everything is still alive and swimming, and therefore super fresh. The vegetables are also very enticing.

There are usually indoor and outdoor wet markets in every major district. The more well known ones are in Tai Po, Tsuen Wan, Kowloon City, Sheung Wan, and Wan Chai.

Besides food-centric wet markets, which are arguably the most famous of them all, there are also a variety of street-side markets and stalls that specialize in different themes and items, from costumes to souvenirs.

1. Yau Ma Tei magazine vendor, at dusk
2. Top-down view of fruit vendor by the Mid-Levels escalators
3. Vegetable stall on Stanley Street in Central
4. Dried goods stall on Stanley Street in Central
5. Fa Yuen Street fruit stand
6. Wan Chai Market
7. Live seafood stall in Sai Kung
8. Souvenir stalls on Fa Yuen Street
9. A market on Graham Street in Central
10. Around Stone Nullah Street in Wan Chai
11. Pedder Street in Central

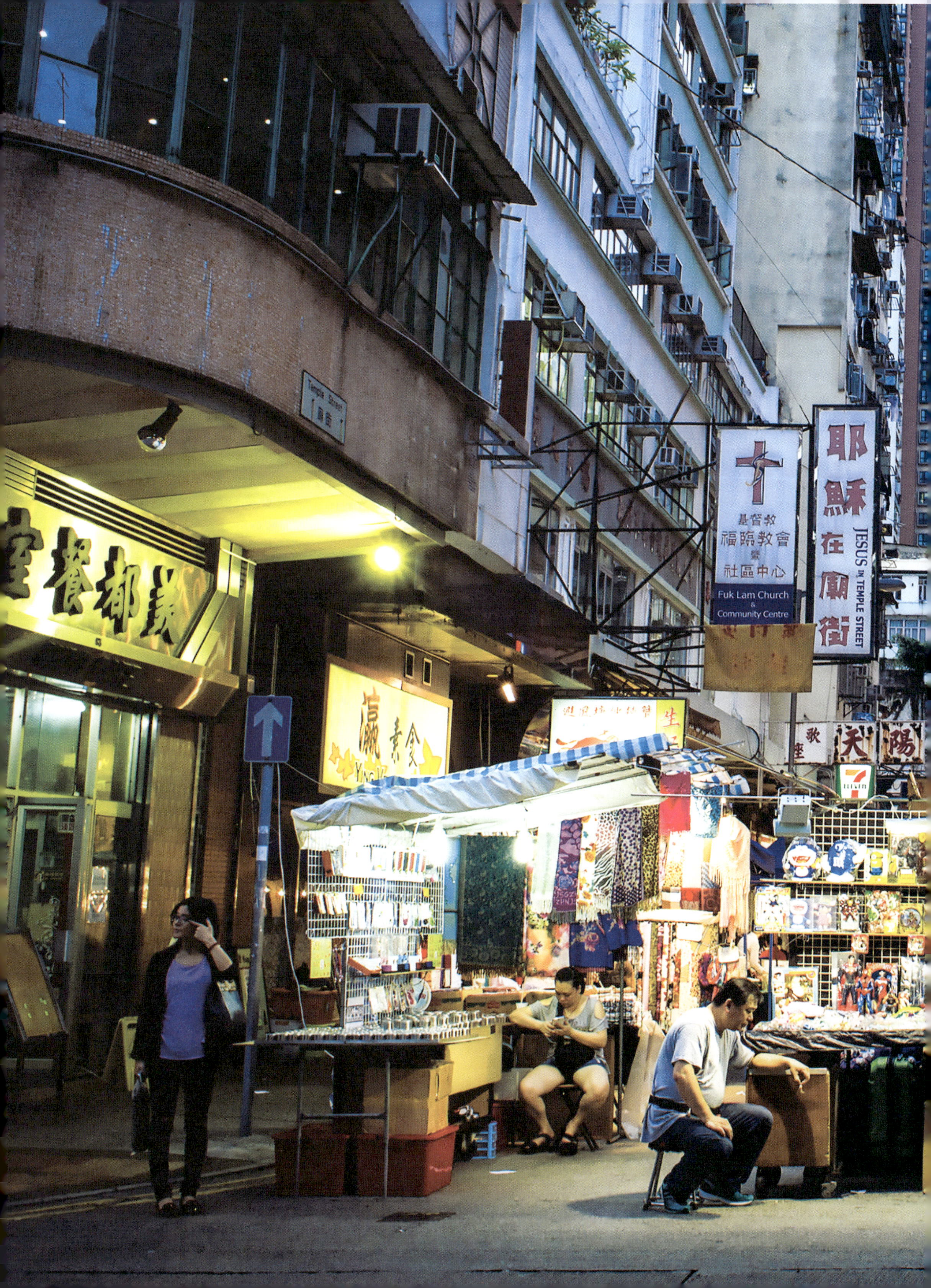
美都餐室
基督教
福臨教會
暨
社區中心
Fuk Lam Church
&
Community Centre
耶穌在廟街
JESUS IN TEMPLE STREET

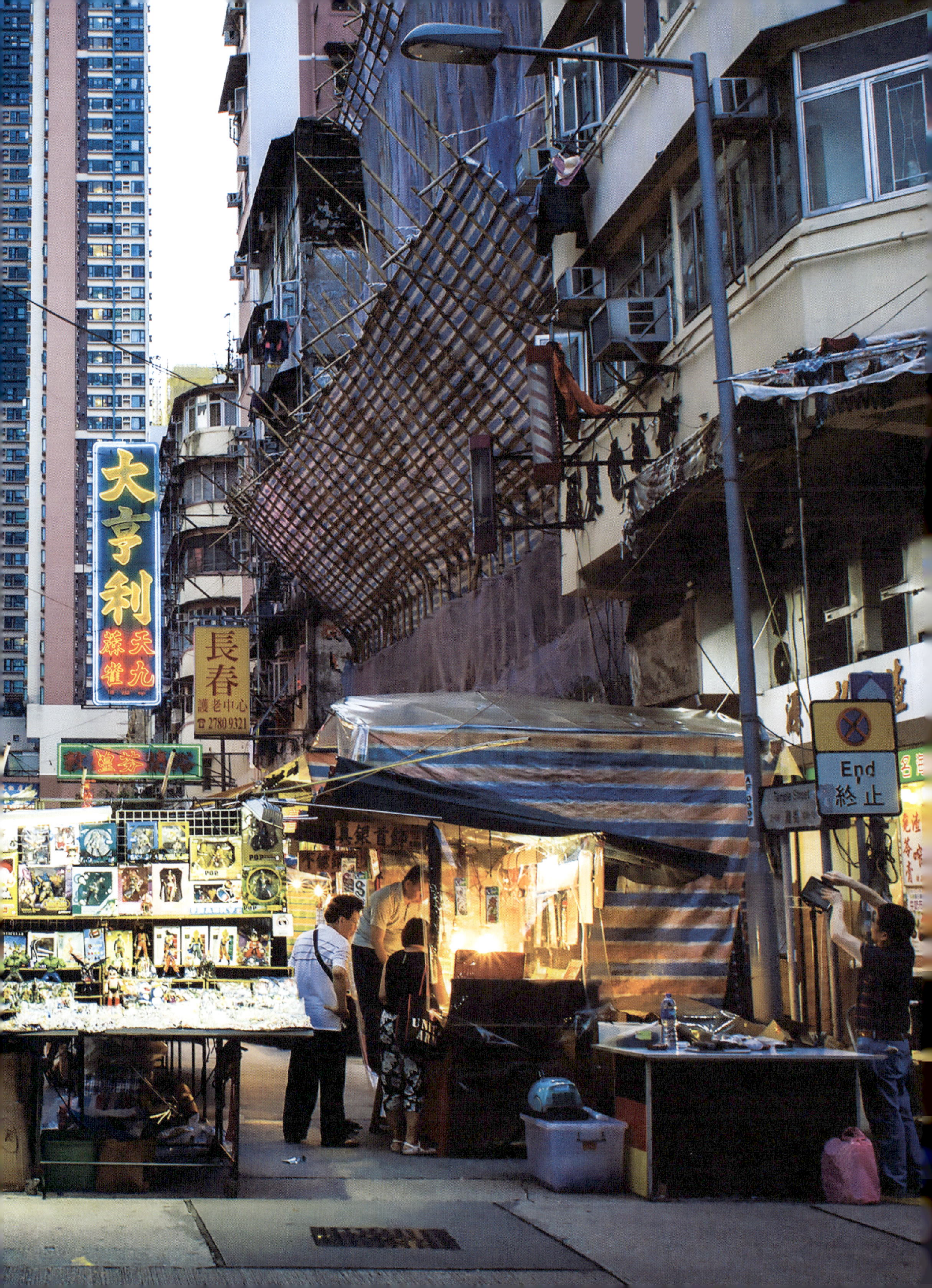
大亨利
天九 麻雀
長春
護老中心
2780 9321
End
終止

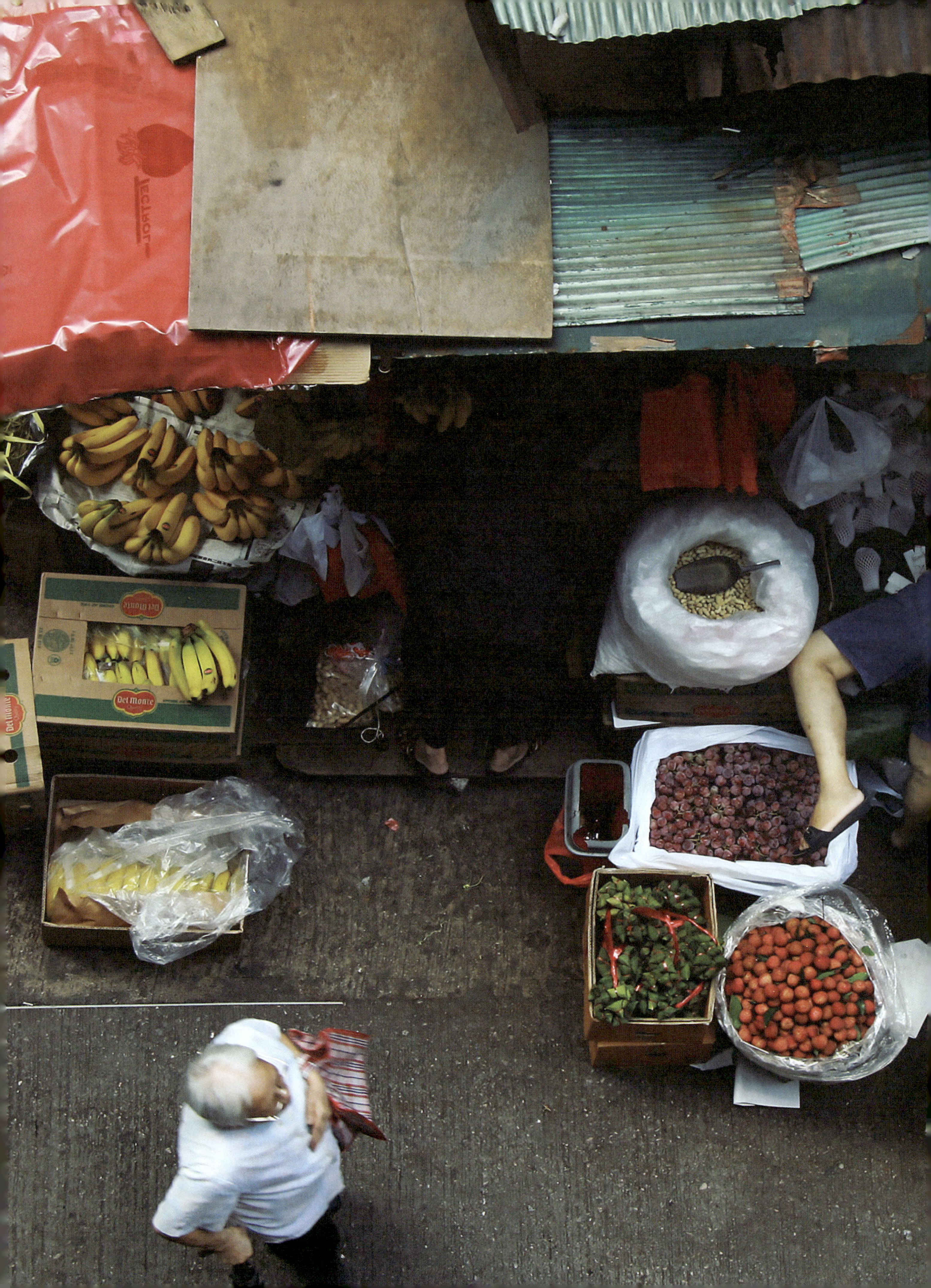
Del Monte

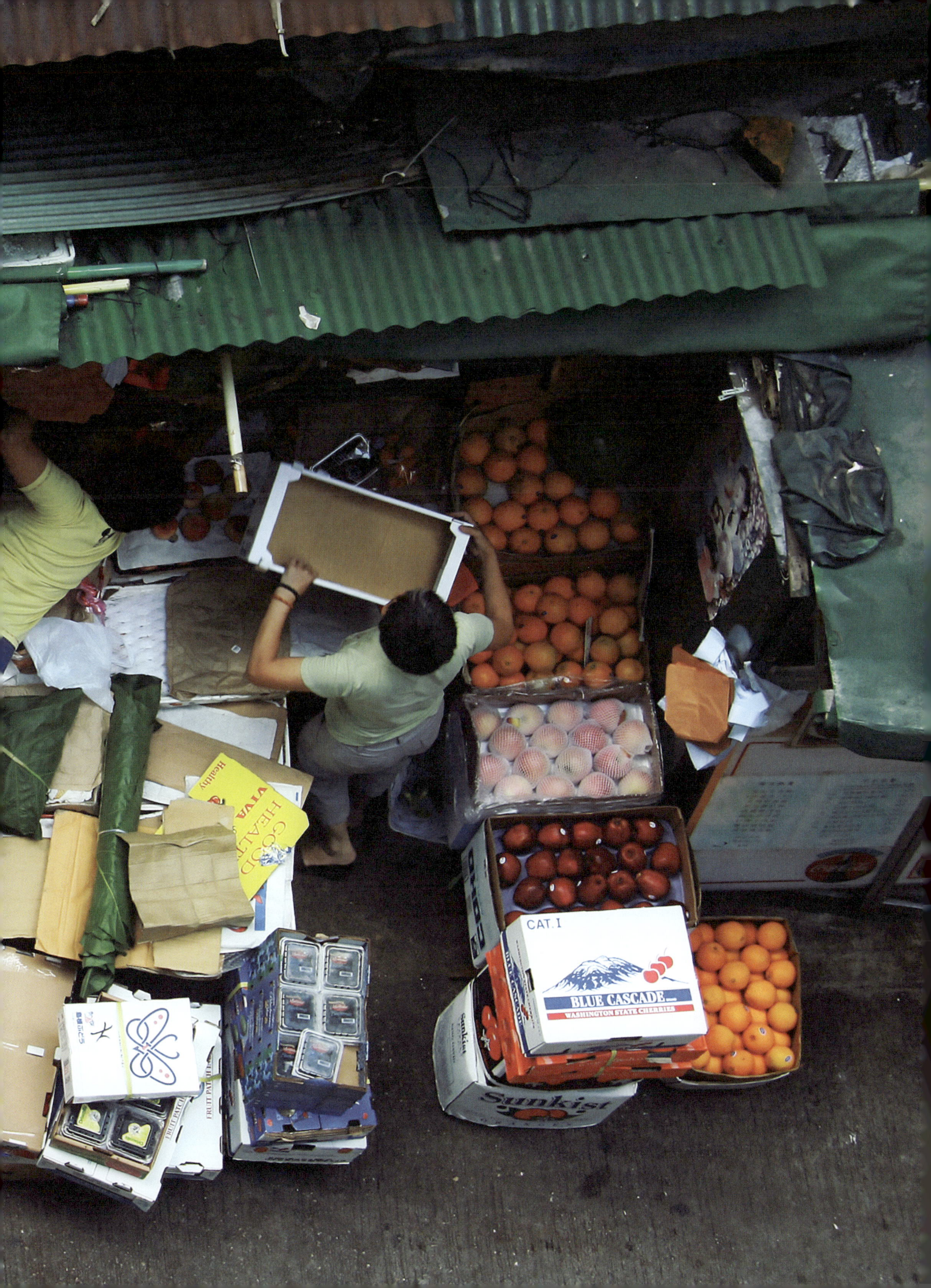
CAT.I
BLUE CASCADE
WASHINGTON STATE CHERRIES
Sunkist

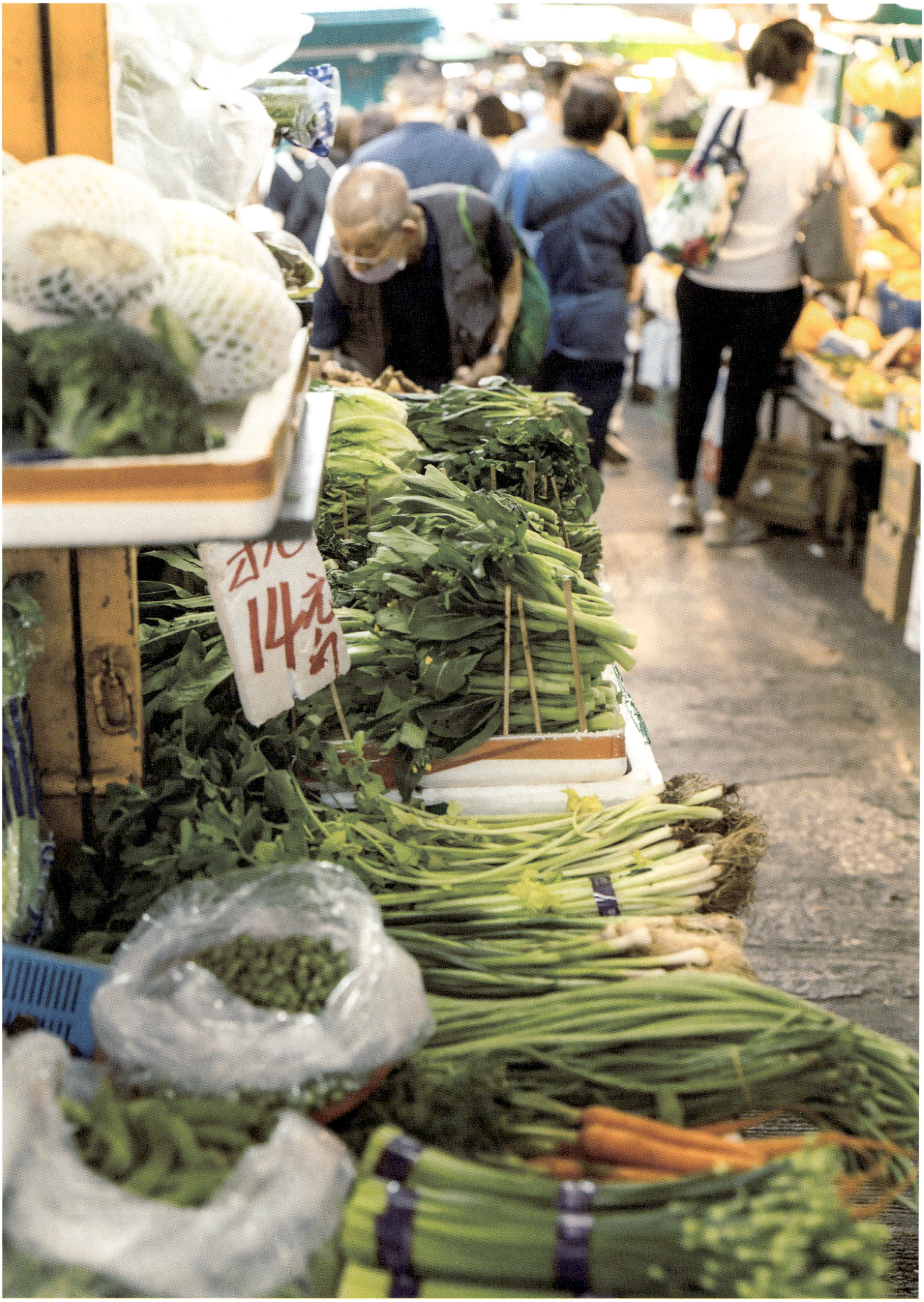

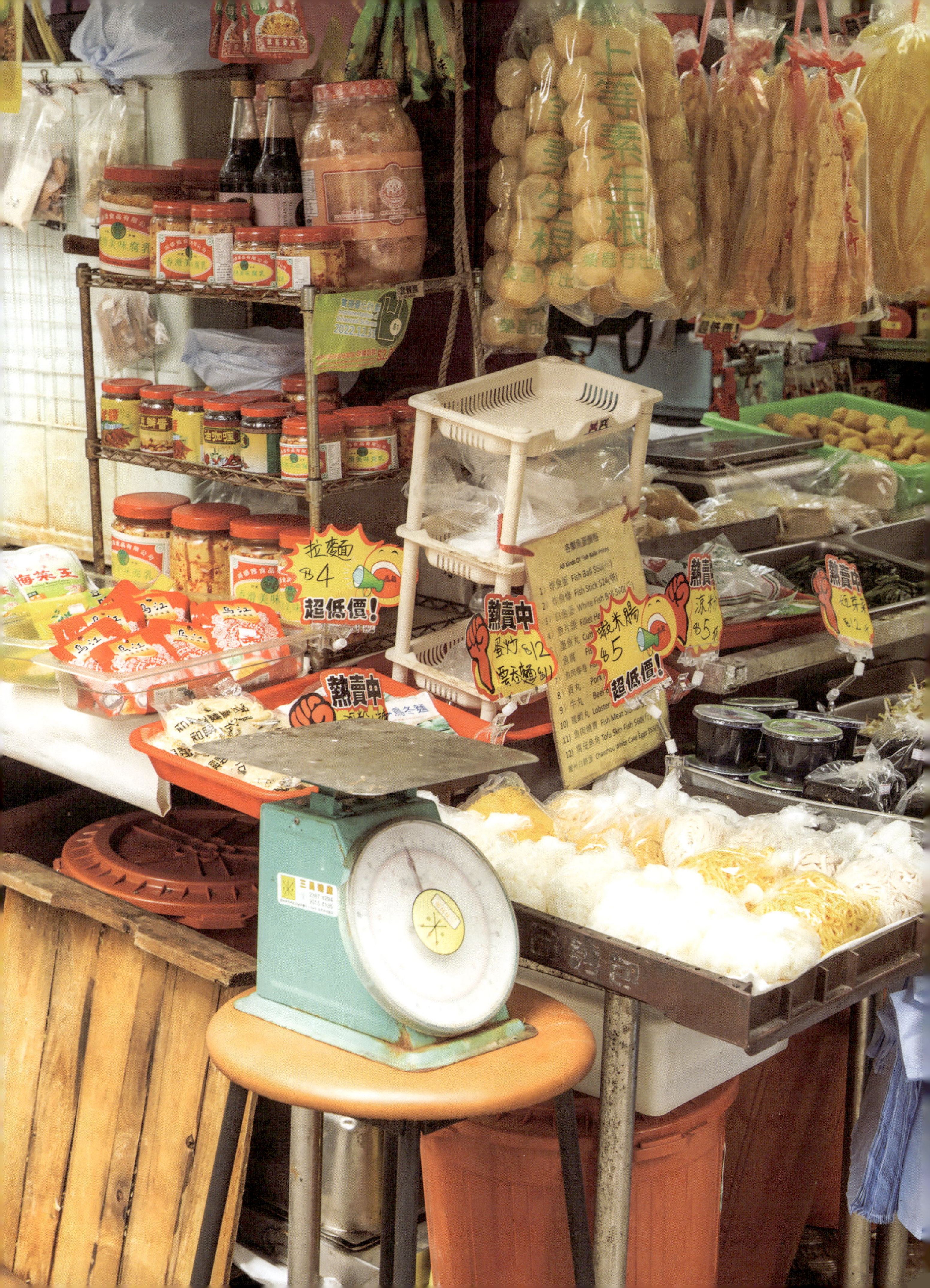
上等素生根
梅菜王
烏江
拉麵
$4
超低價!
熱賣中
蝦米腸
$5
超低價!
熱賣中
熱賣中

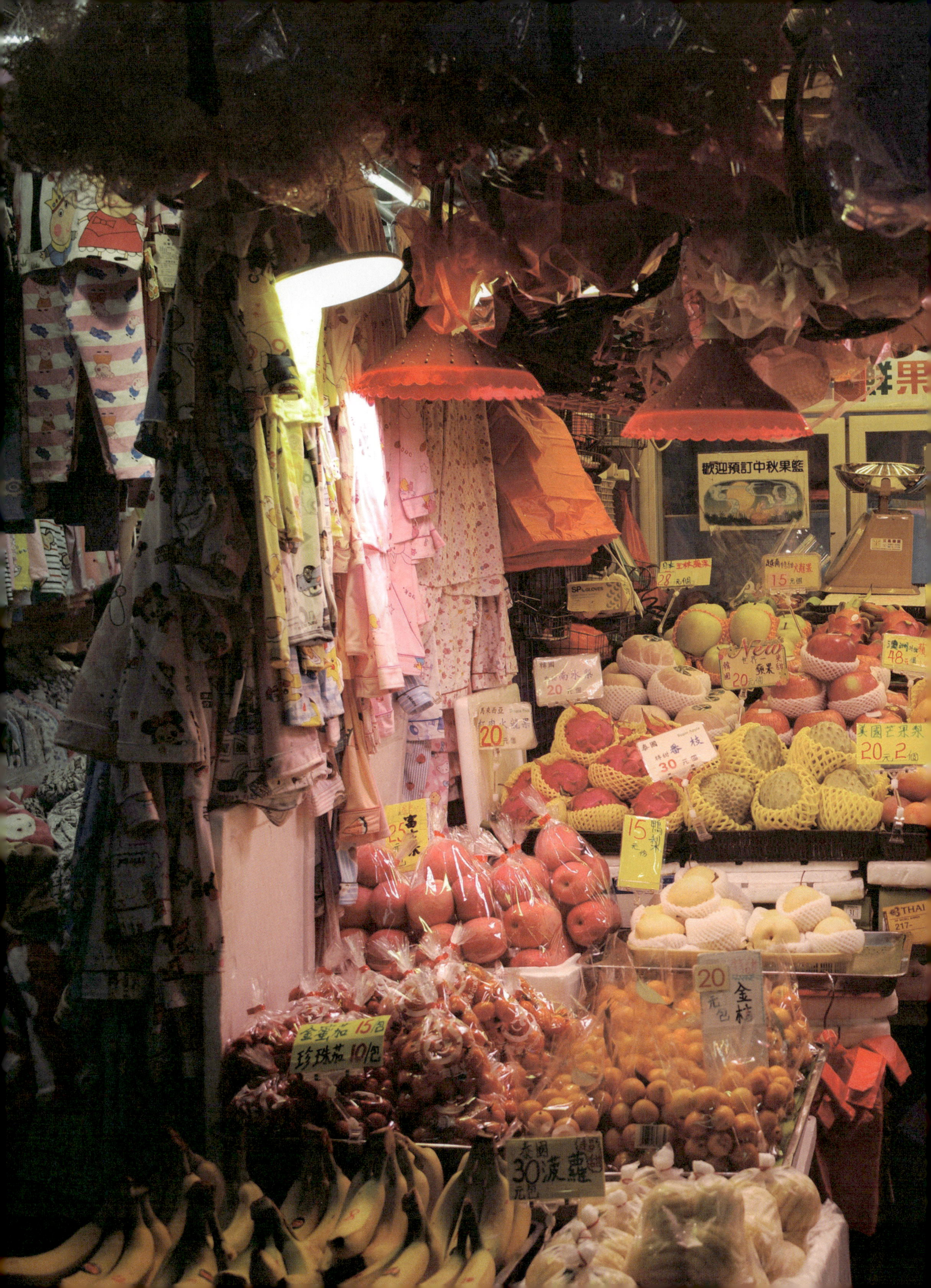
歡迎預訂中秋果籃
美國芒果梨
20元2個
20
元包
金桔

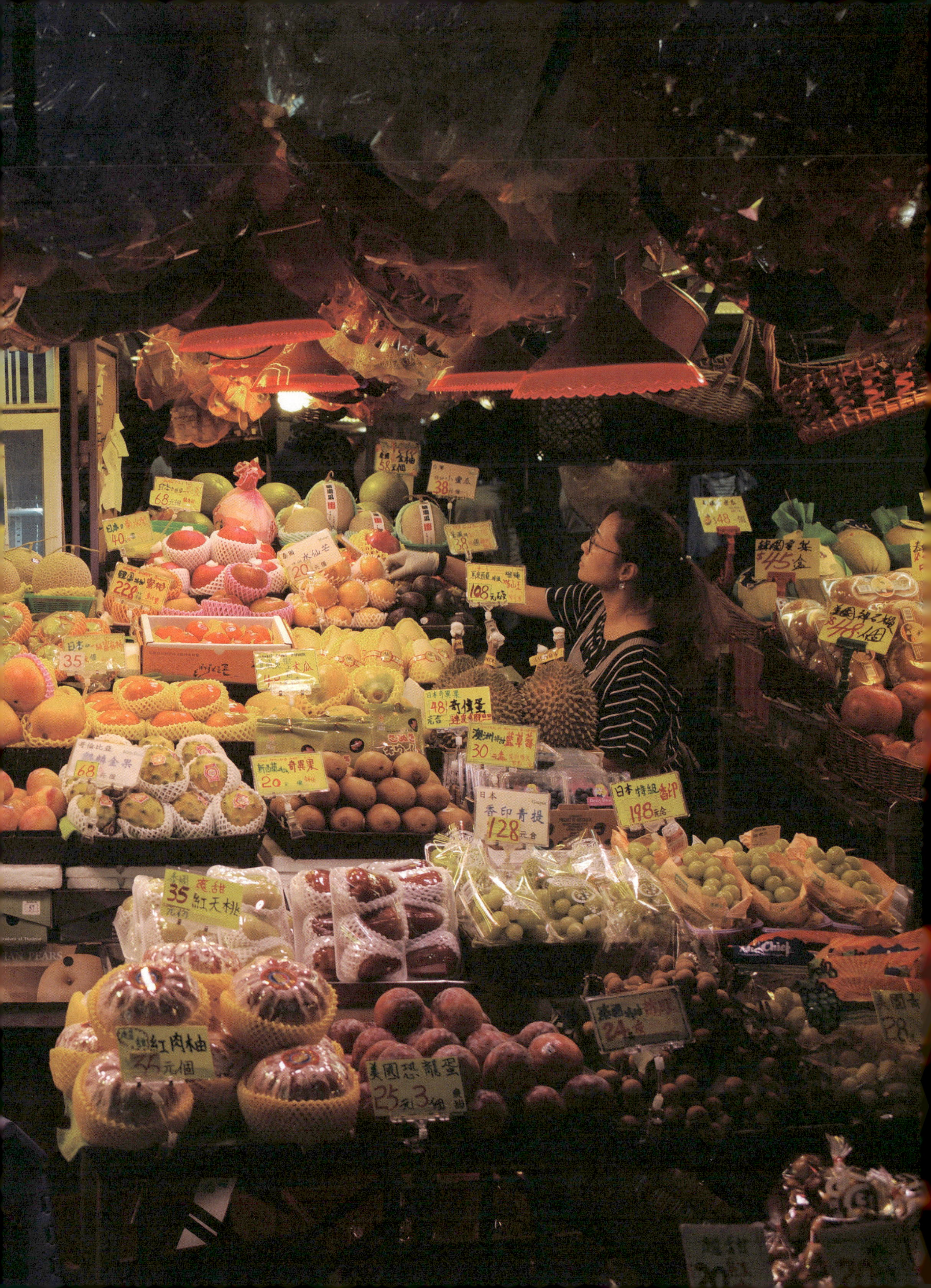

水仙芒
奇異果
20
澳洲
藍莓
30
日本
香印青提
128元盒
日本 特級
198元盒
35
紅天桃
紅肉柚
美國恐龍蛋
25元3個

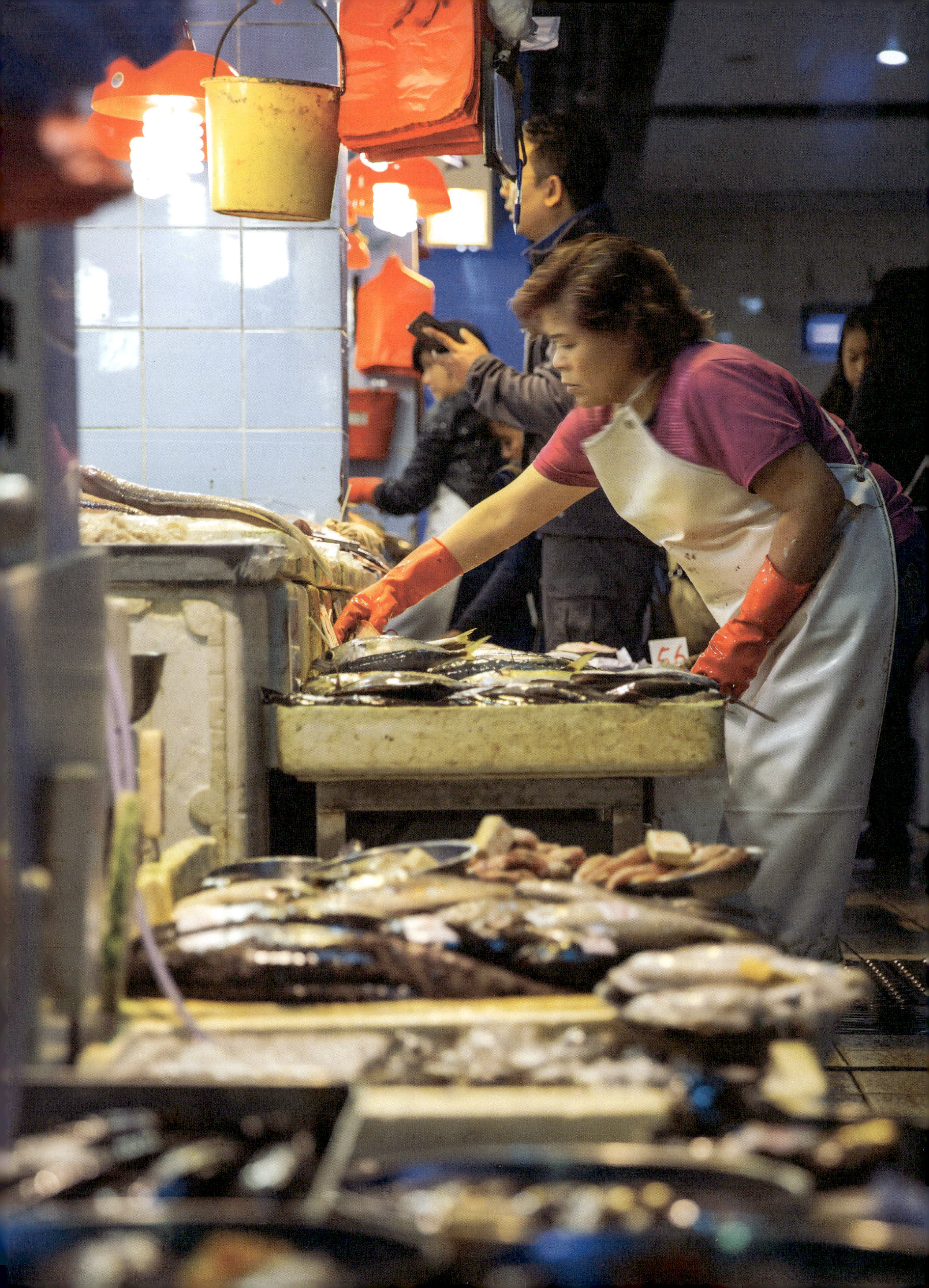
56

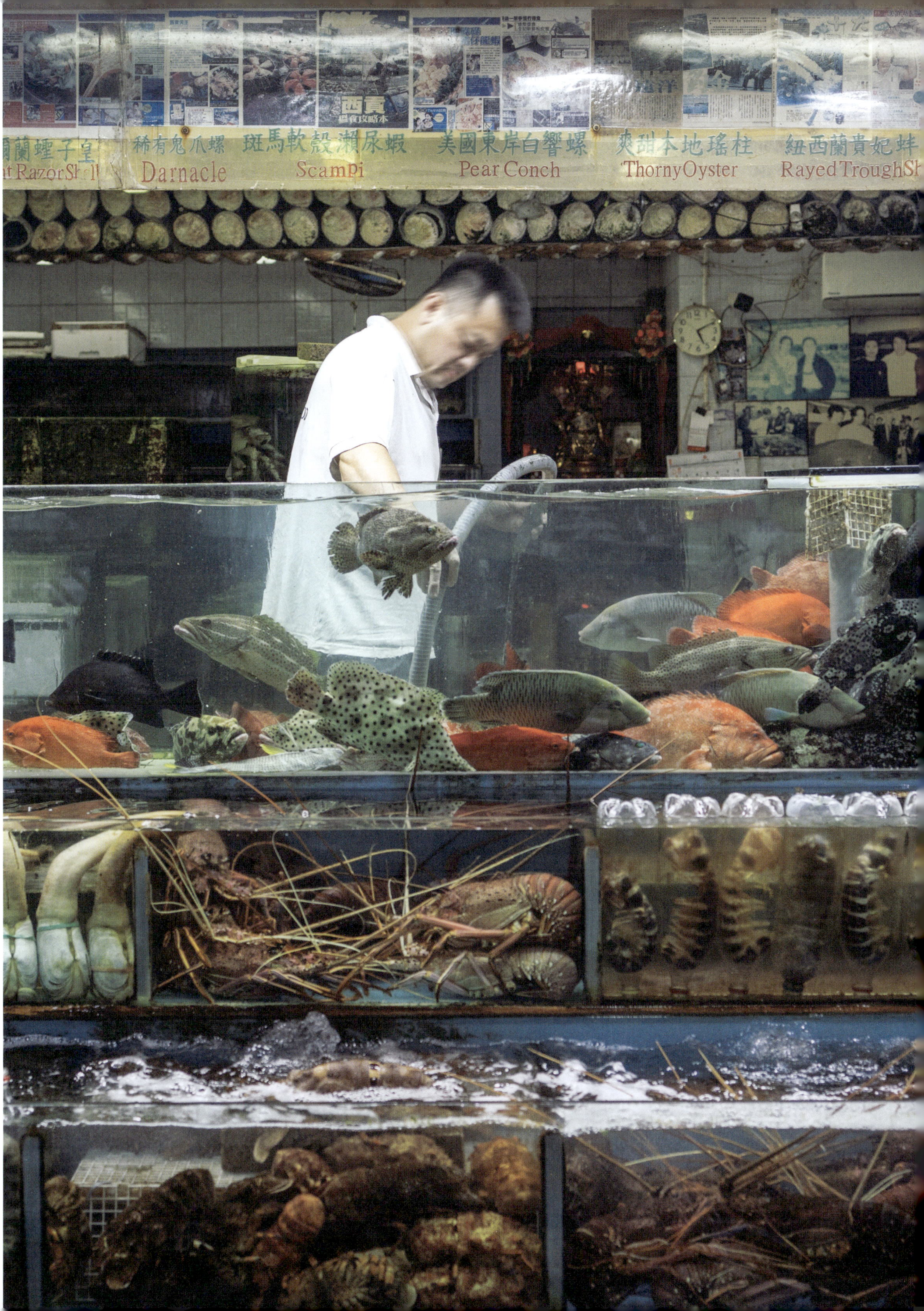

稀有鬼爪螺
Darnacle
斑馬軟殼瀨尿蝦
Scampi
美國東岸白響螺
Pear Conch
爽甜本地瑤柱
ThornyOyster

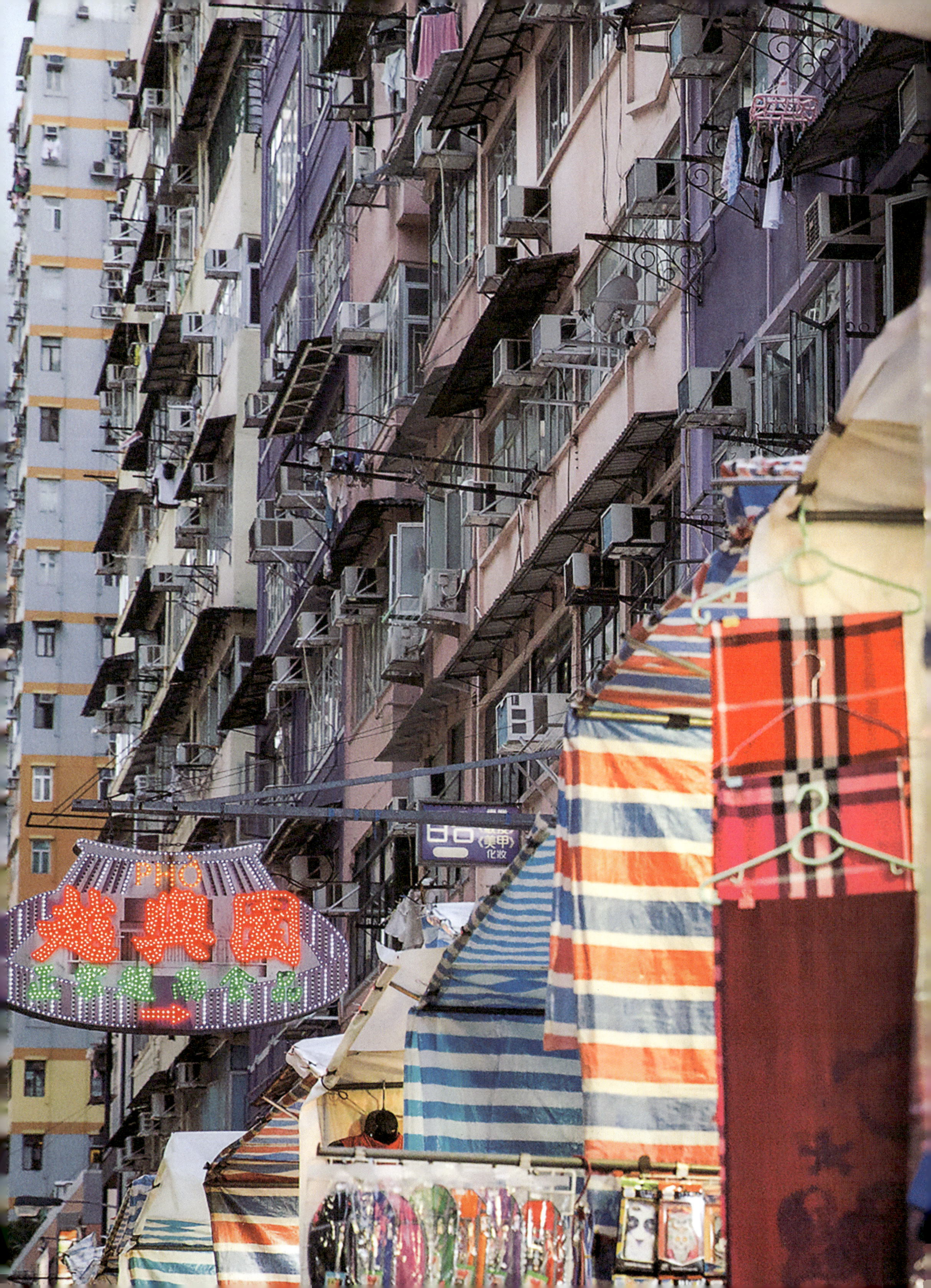
PHỞ
《美甲》
化妝

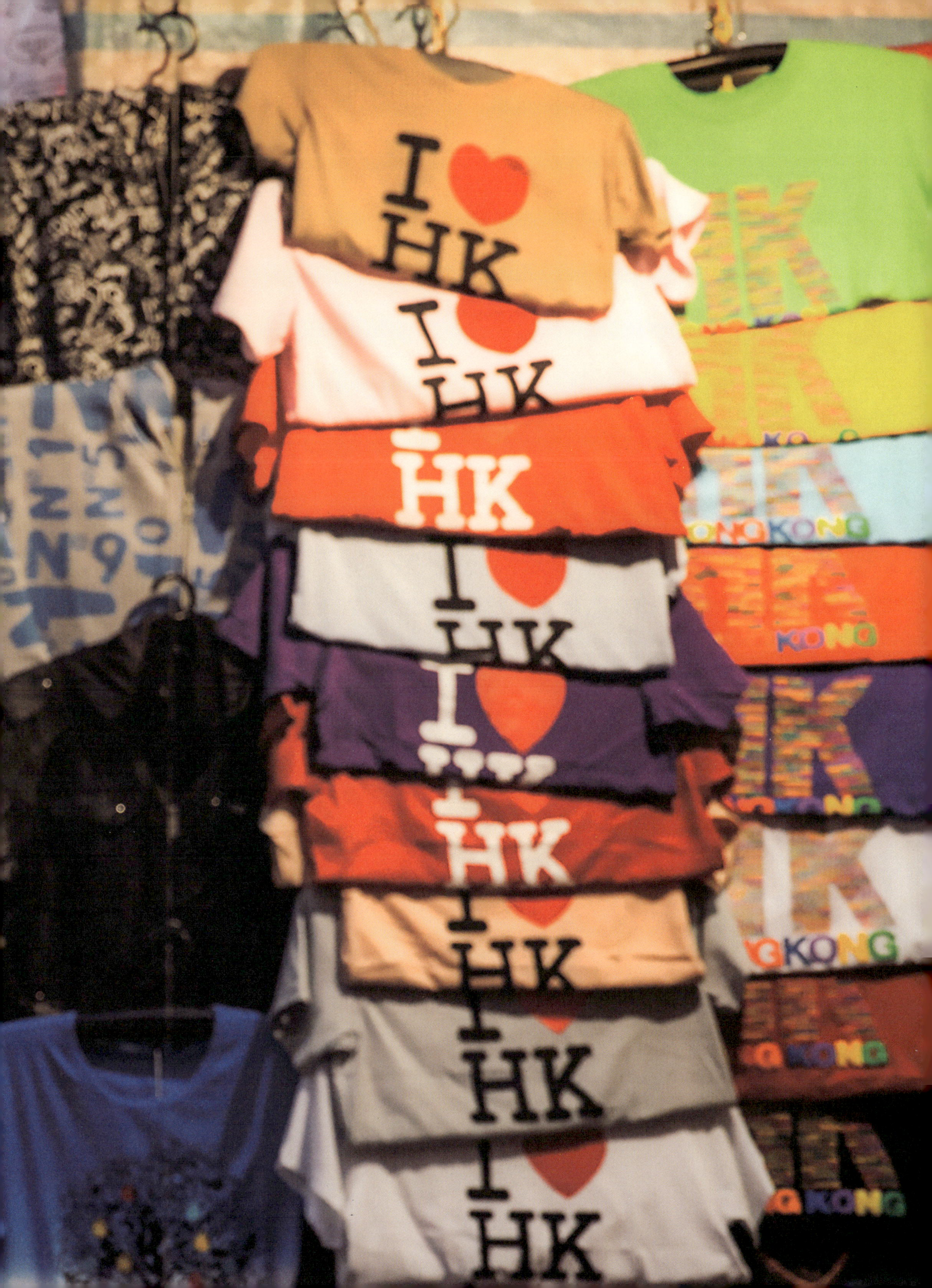

I
HK
KONG

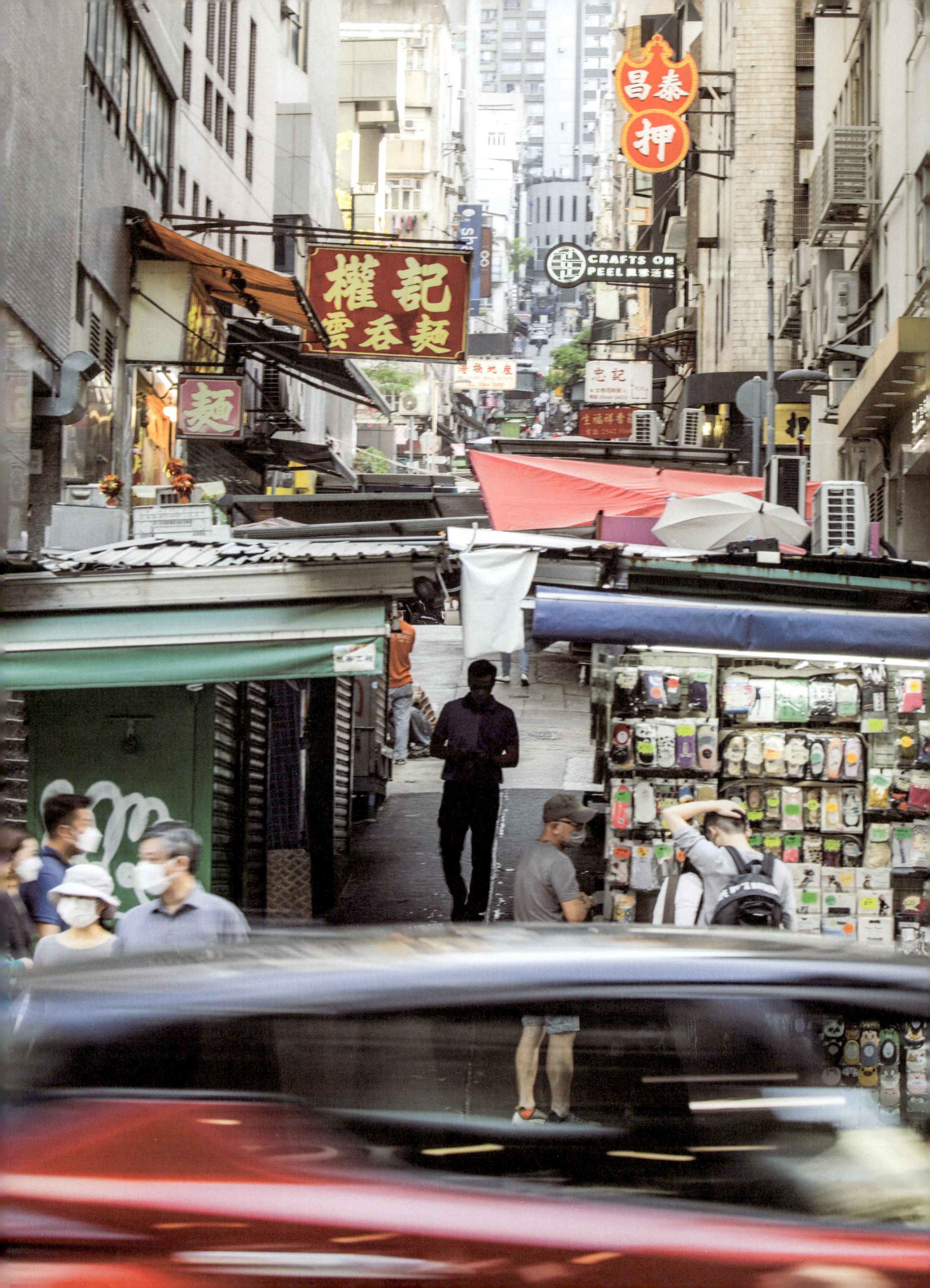

昌泰
押
權記
雲吞麵
麵
CRAFTS ON
PEEL
忠記

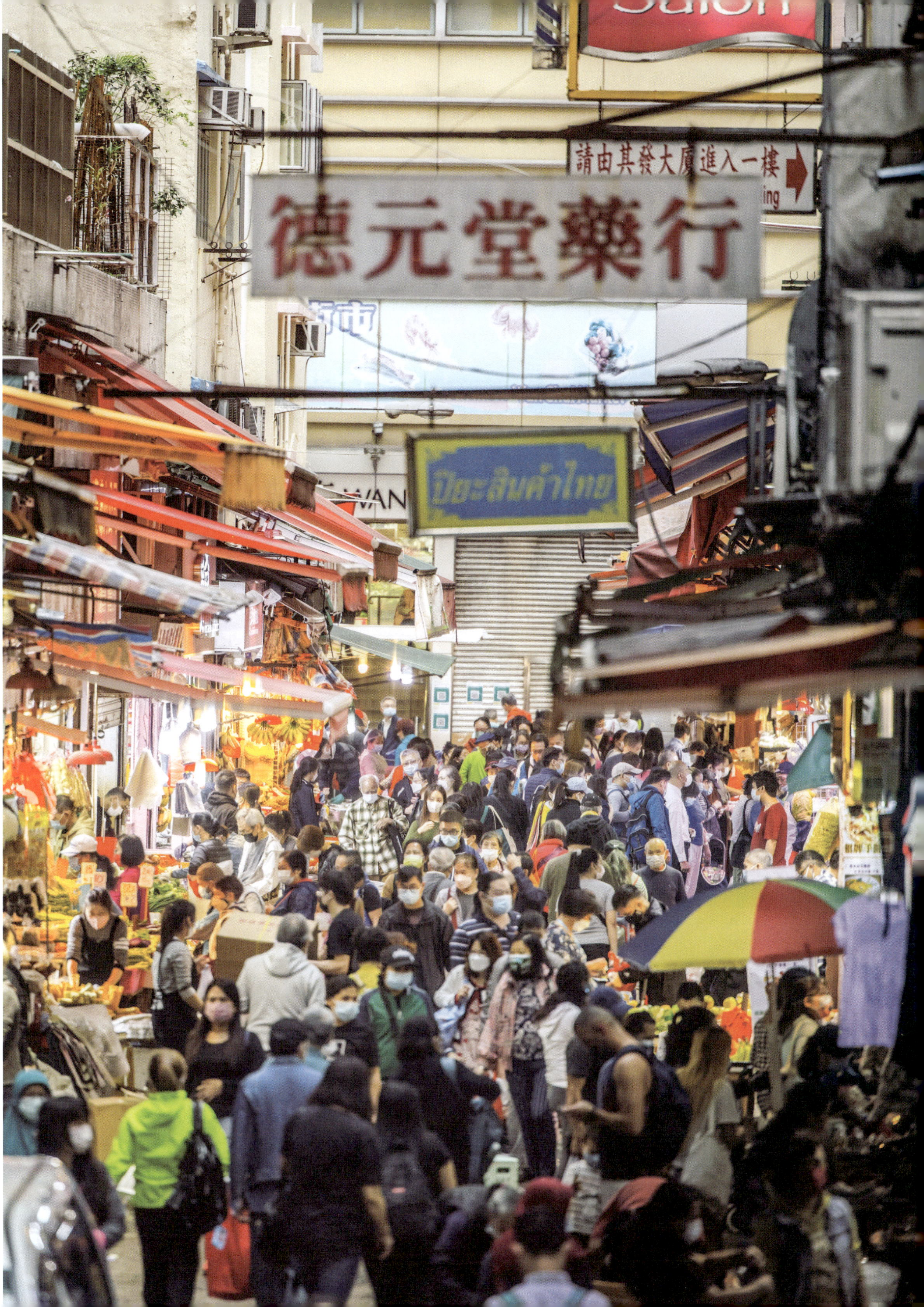
德元堂藥行
請由其發大廈進入一樓
ปิยะสินค้าไทย

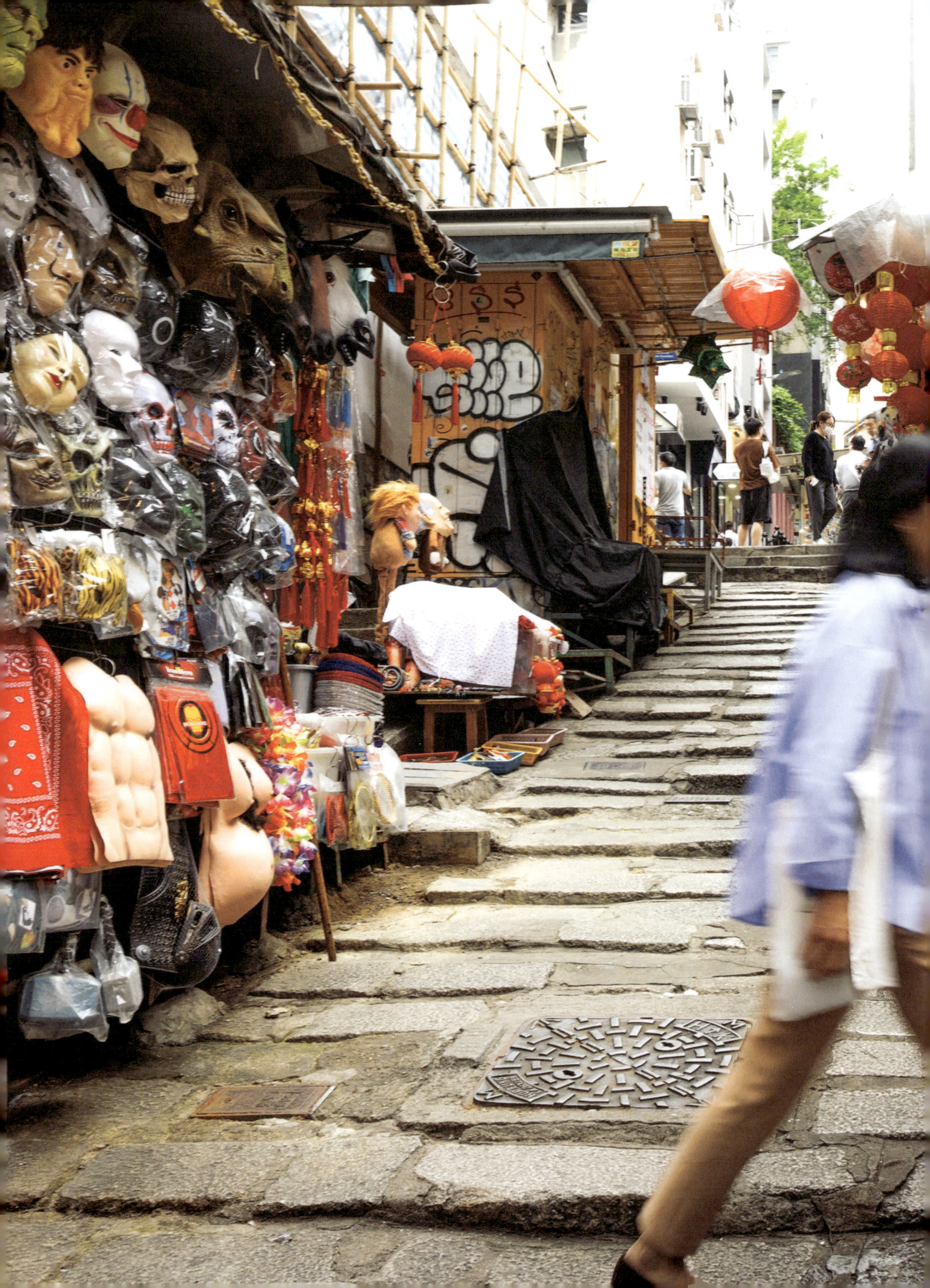

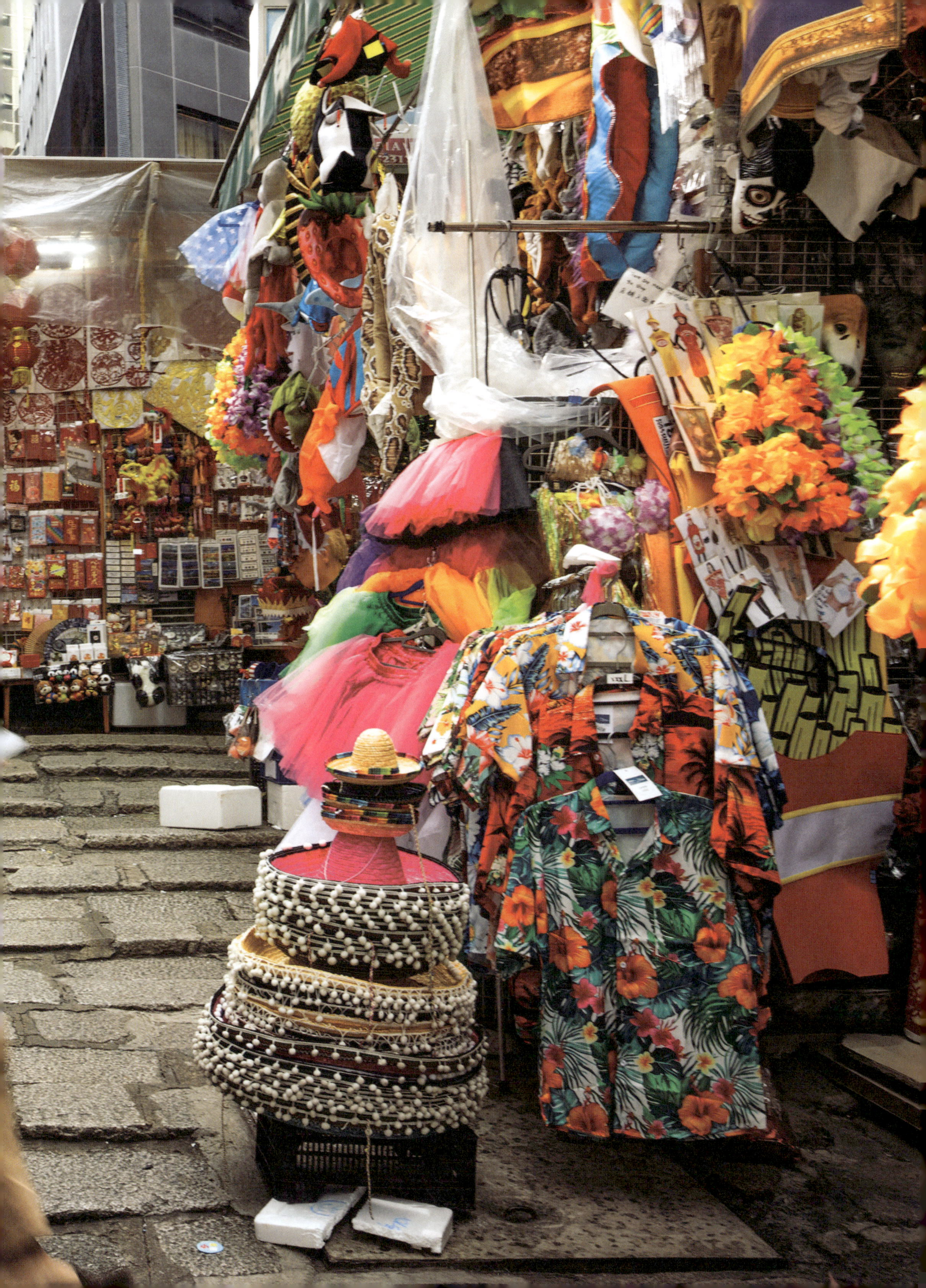

DAILY LIVING

THE STREETS & SHOPS

Hong Kong's streets are full of character — a photographer's dream. You get a nice mixture and contrast of the old and the new, of patterns and textures, of people and vehicular interactions, of the colorful shops and the vibrant signs hanging off of buildings.

I have conducted street photography tours in the city's various districts. I enjoy walking around everywhere, and always find something different to shoot every time.

12. Sugarcane juice shopfront on Hollywood Road in Central
13. Staunton Street in Central
14. Hennessy Road and Fleming Road crossing in Wan Chai
15. Cat at a shop in Sai Kung
16. Cat at a dried seafood store on Des Voeux Road West in Sai Ying Pun
17. Seafood store in Cheung Chau
18. Birdcage shop in Mong Kok's Yuen Po Street Bird Garden
19. Wan Chai Market, outside
20. Tak Wing Pawn Shop in Central
21. Central — Mid-Levels Escalators
22. Pedder Street in Central
23. Tang Lung Street in Causeway Bay

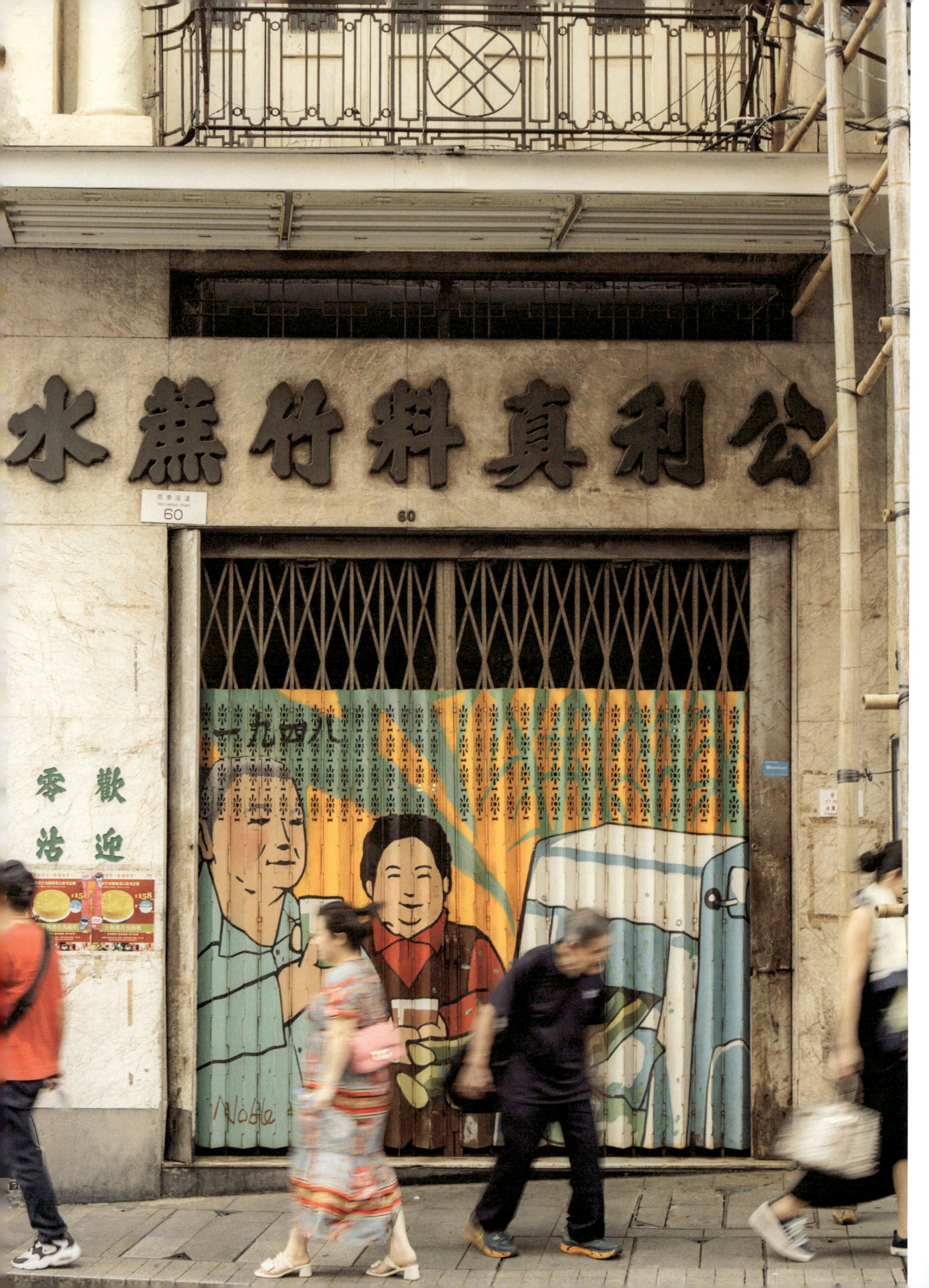

公利真料竹蔗水
60
歡迎
零沽
一九四八

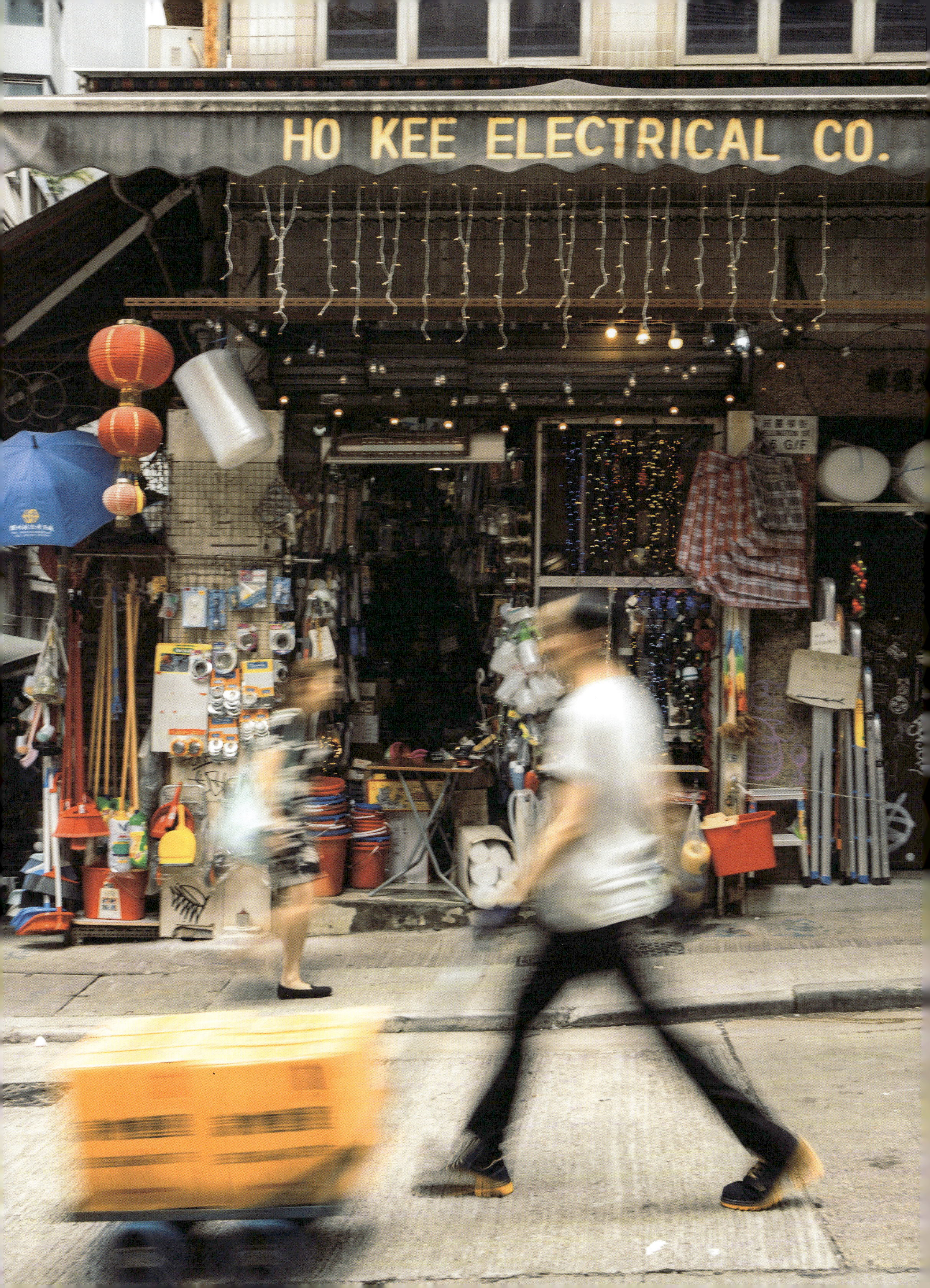
HO KEE ELECTRICAL CO.

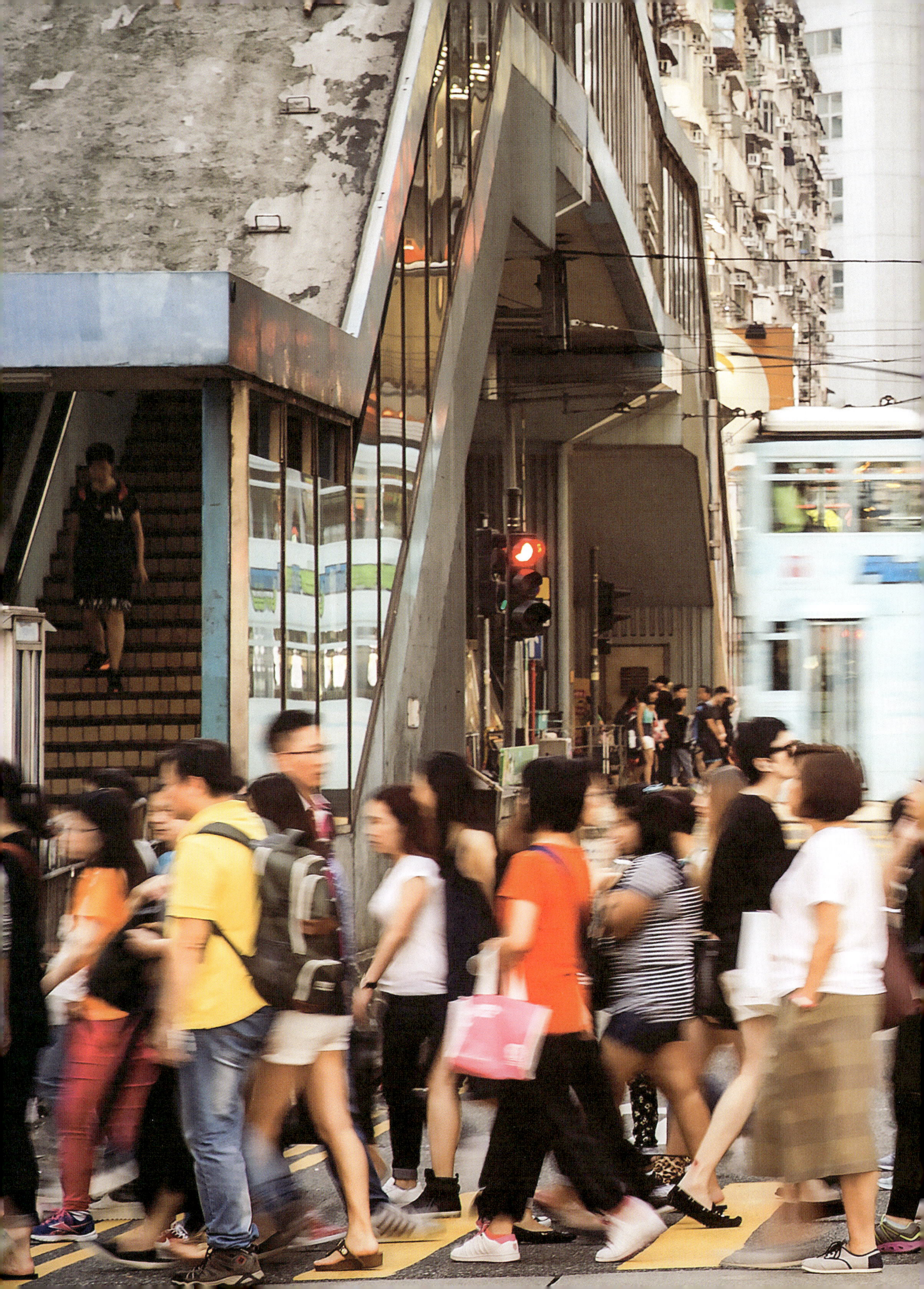

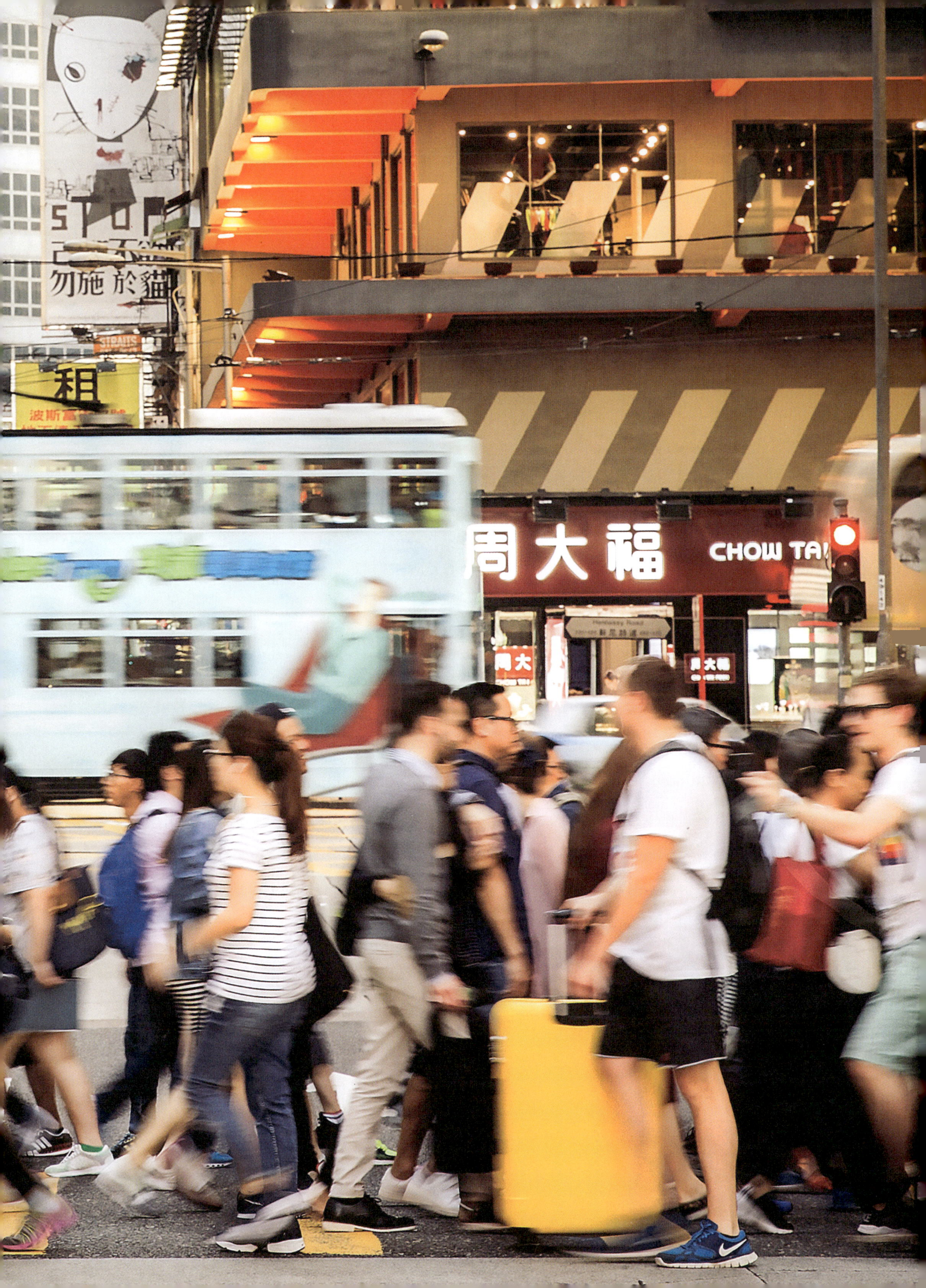
勿施於貓
租
周大福
CHOW TA

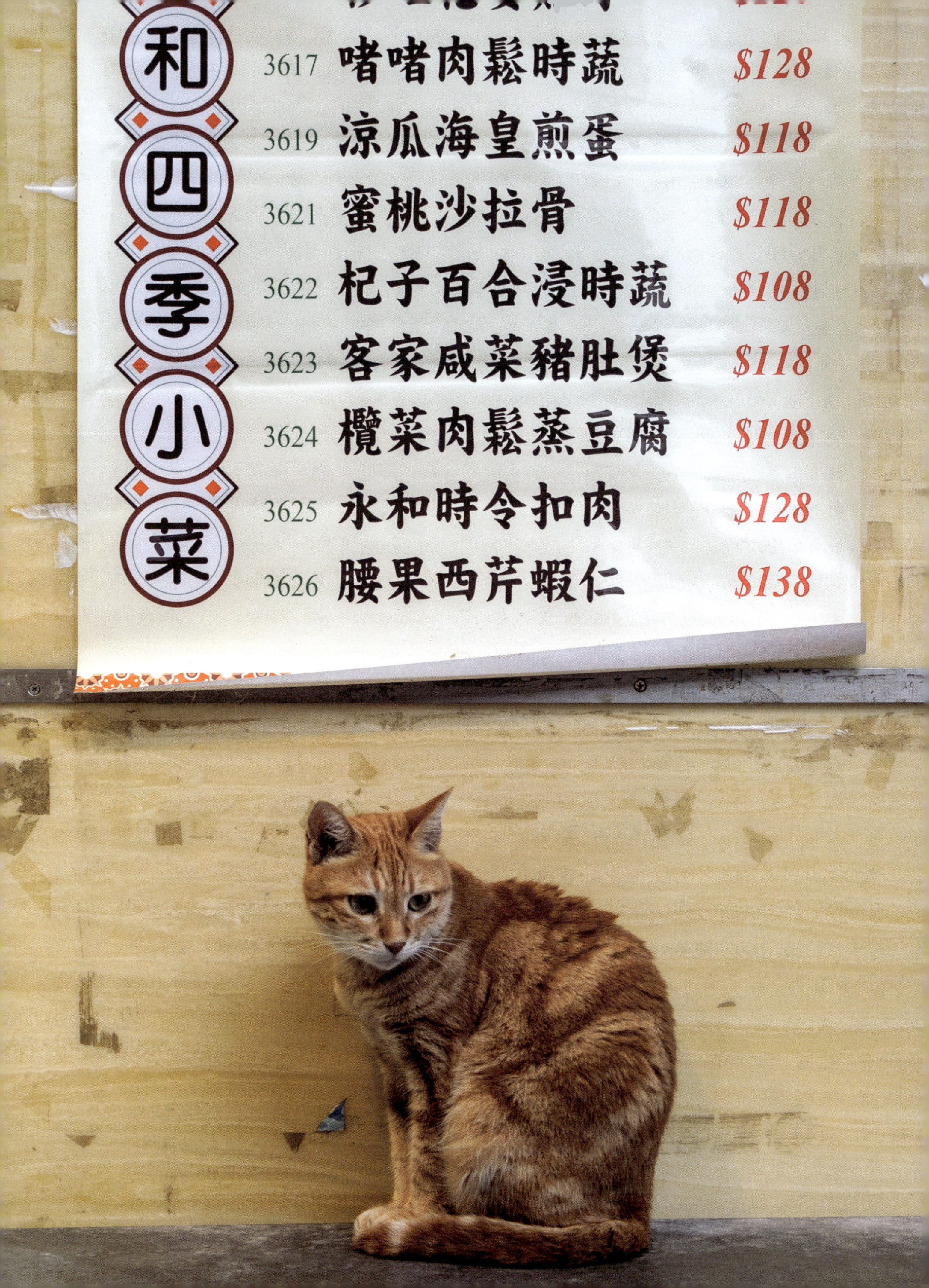
和四季小菜
3617 啫啫肉鬆時蔬 $128
3619 涼瓜海皇煎蛋 $118
3621 蜜桃沙拉骨 $118
3622 杞子百合浸時蔬 $108
3623 客家咸菜豬肚煲 $118
3624 欖菜肉鬆蒸豆腐 $108
3625 永和時令扣肉 $128
3626 腰果西芹蝦仁 $138

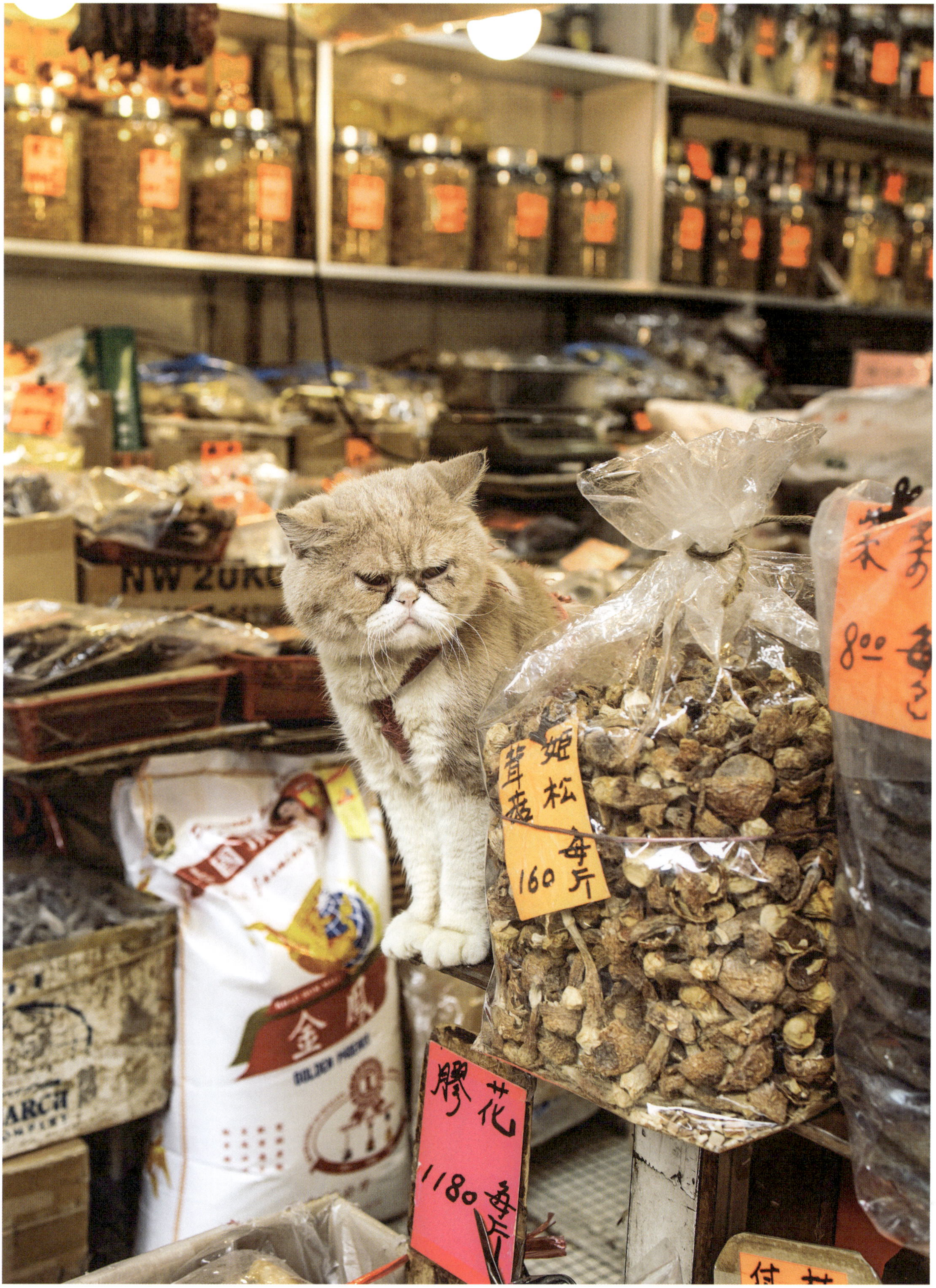
姬松茸菇 每斤 160
膠花 1180 每斤
金鳳

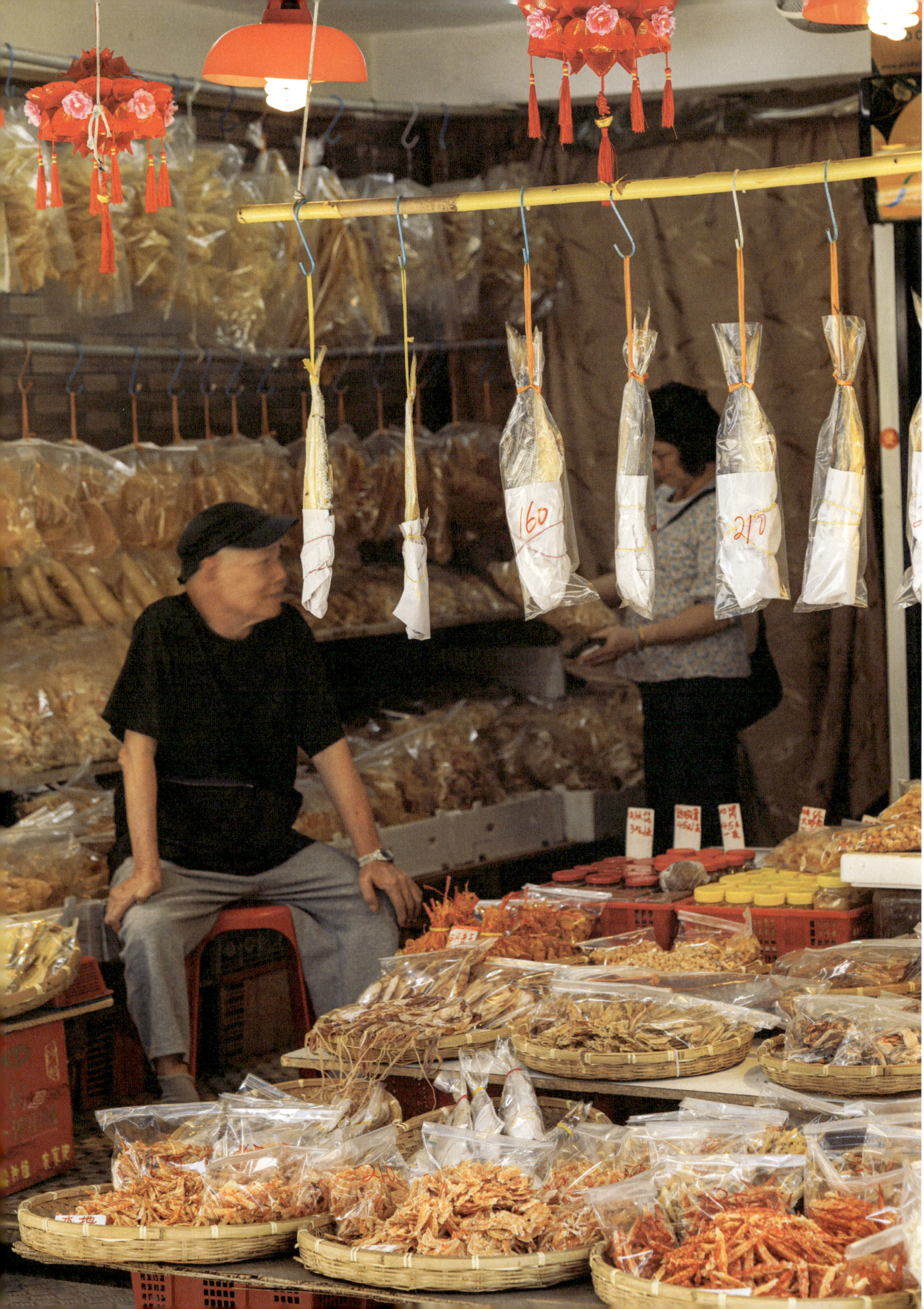
160
210

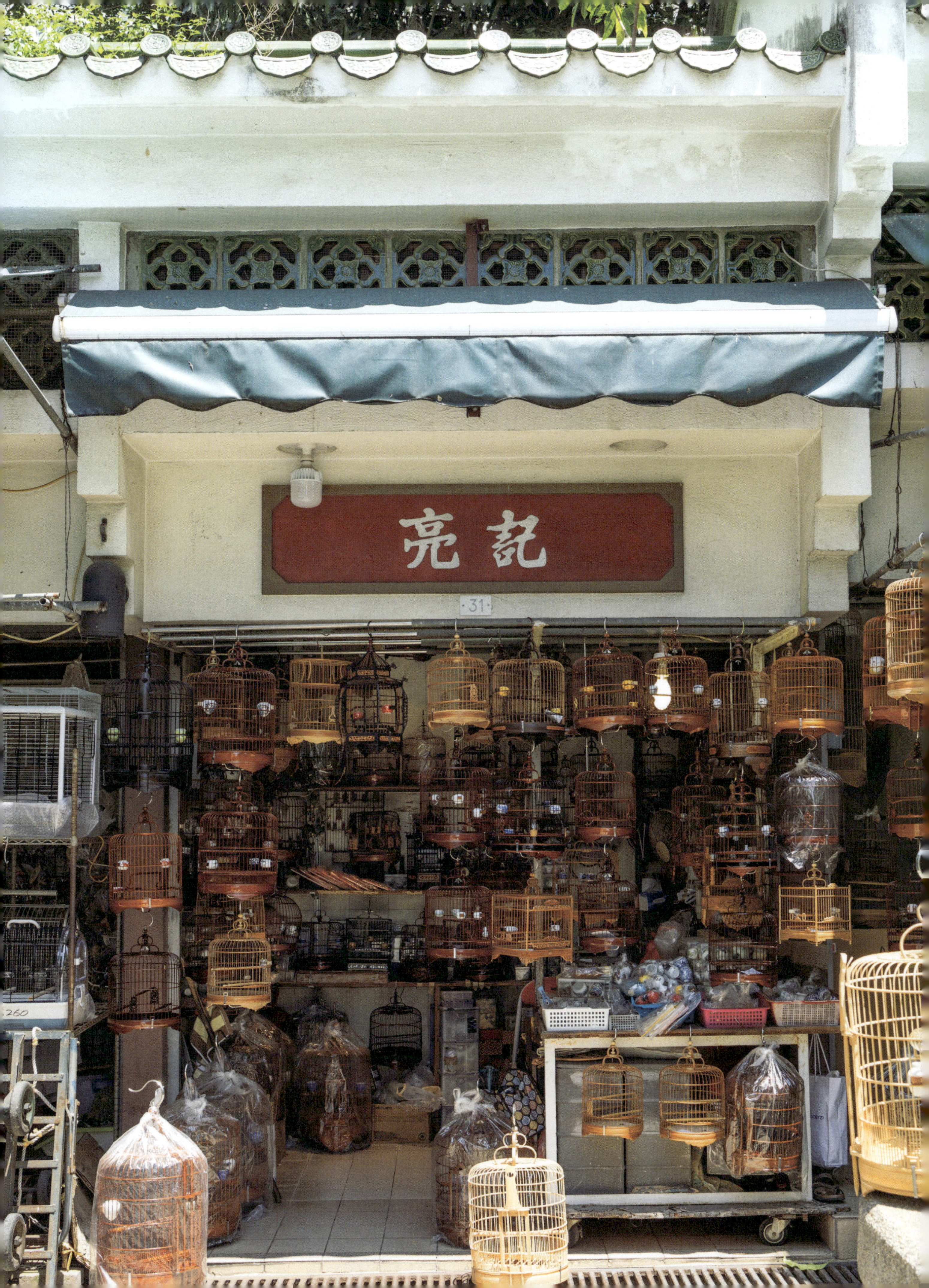
亮記
31

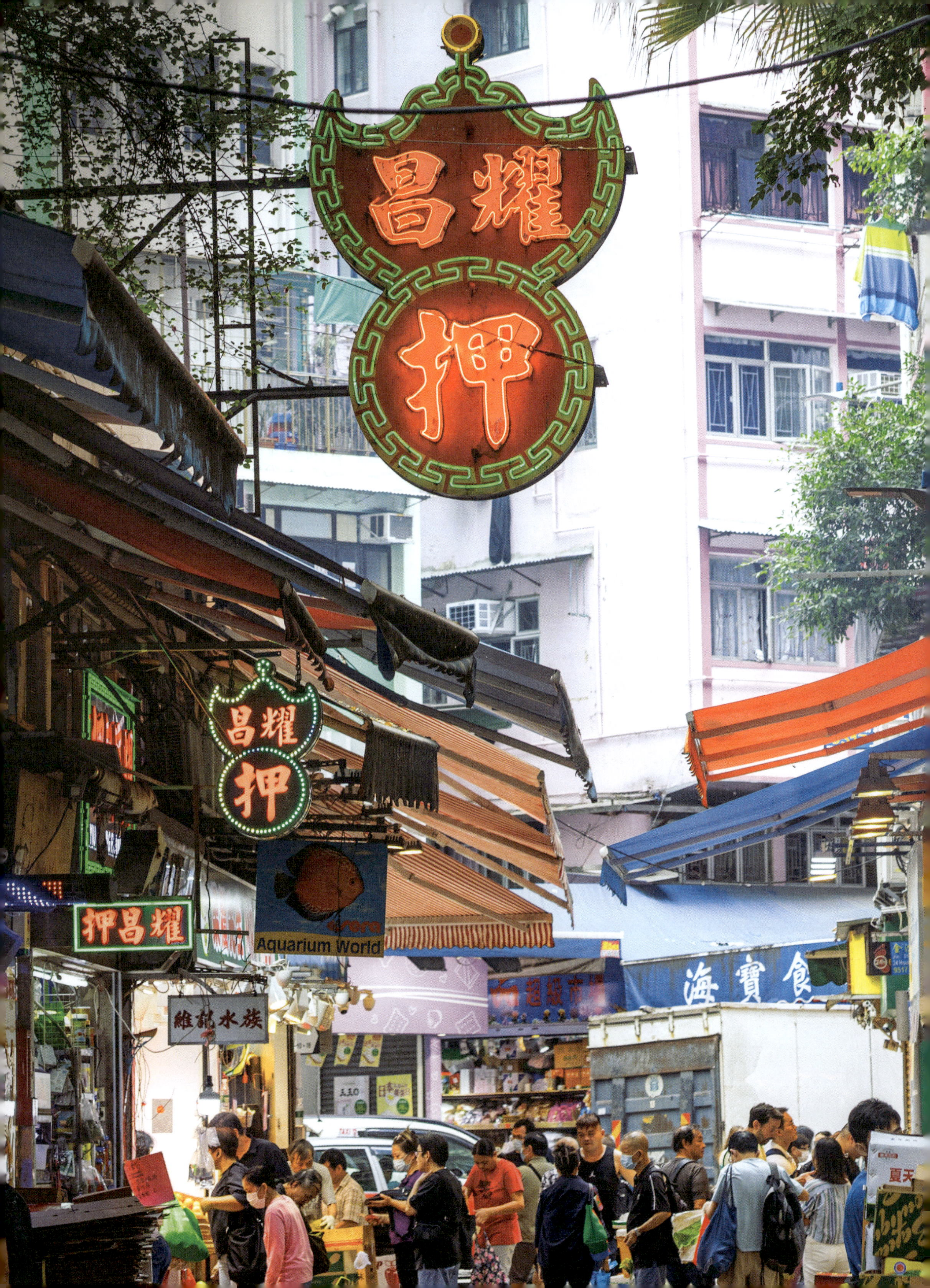

耀昌
押
耀昌
押
押昌耀
Aquarium World
維記水族
海寶食

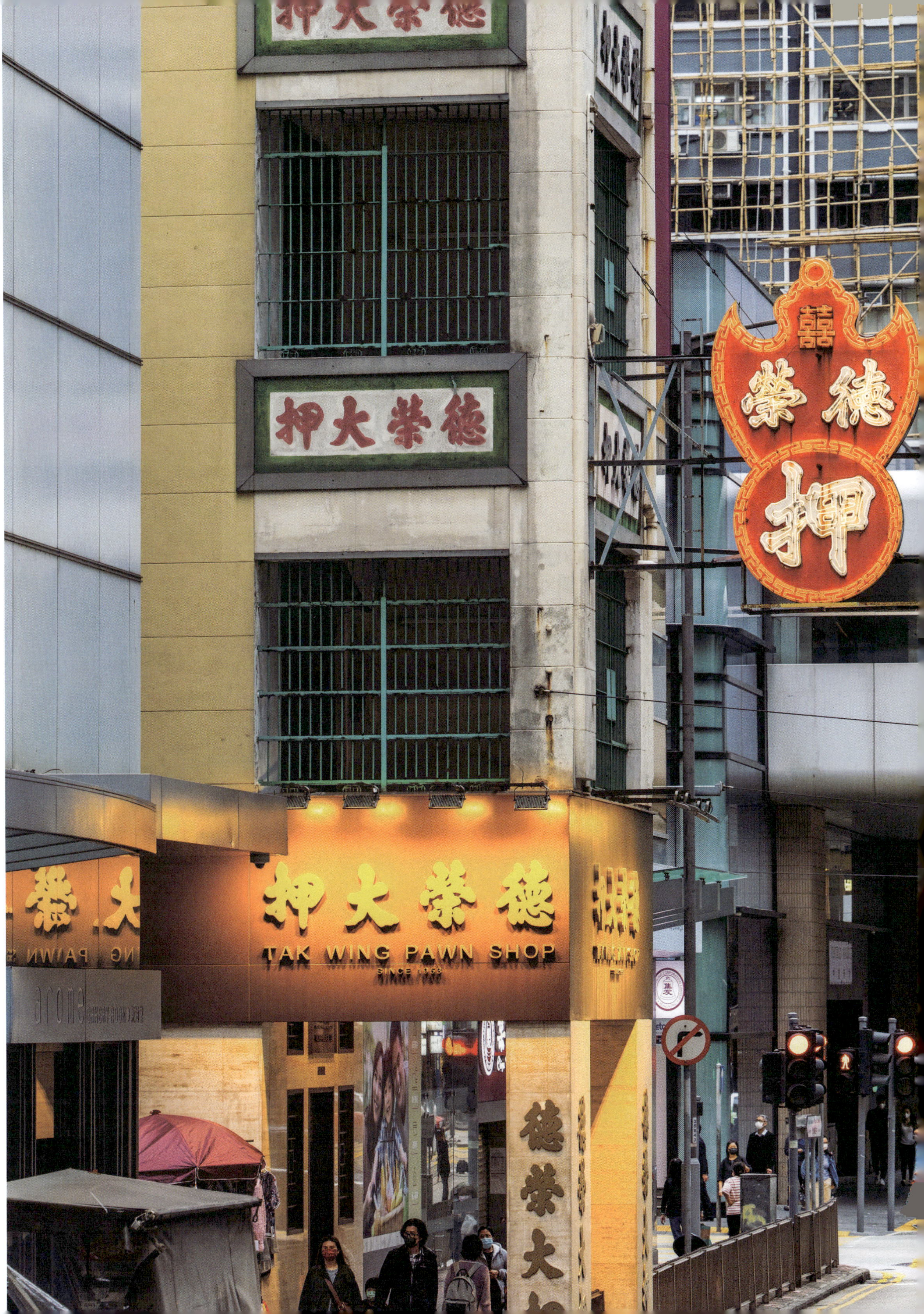

押大榮德
囍
德榮
押
押大榮德
TAK WING PAWN SHOP
德榮大

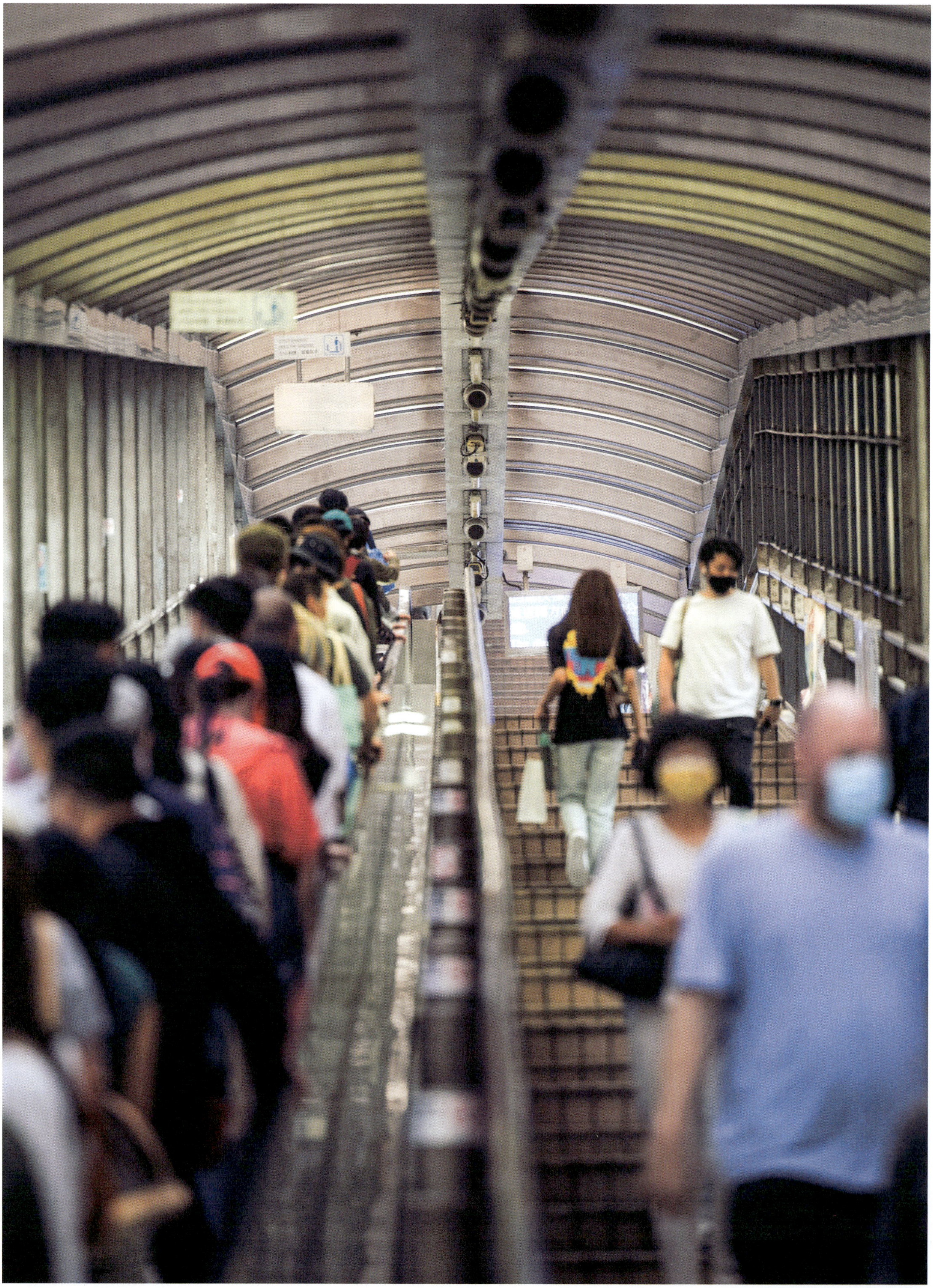

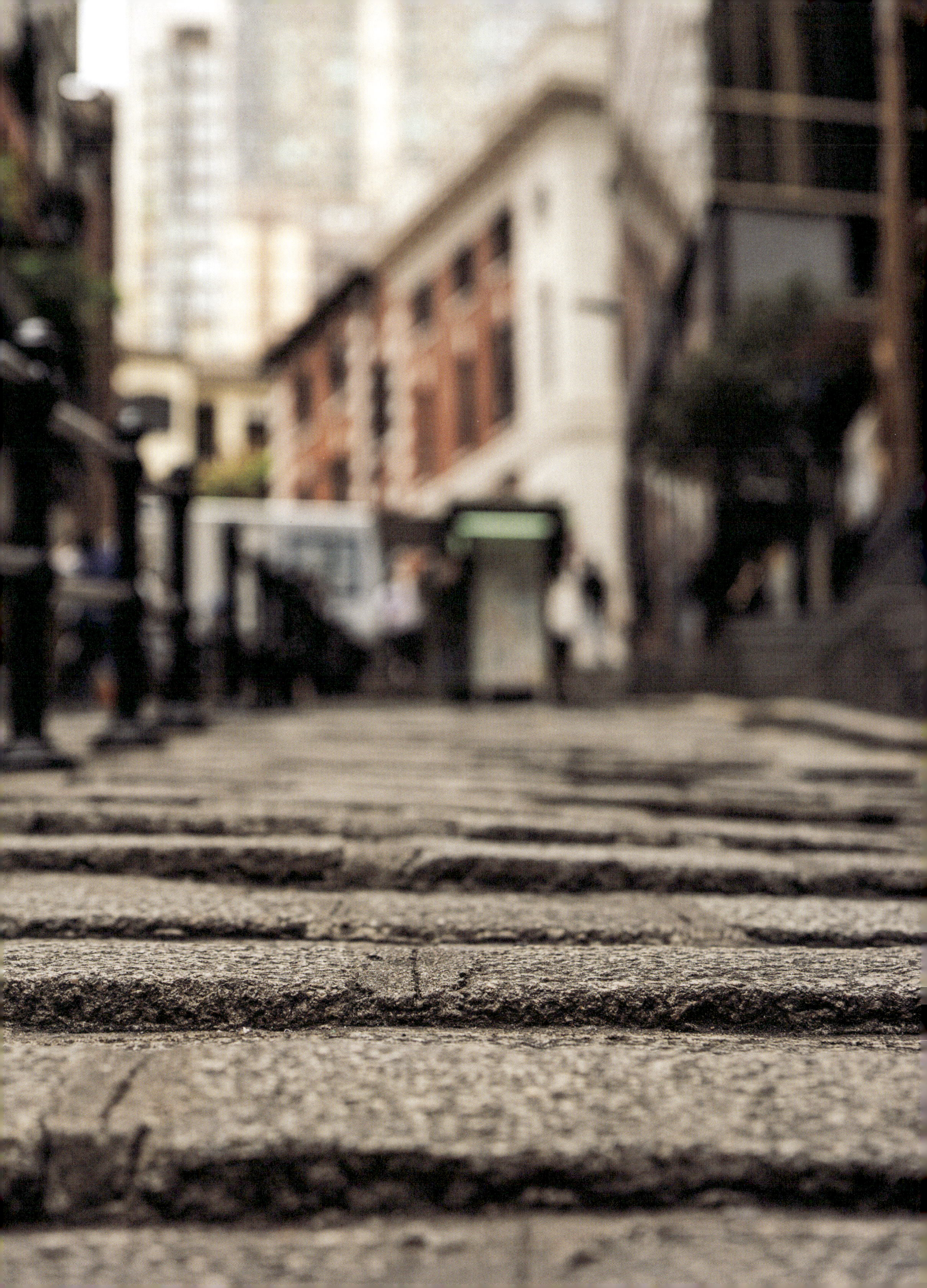

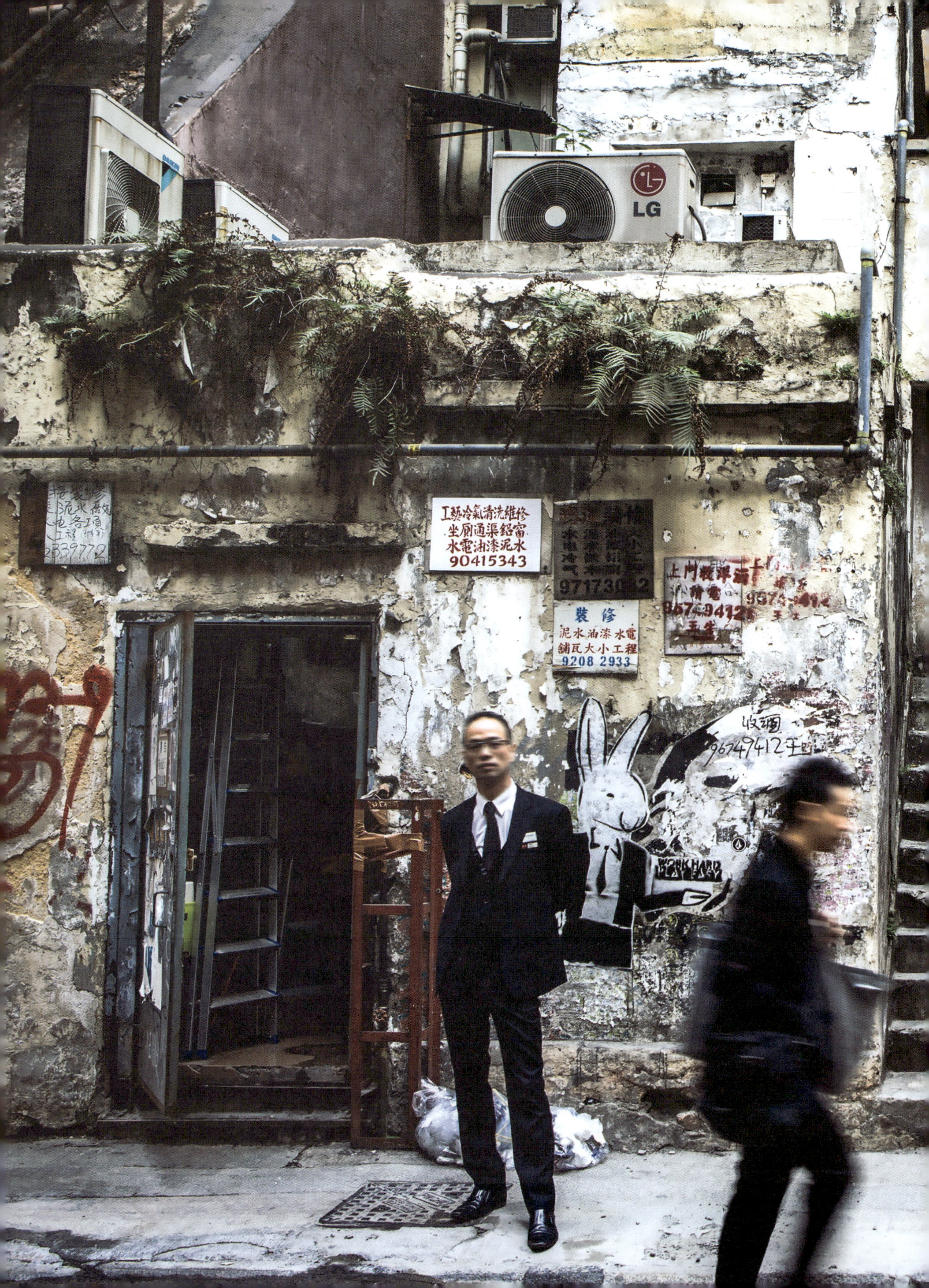
LG
工藝冷氣清洗維修
坐厠通渠鋁窗
水電油漆泥水
90415343
裝修
泥水油漆 水電
鋪瓦大小工程
9208 2933
WORK HARD

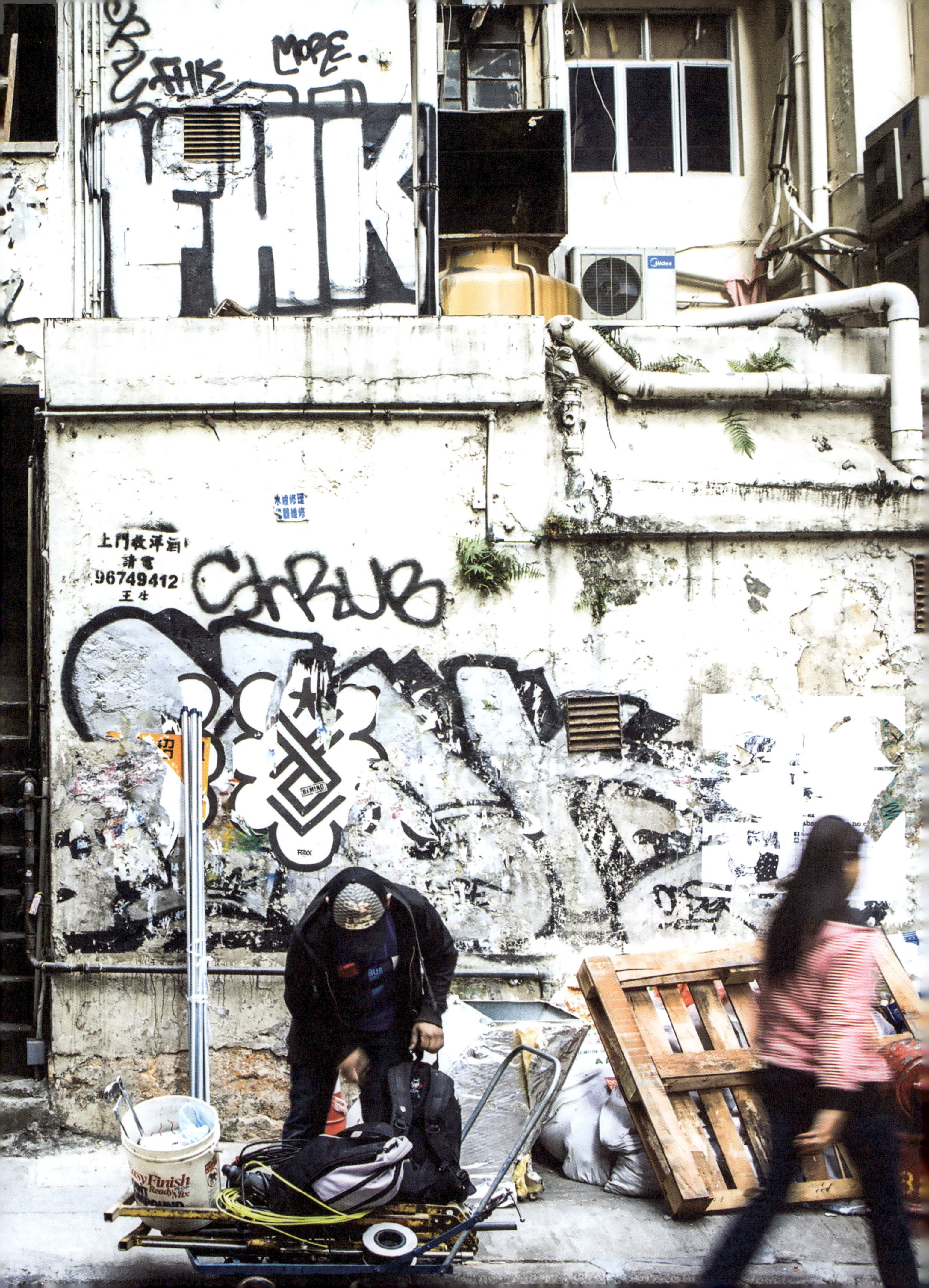
MORE.
上門收洋酒
請電
96749412
王生
水喉修理
電器維修
REMIND
Easy Finish
Ready Mix

DAILY LIVING

THE ACTIVITIES

Hongkongers have plenty of options when it comes to leisurely activities.

Outdoor sports, beach going, mahjong playing, photo taking, and group tai-chi count as common pastimes. Fishing along the harbor or ferry piers is another particularly Hong Kong hobby. In short: anything goes.

24. Man fishing in Ap Lei Chau
25. People playing mahjong at Wu Kai Sha Beach
26. Photographers at Wu Kai Sha Beach
27. Revelers at Wu Kai Sha Beach
28. A dog strolling along Hoi Ha beach in Sai Kung
29. Couple enjoying the views near Sai Kung Pier
30. Cross Harbour Race at Victoria Harbour
31. Biker walking along Wu Kai Sha Pier
32. Runner at the Central Ferry Piers
33. People exercising outside Taikoo Shing

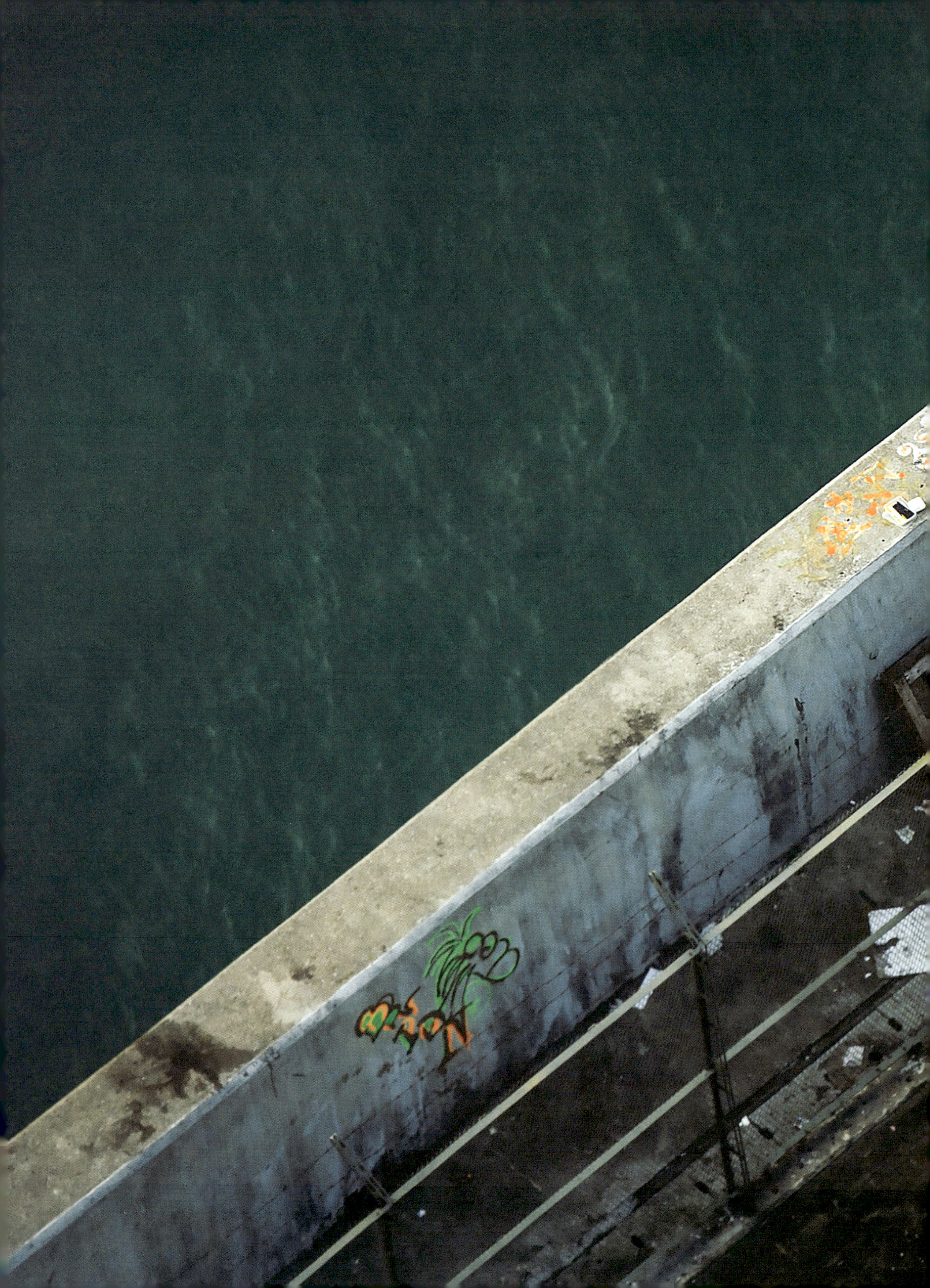

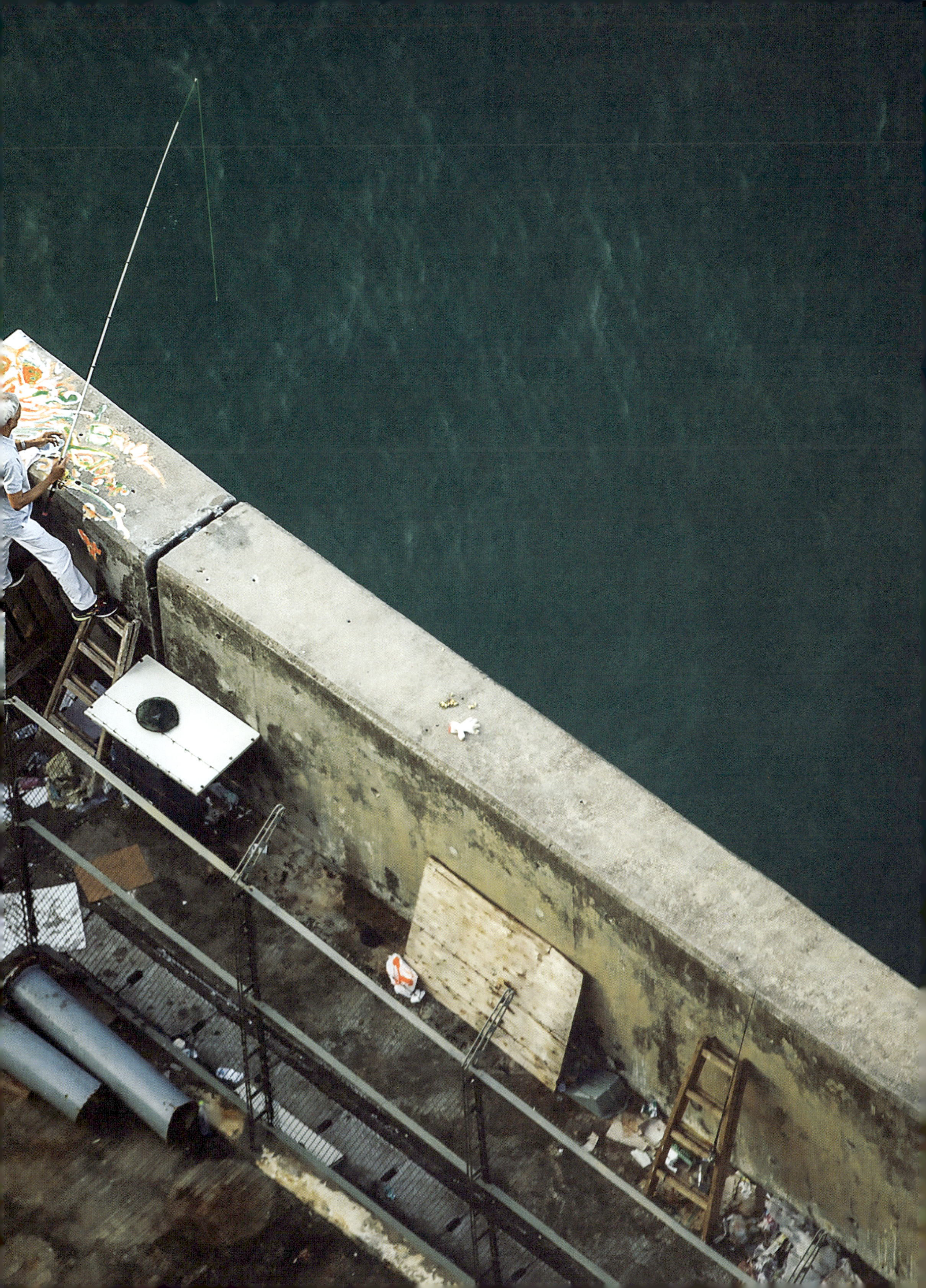

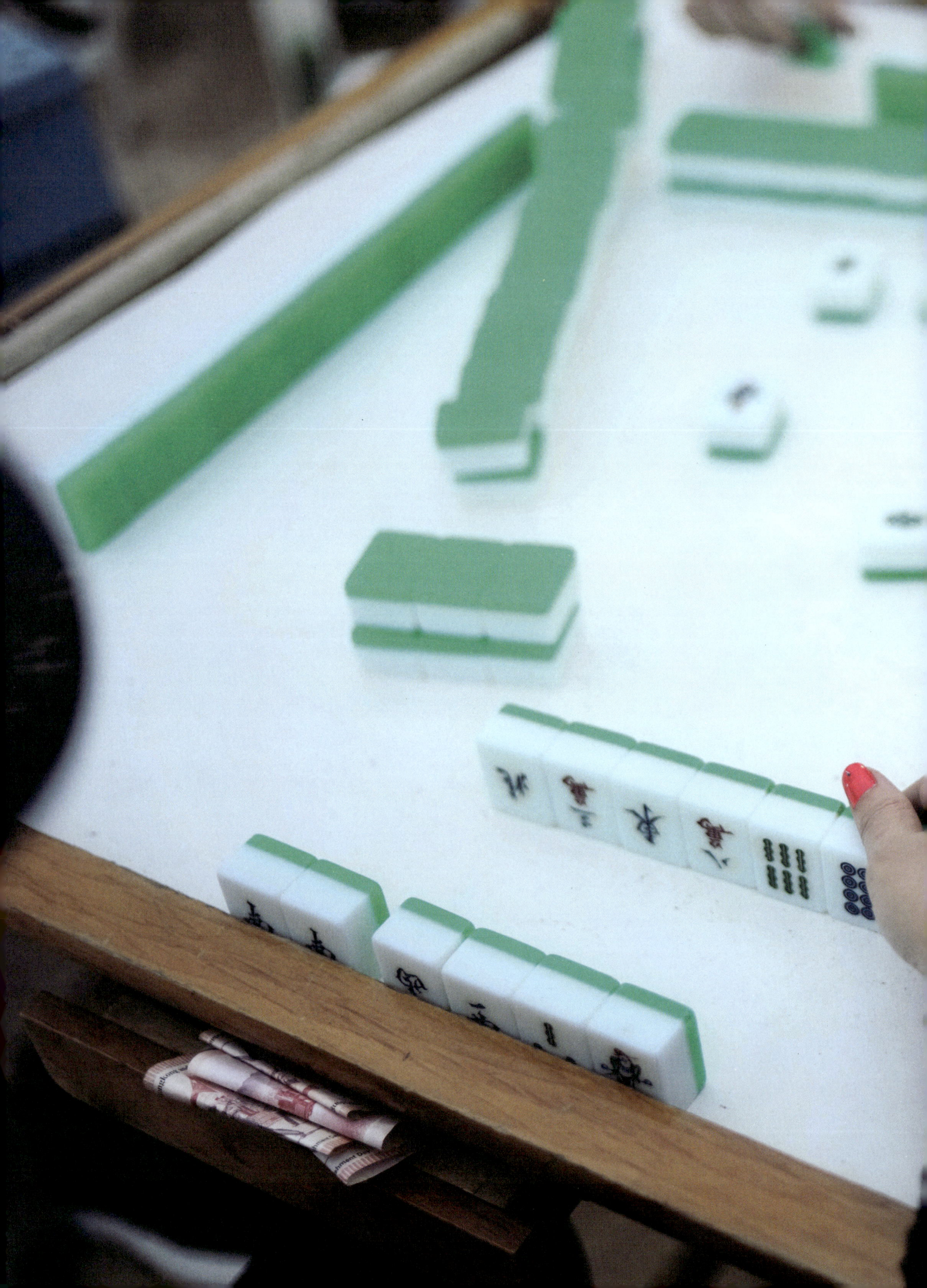

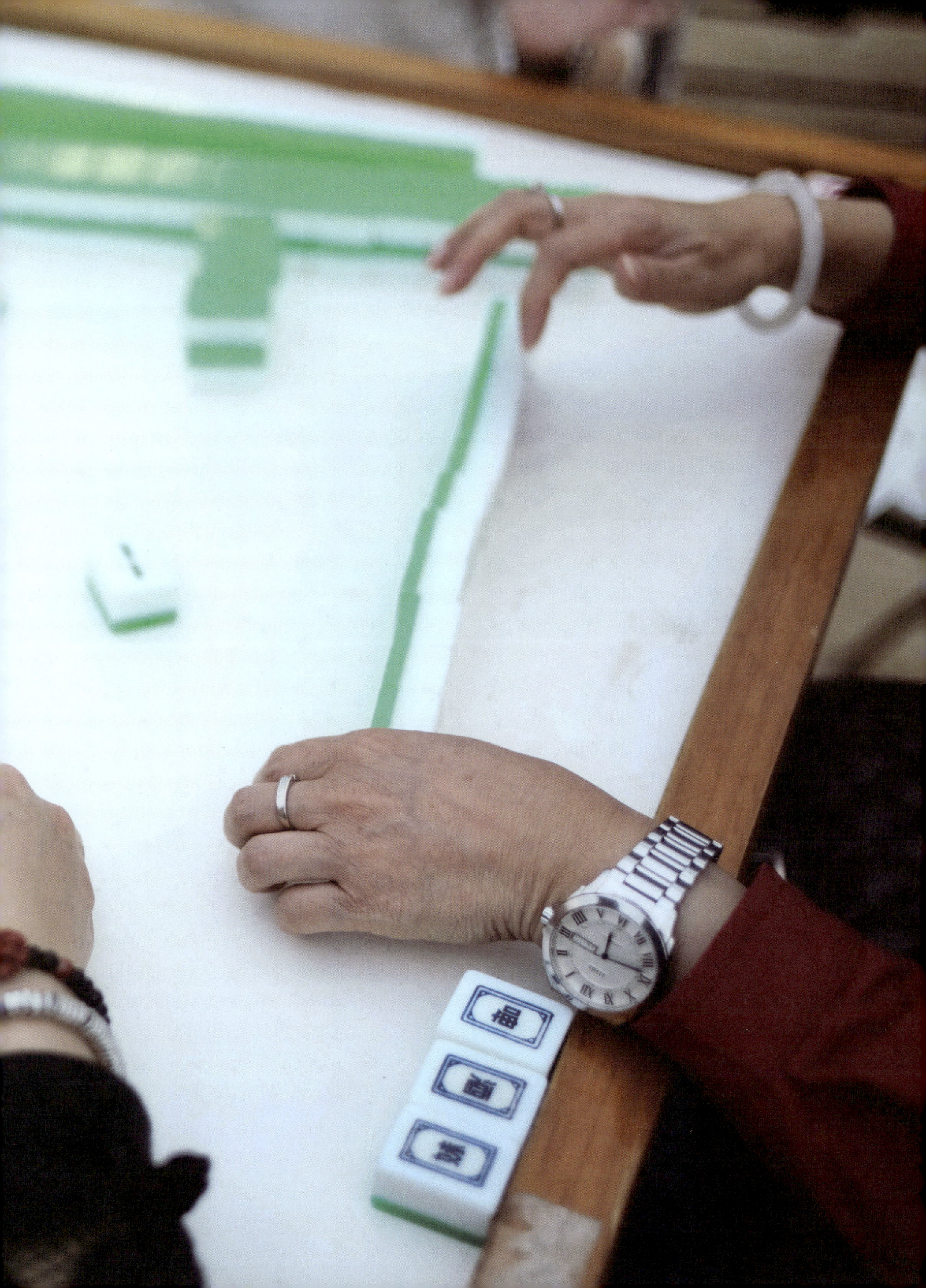

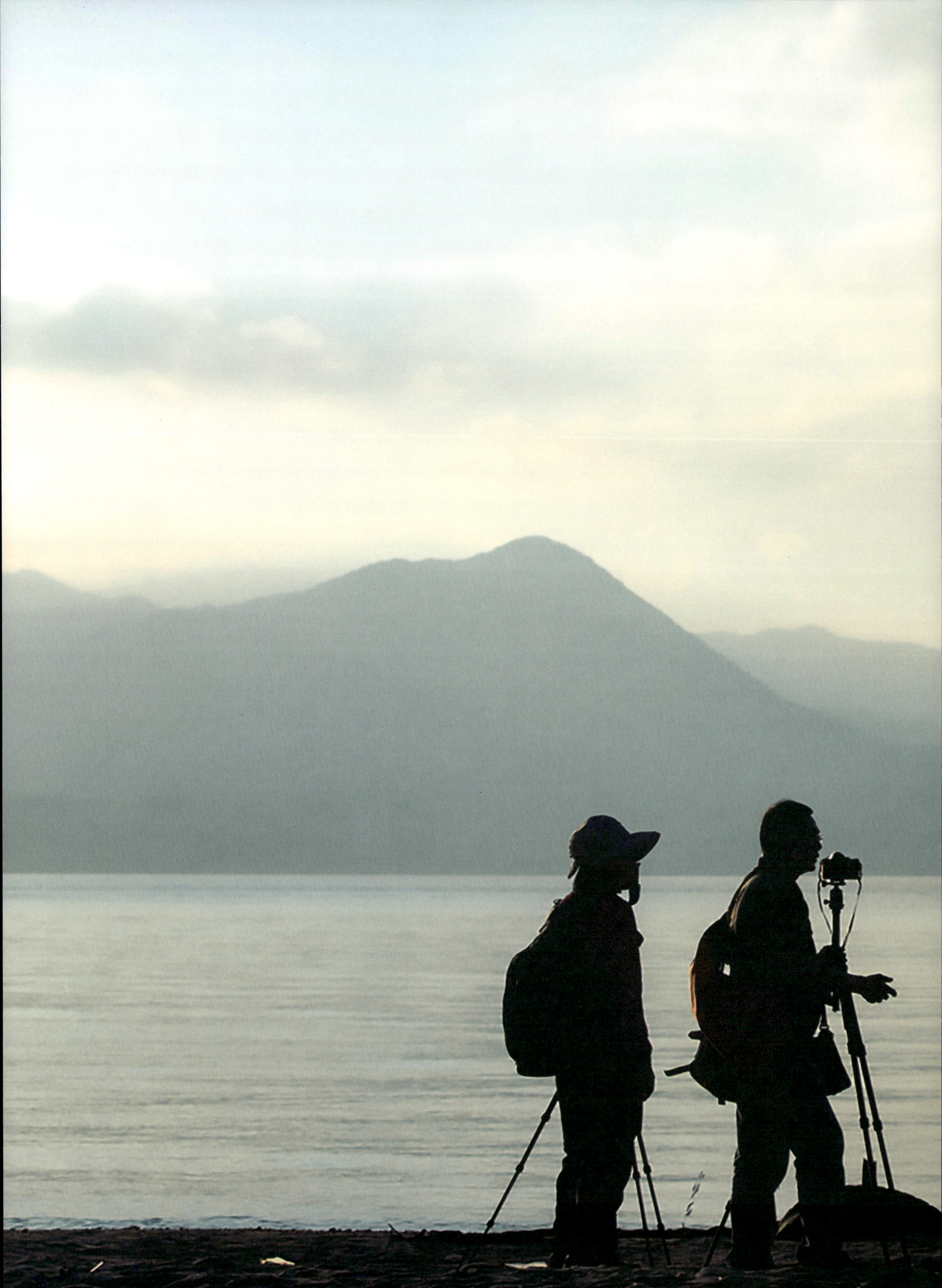

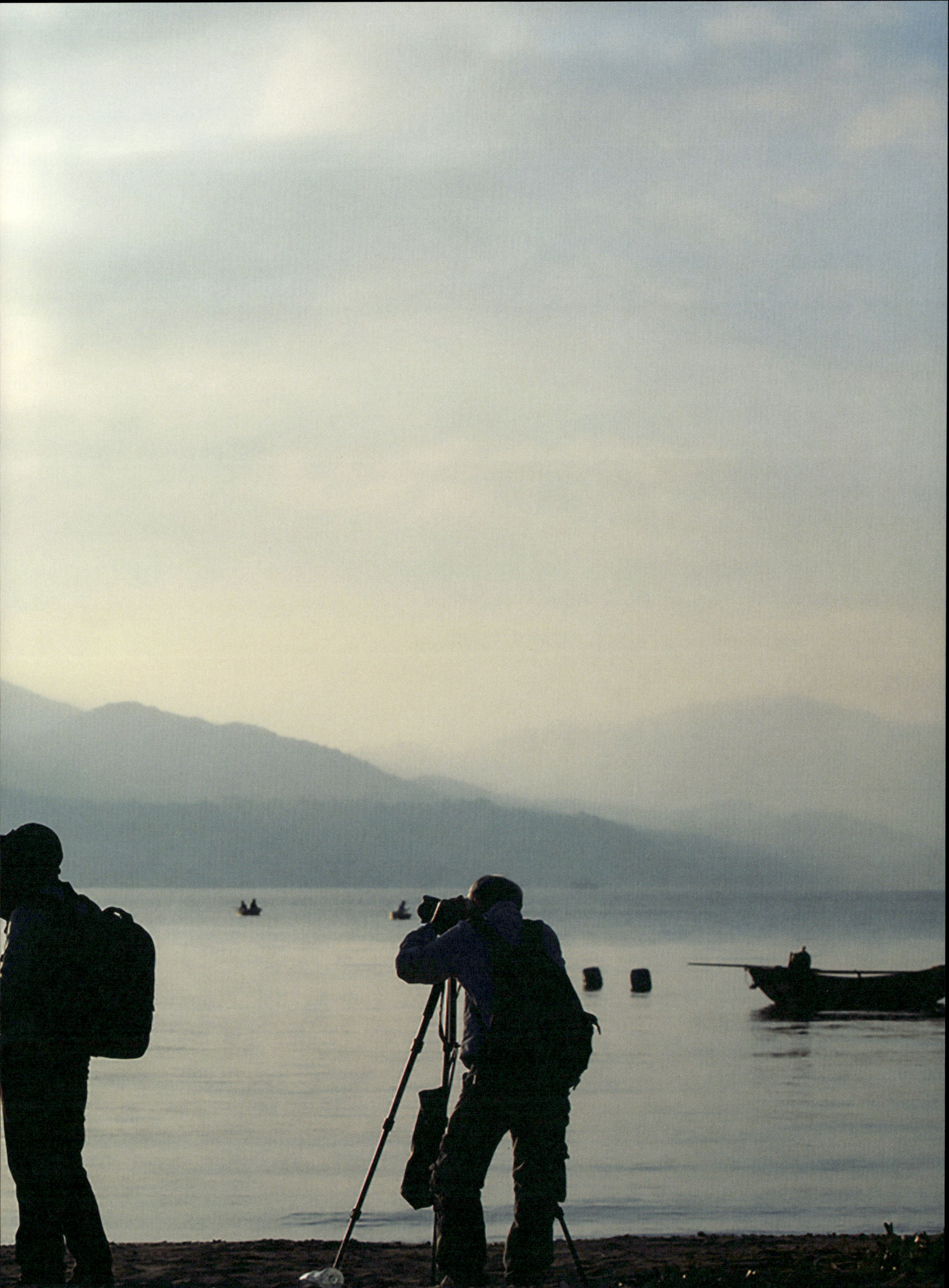

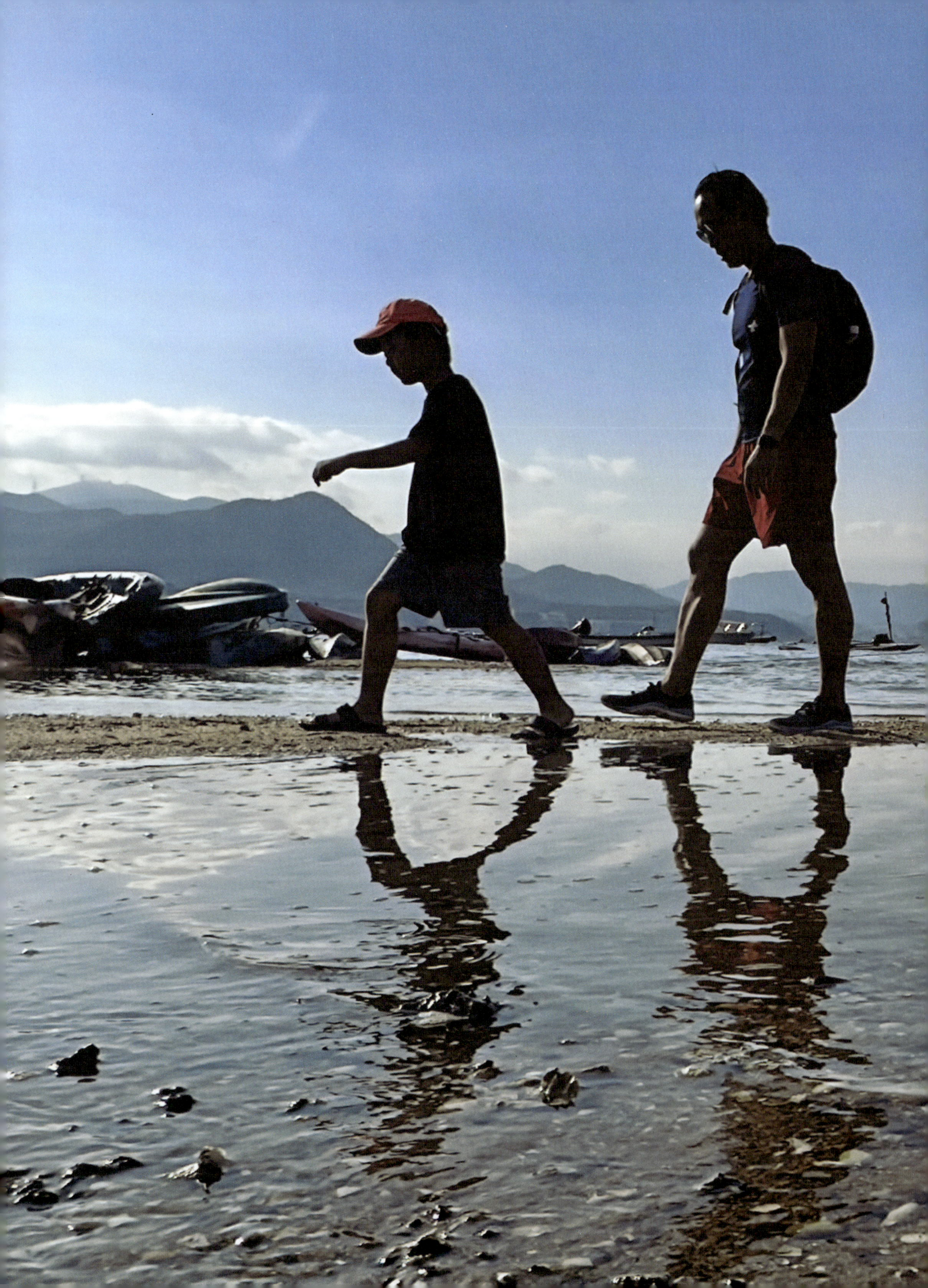

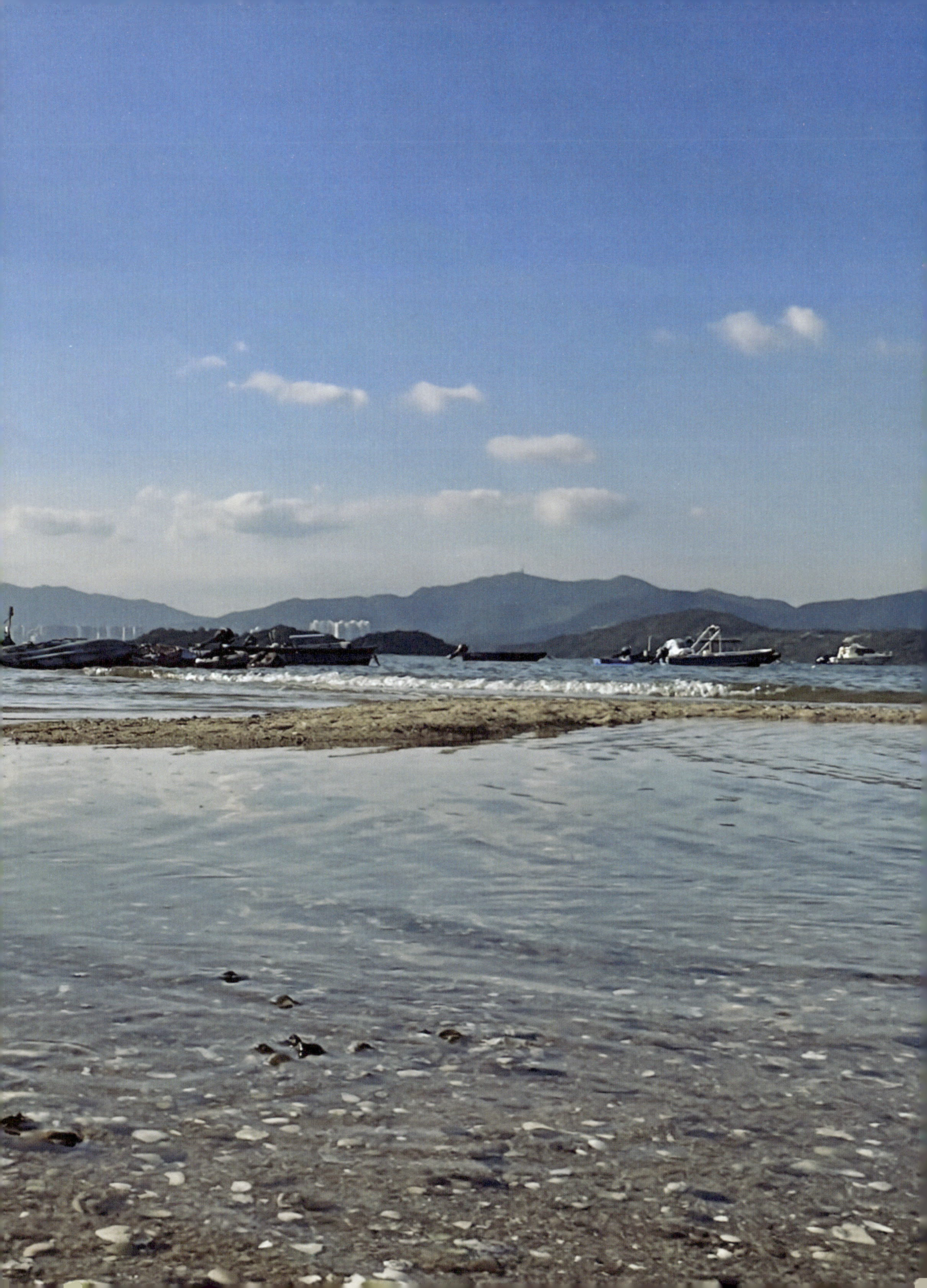

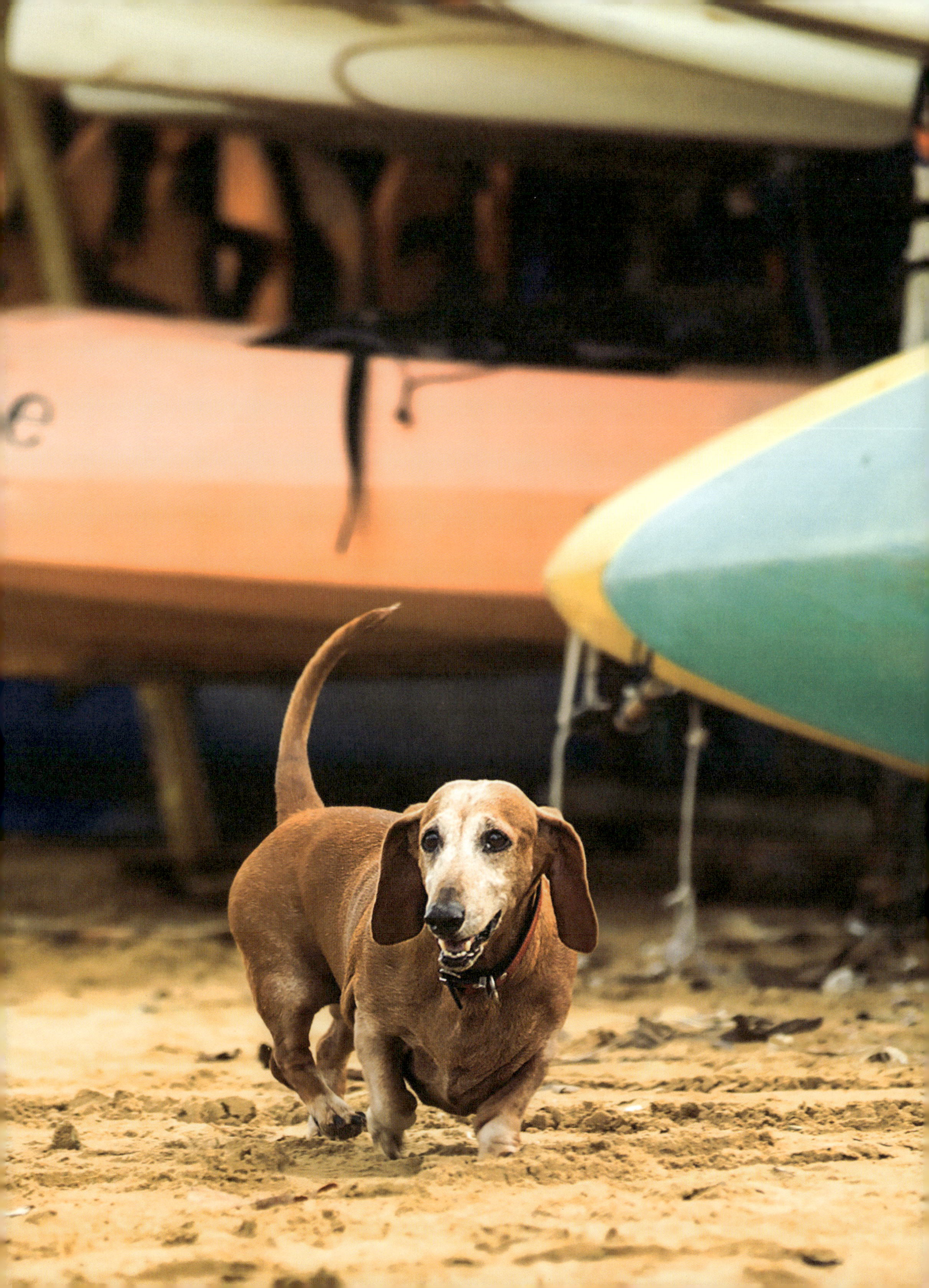

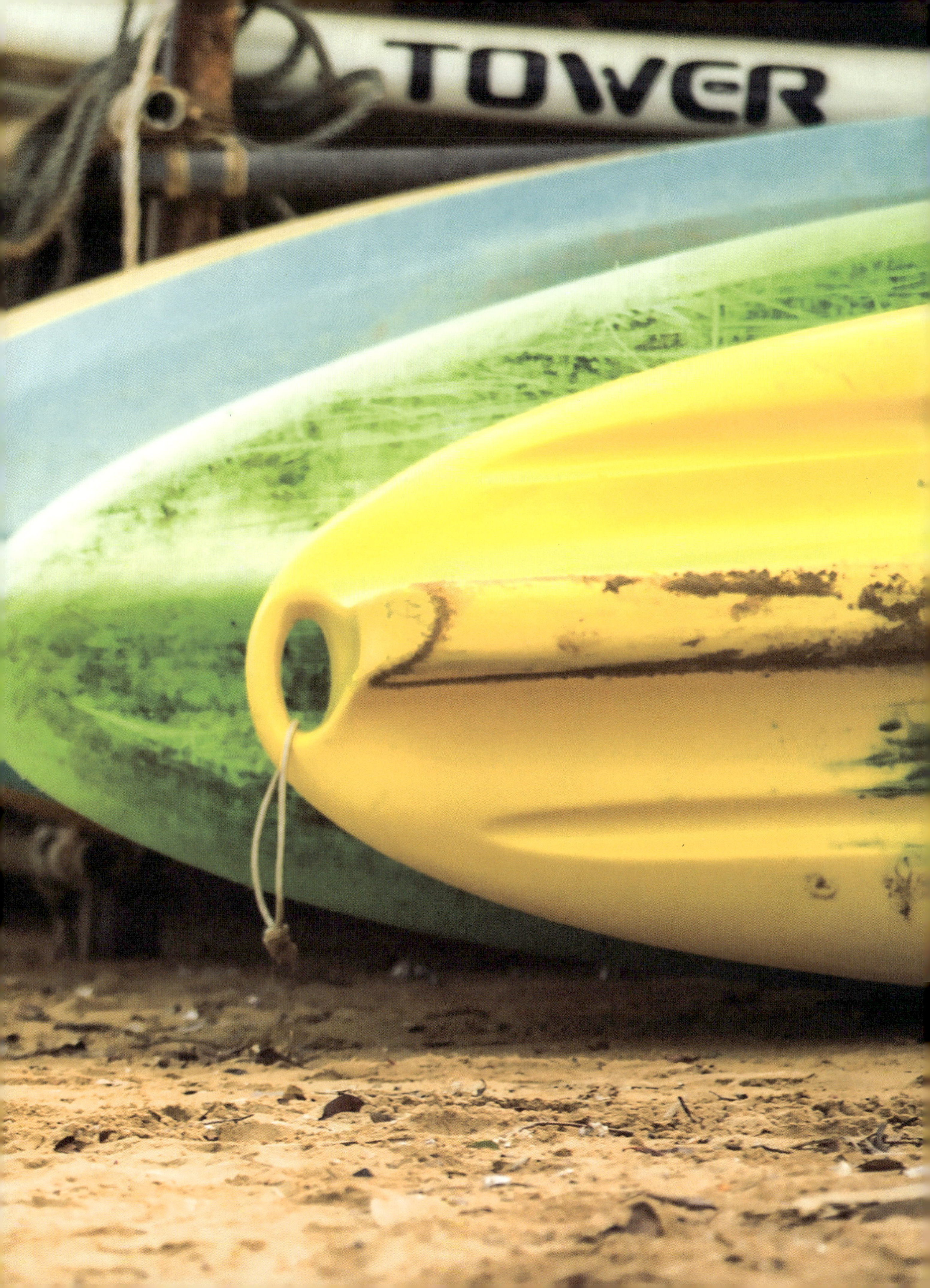
TOWER

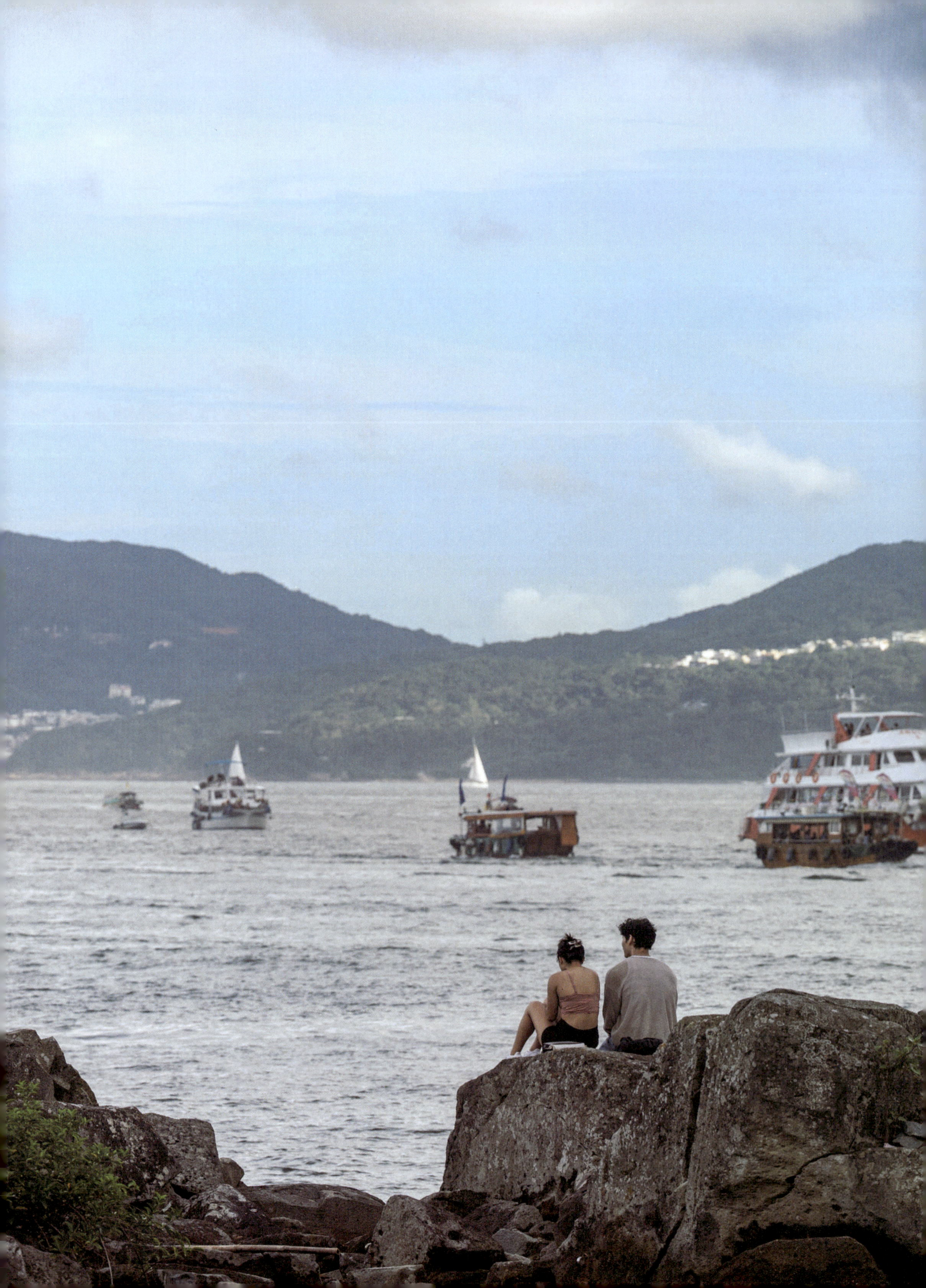

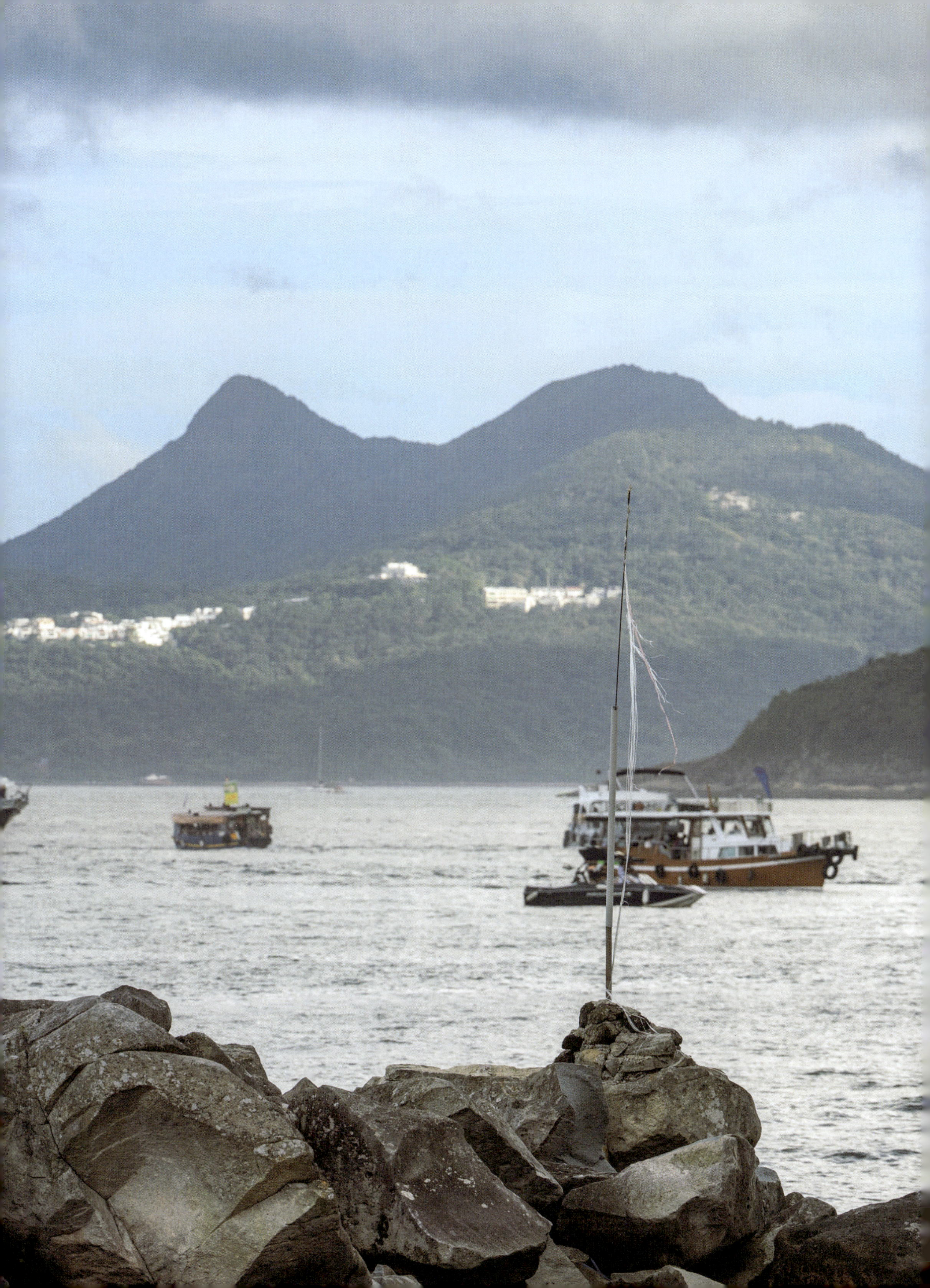

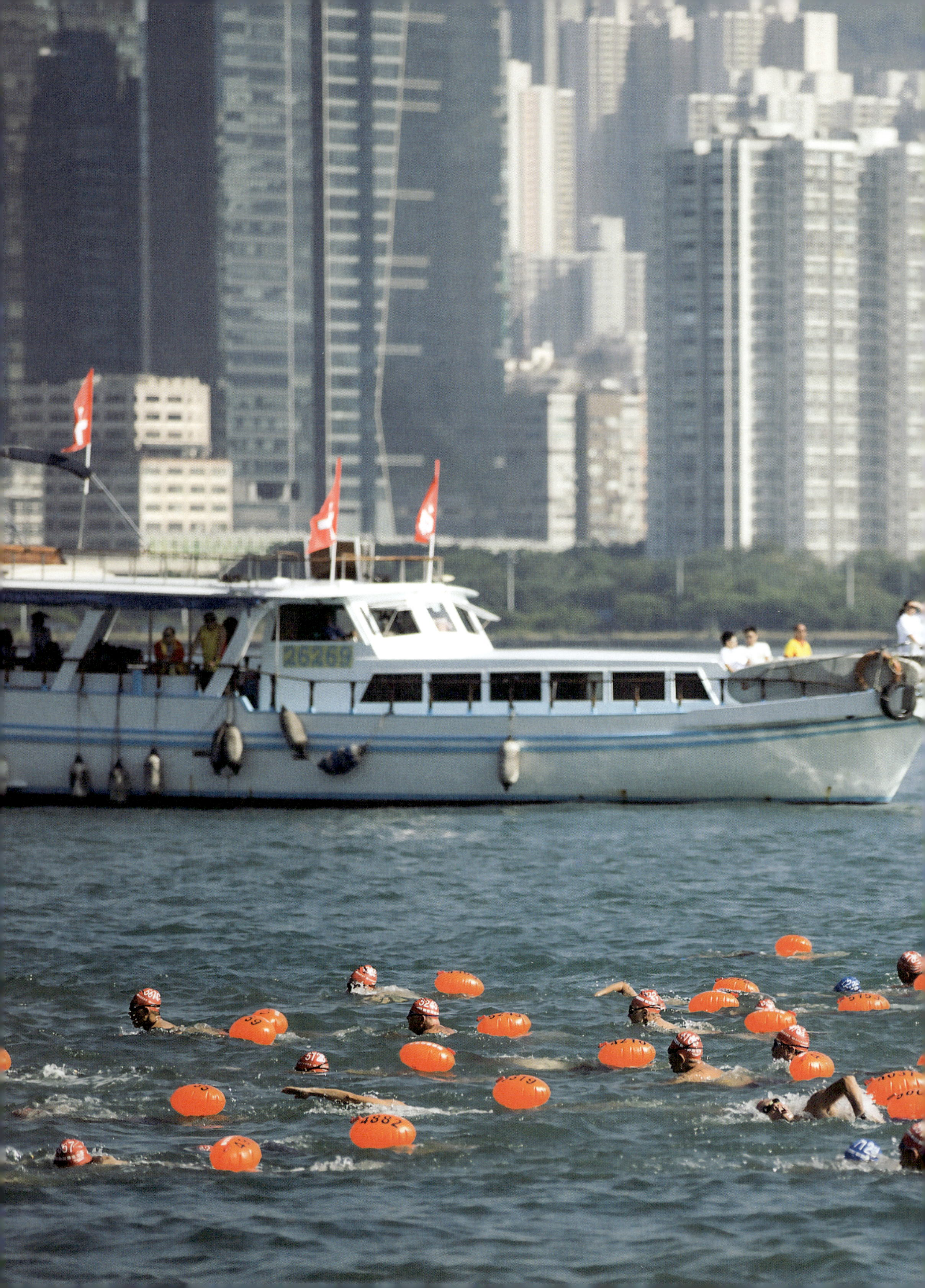

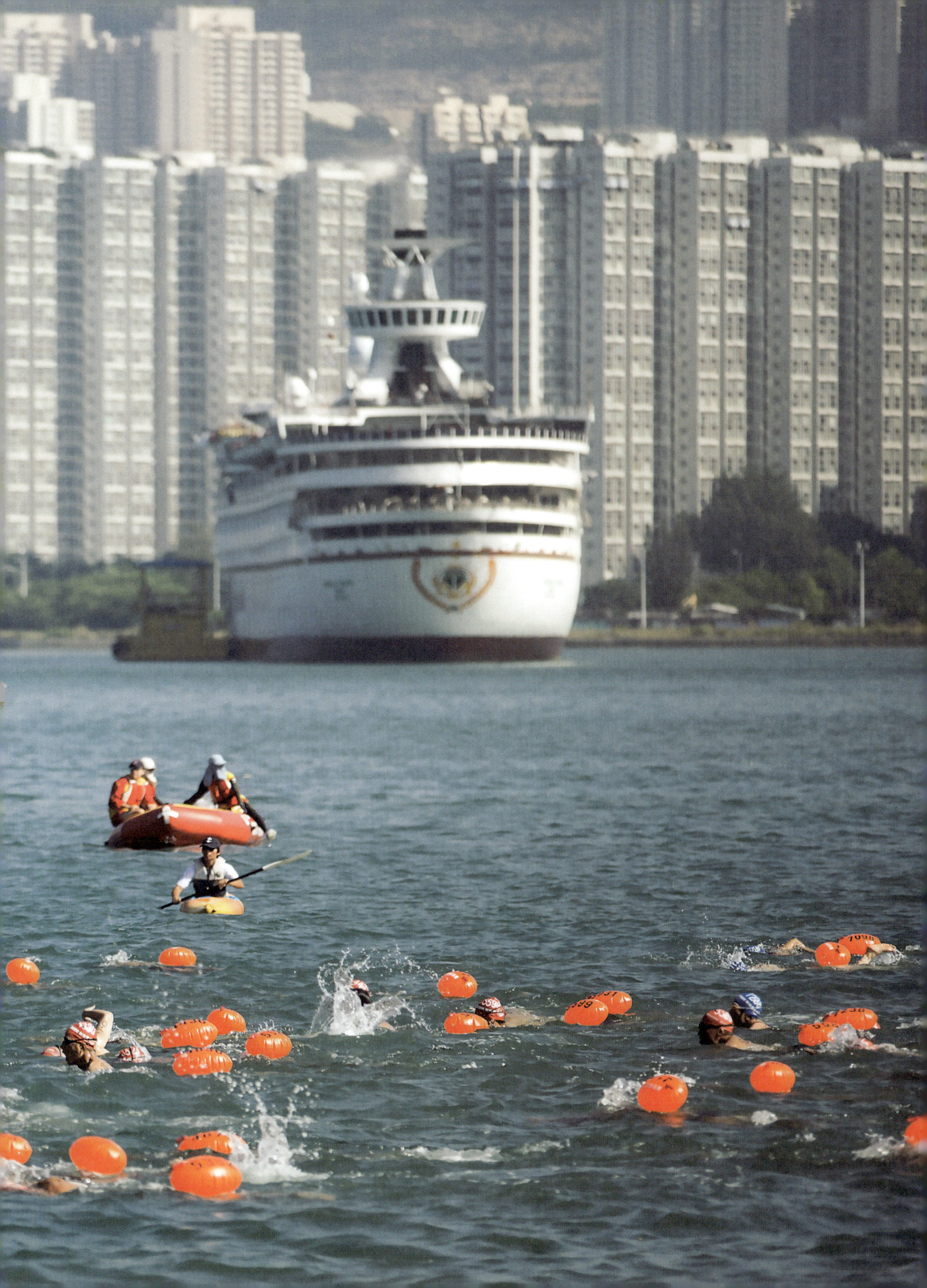

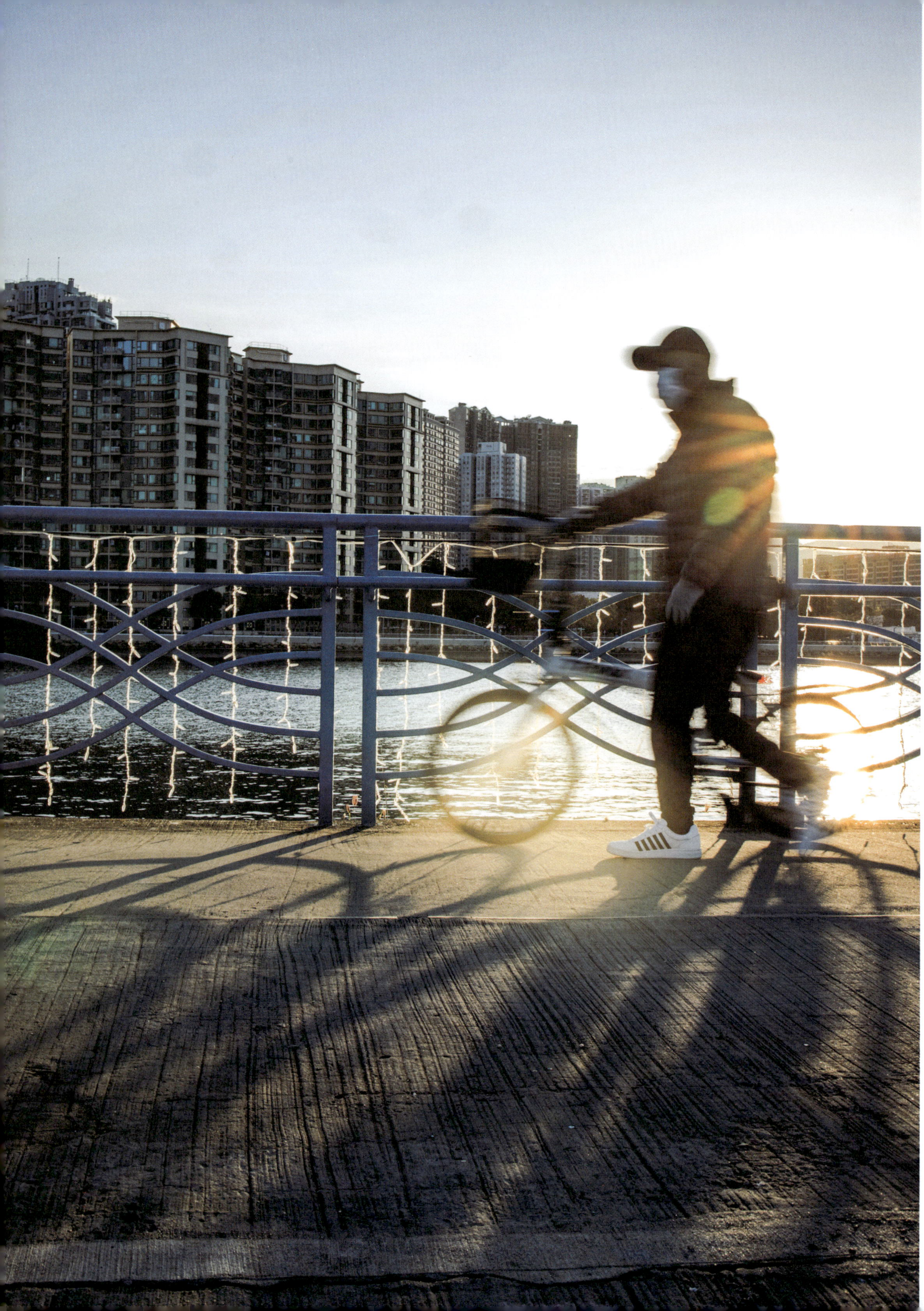

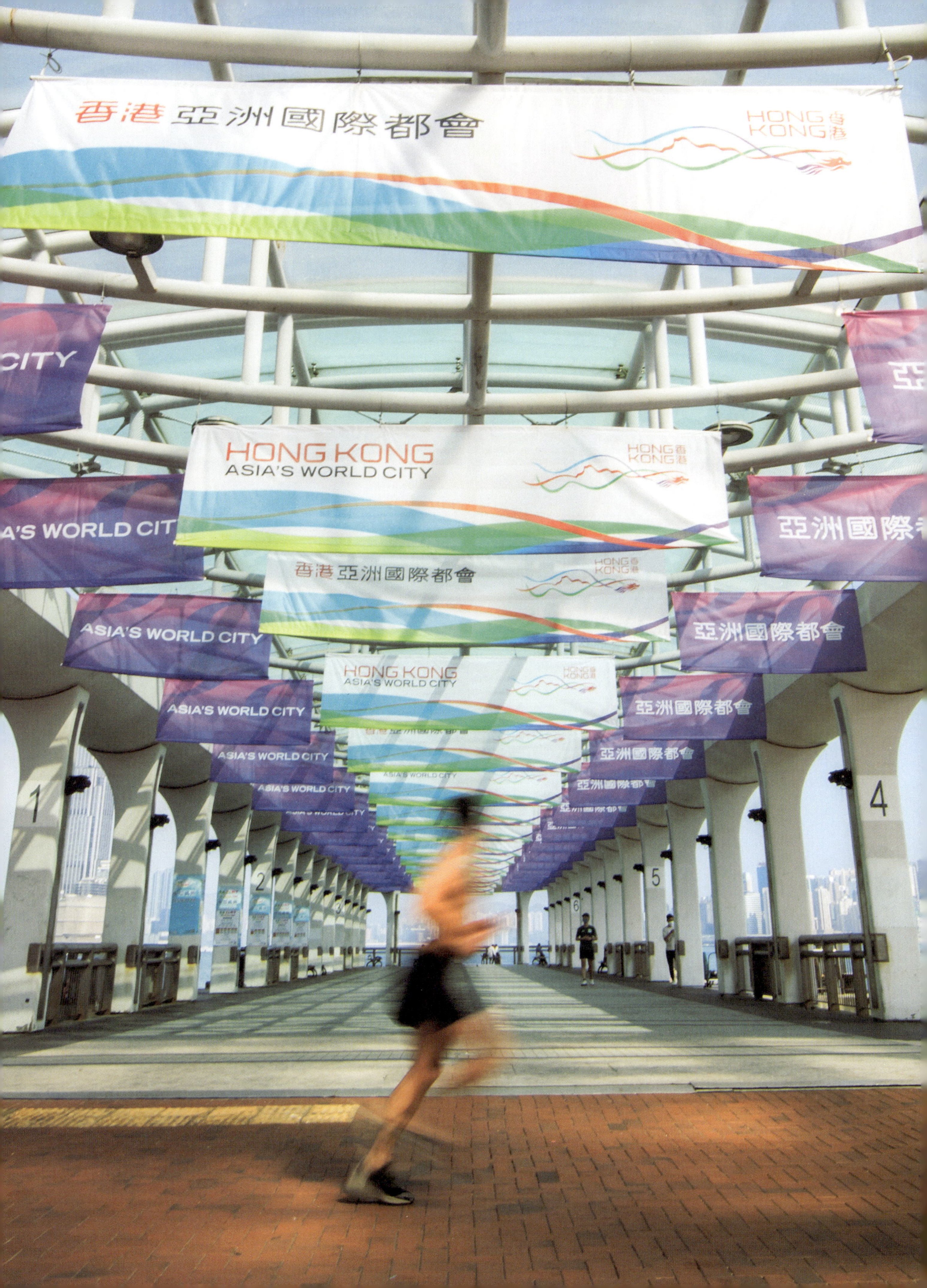
香港 亞洲國際都會
HONG KONG 香港
HONG KONG
ASIA'S WORLD CITY
ASIA'S WORLD CITY
亞洲國際都會

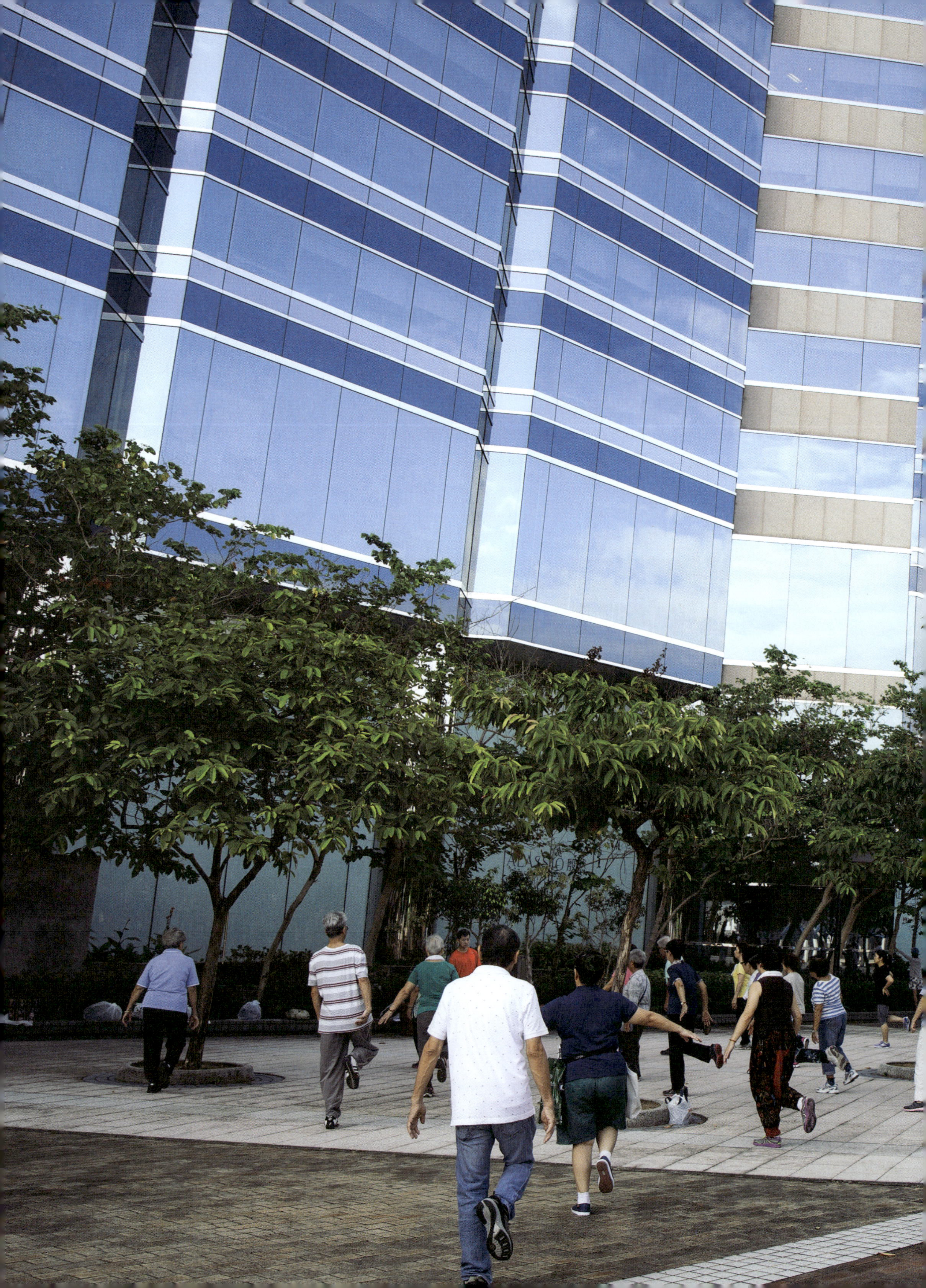

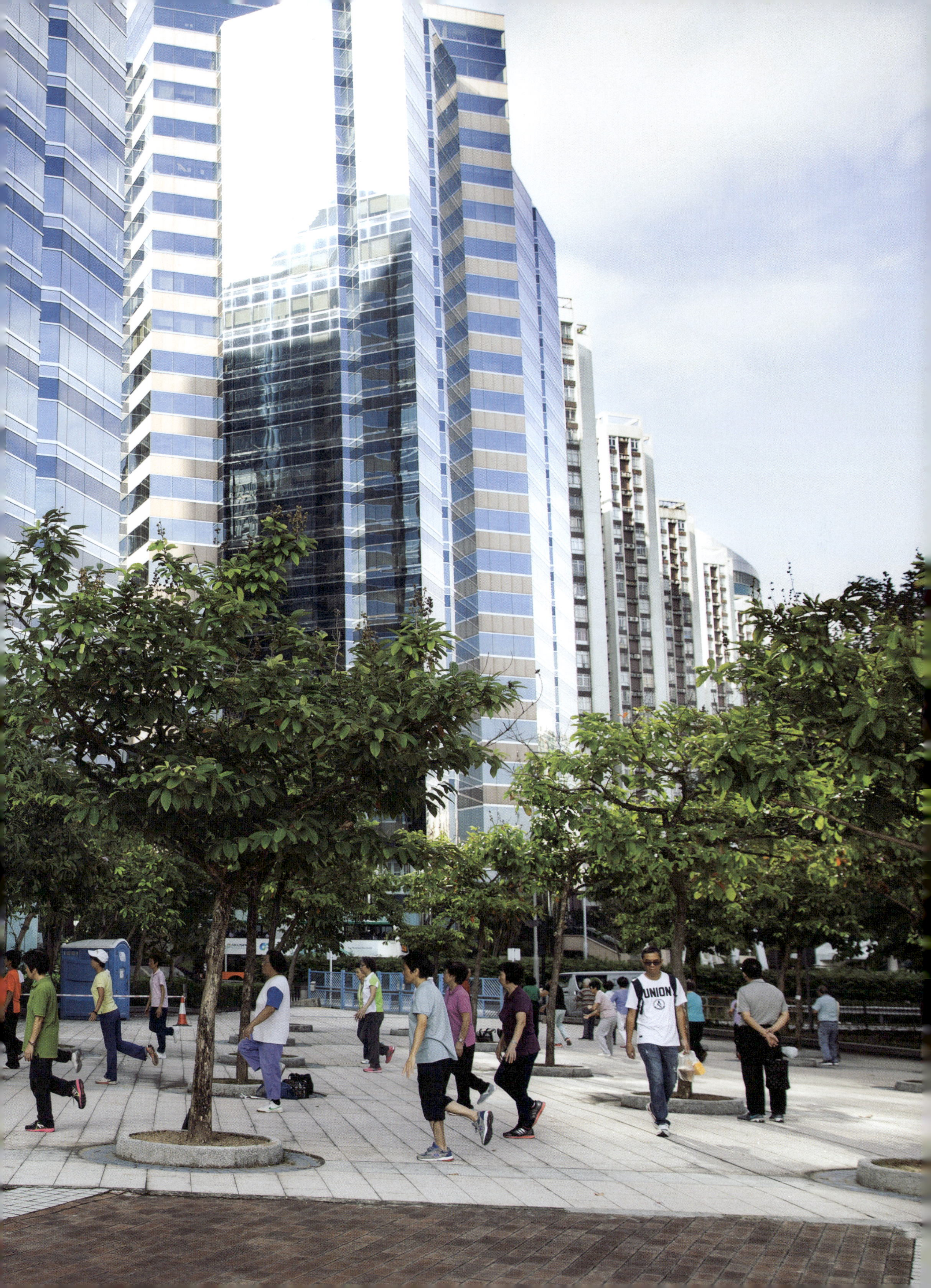
UNION

DAILY LIVING

THE RAIN

Hong Kong's climate is subtropical and monsoonal. It's cool and dry in the winter, and hot and humid during spring and summer. We typically have multiple typhoons in the summer-fall months.

When I was around six or seven years old, I remember there was a typhoon one day that came with major rainfall, but we still had to go to school. It was starting to flood in Quarry Bay, near where we lived, and my mom ended up having to piggyback me across the flooded roads all the way to school.

Nowadays, the streets are often quickly drained, public transportation is still available, and shops are still open until Typhoon 8 (one of the highest typhoon signals) or above hits our city, allowing Hong Kong to be operational even during inclement weather conditions. That is, unless a once-in-a-lifetime storm takes us by surprise — which seems to be happening much more frequently than once in a lifetime these days.

34. View from a footbridge in Causeway Bay
35. Another view from a footbridge in Causeway Bay
36. Taxi in Wu Kai Sha
37. Motorcycle in Sheung Wan

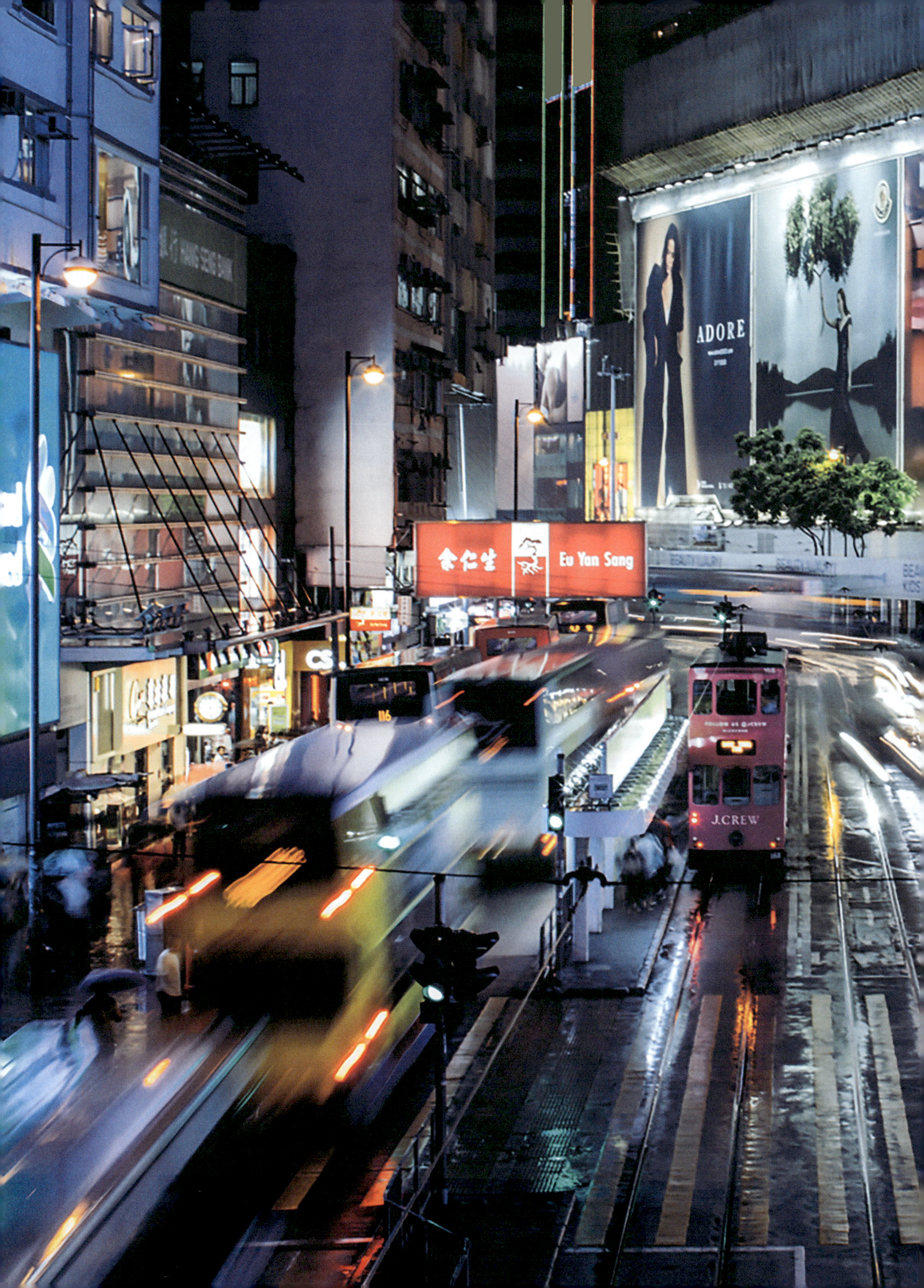
ADORE
余仁生
Eu Yan Sang
116
J.CREW

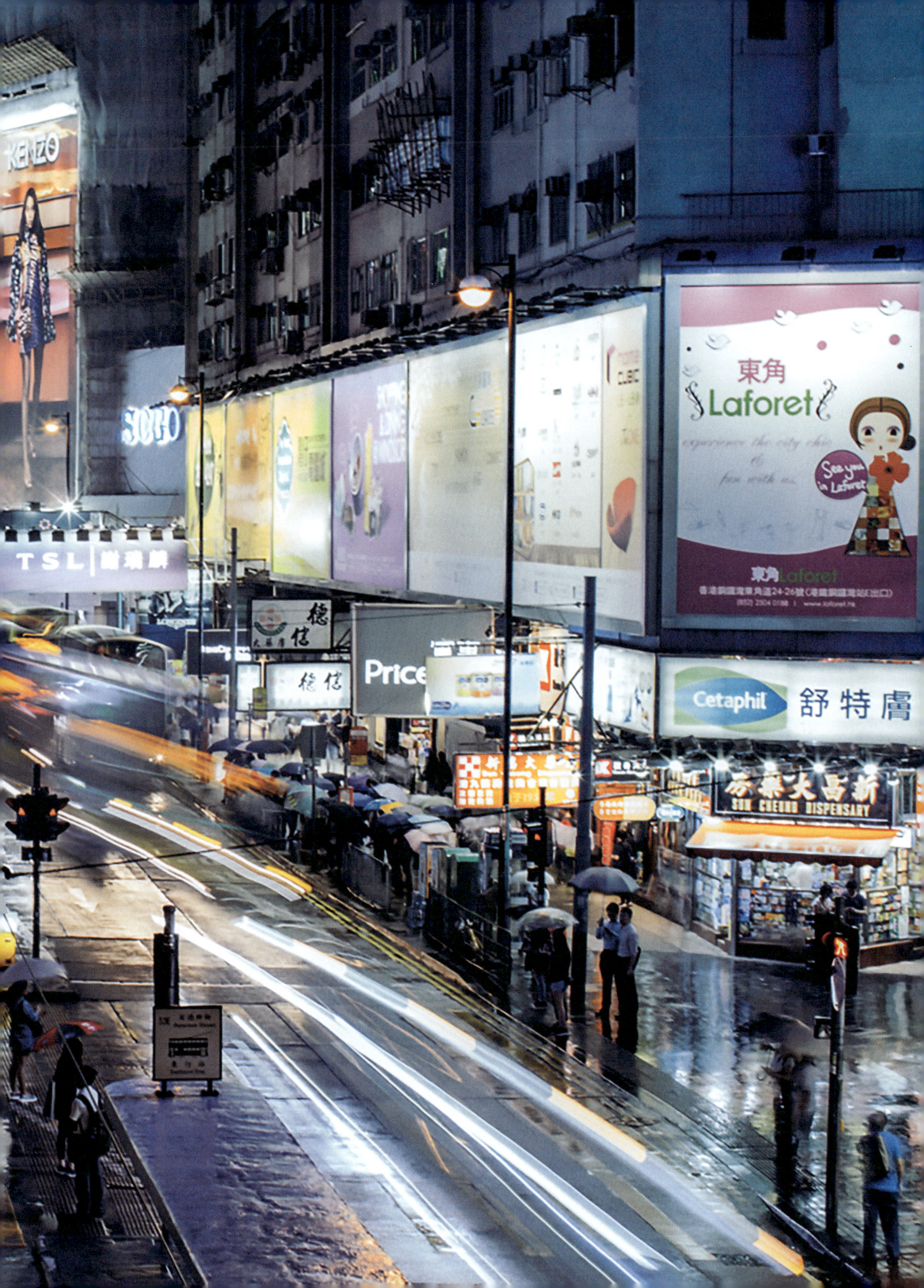
KENZO
SOGO
TSL 謝瑞麟
東角
Laforet
東角Laforet
Price
Cetaphil
舒特膚
新昌大藥房
SUN CHEONG DISPENSARY

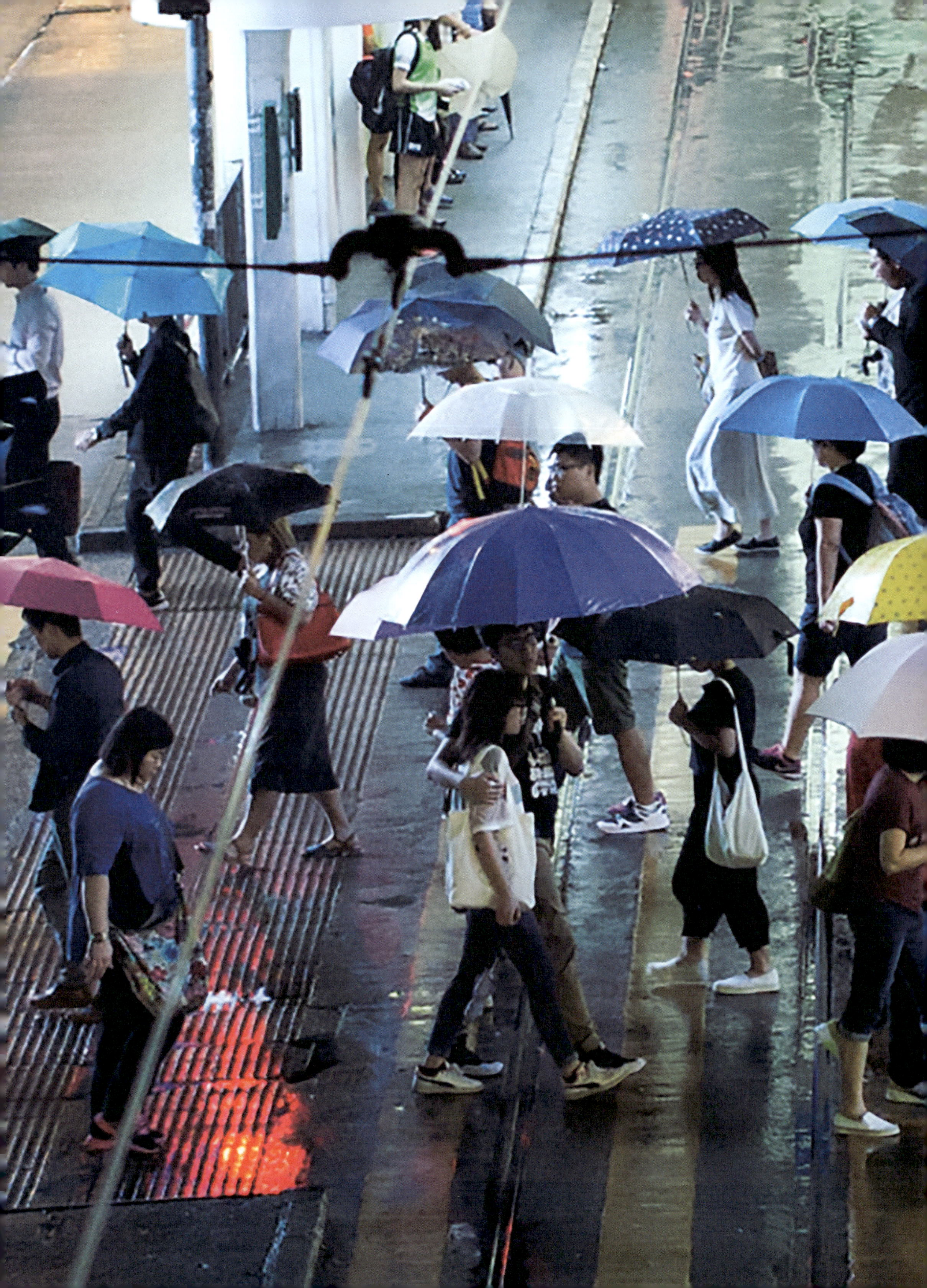

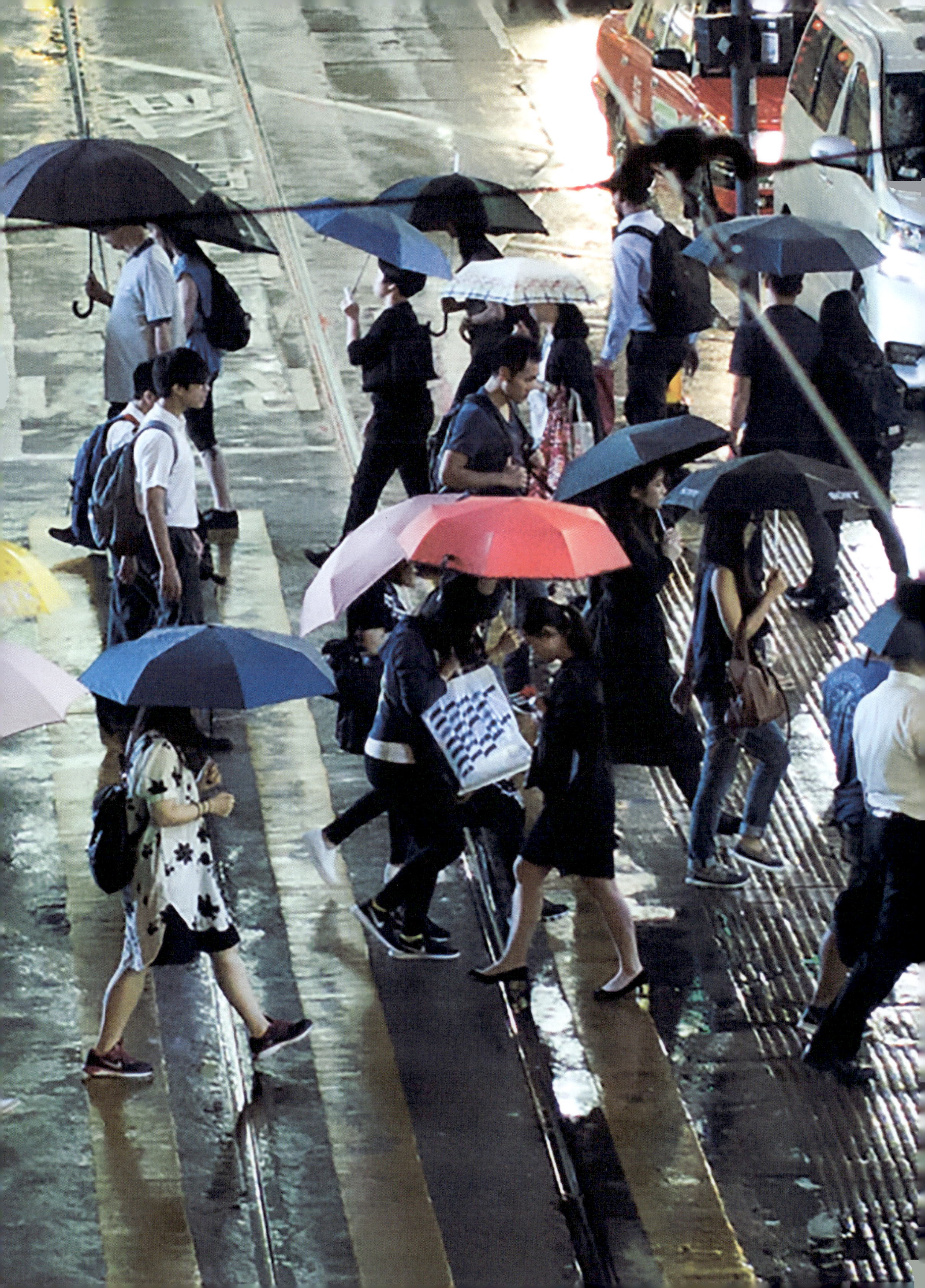

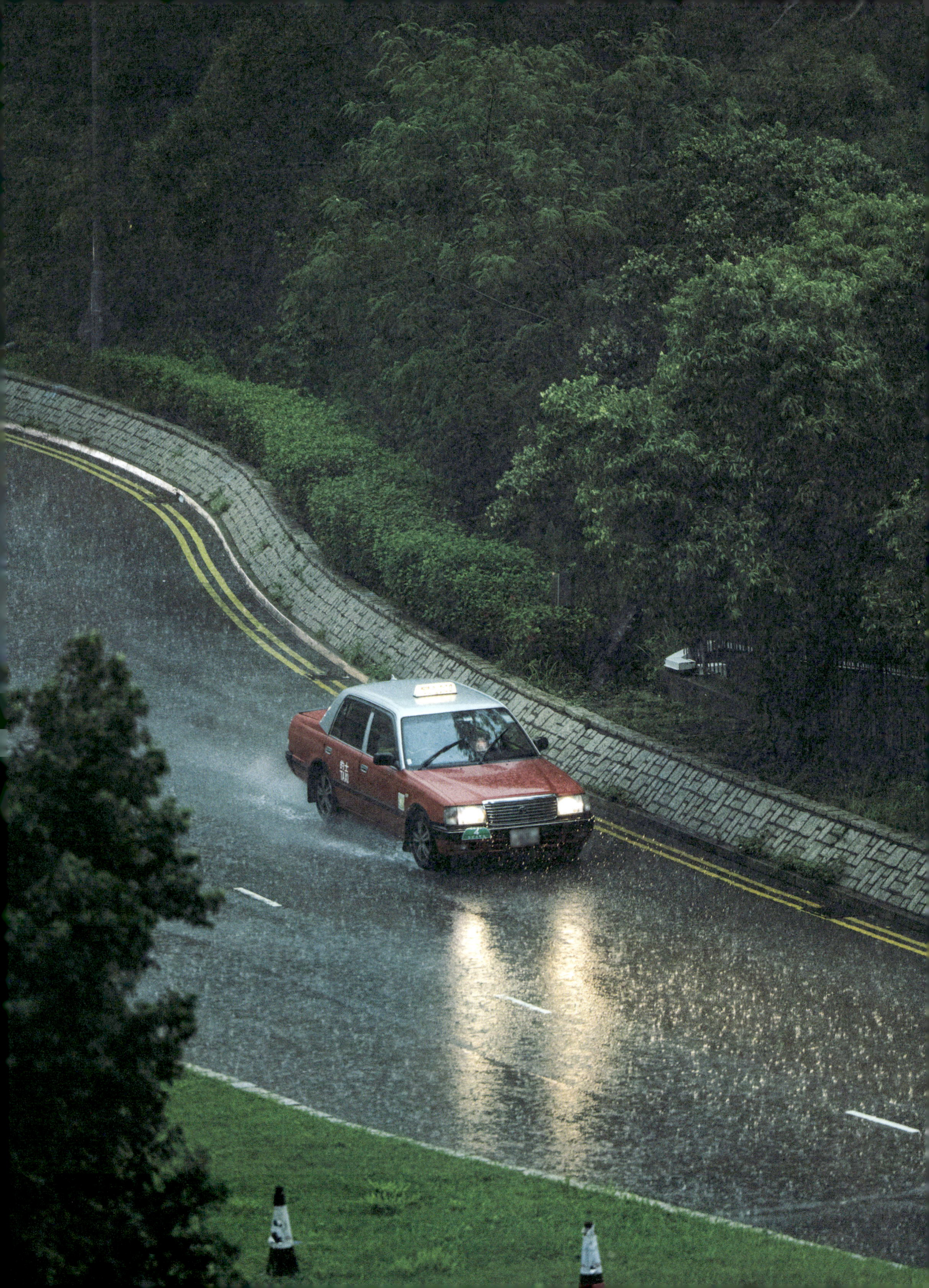

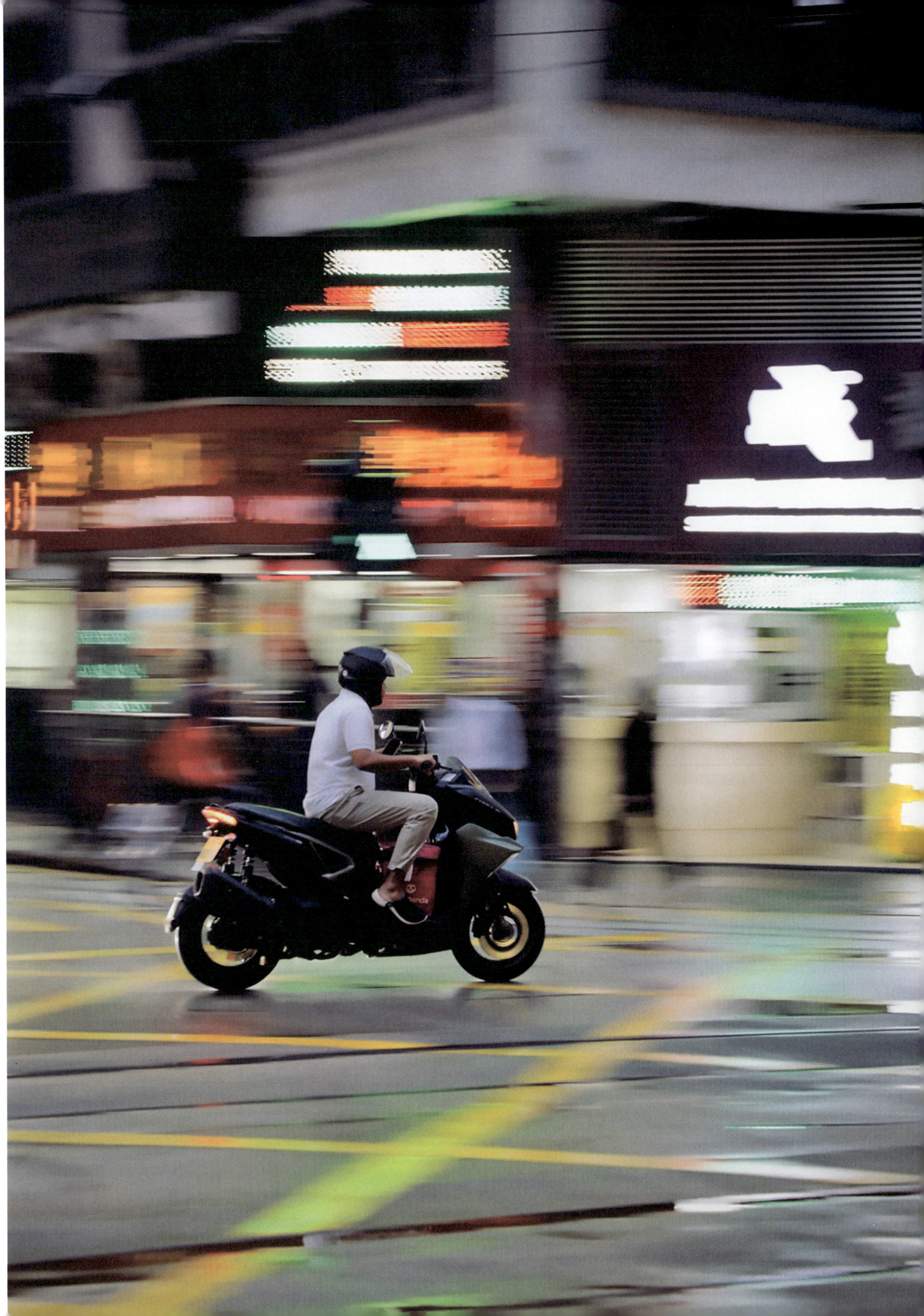

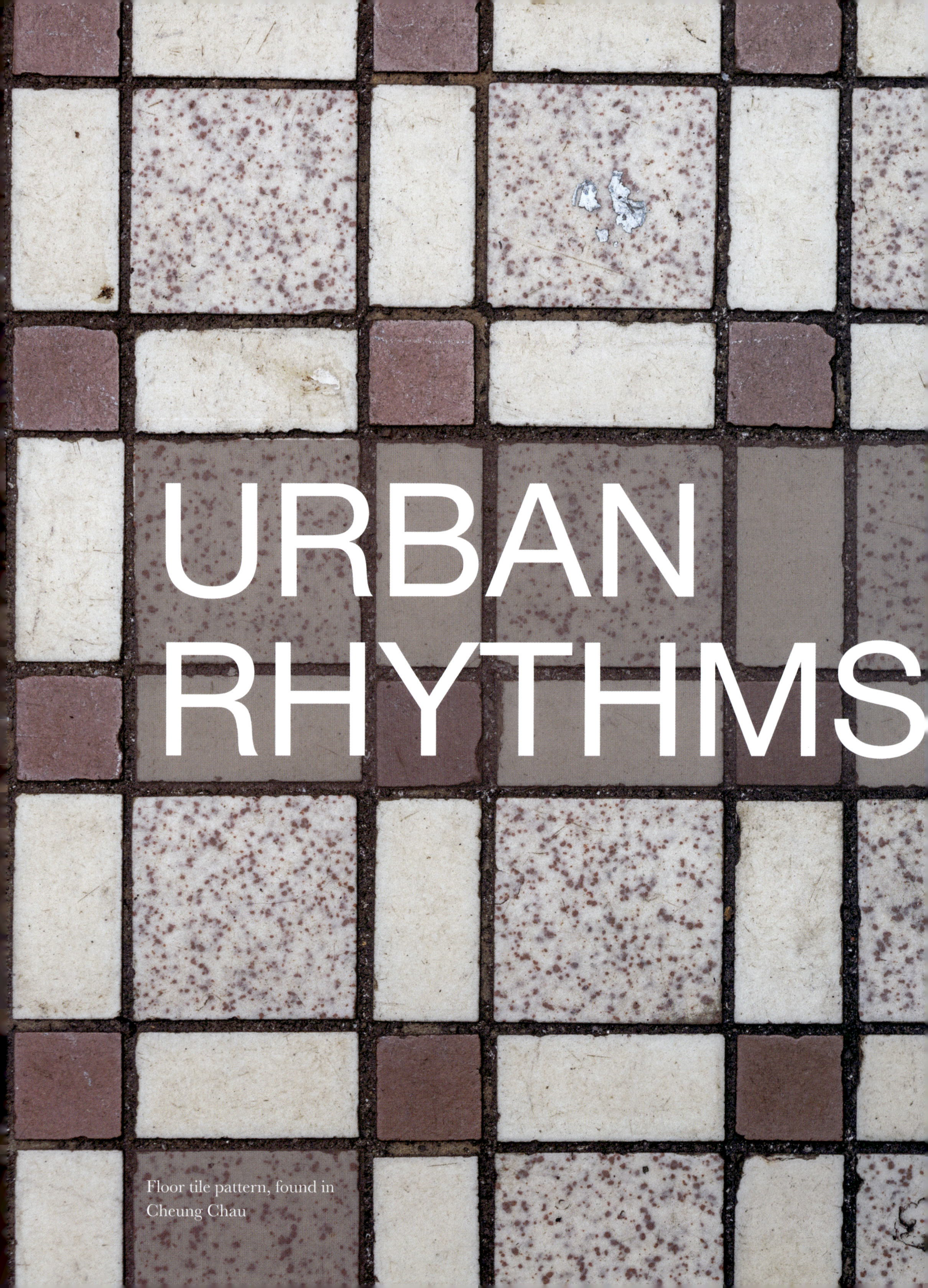

URBAN RHYTHMS

Floor tile pattern, found in Cheung Chau

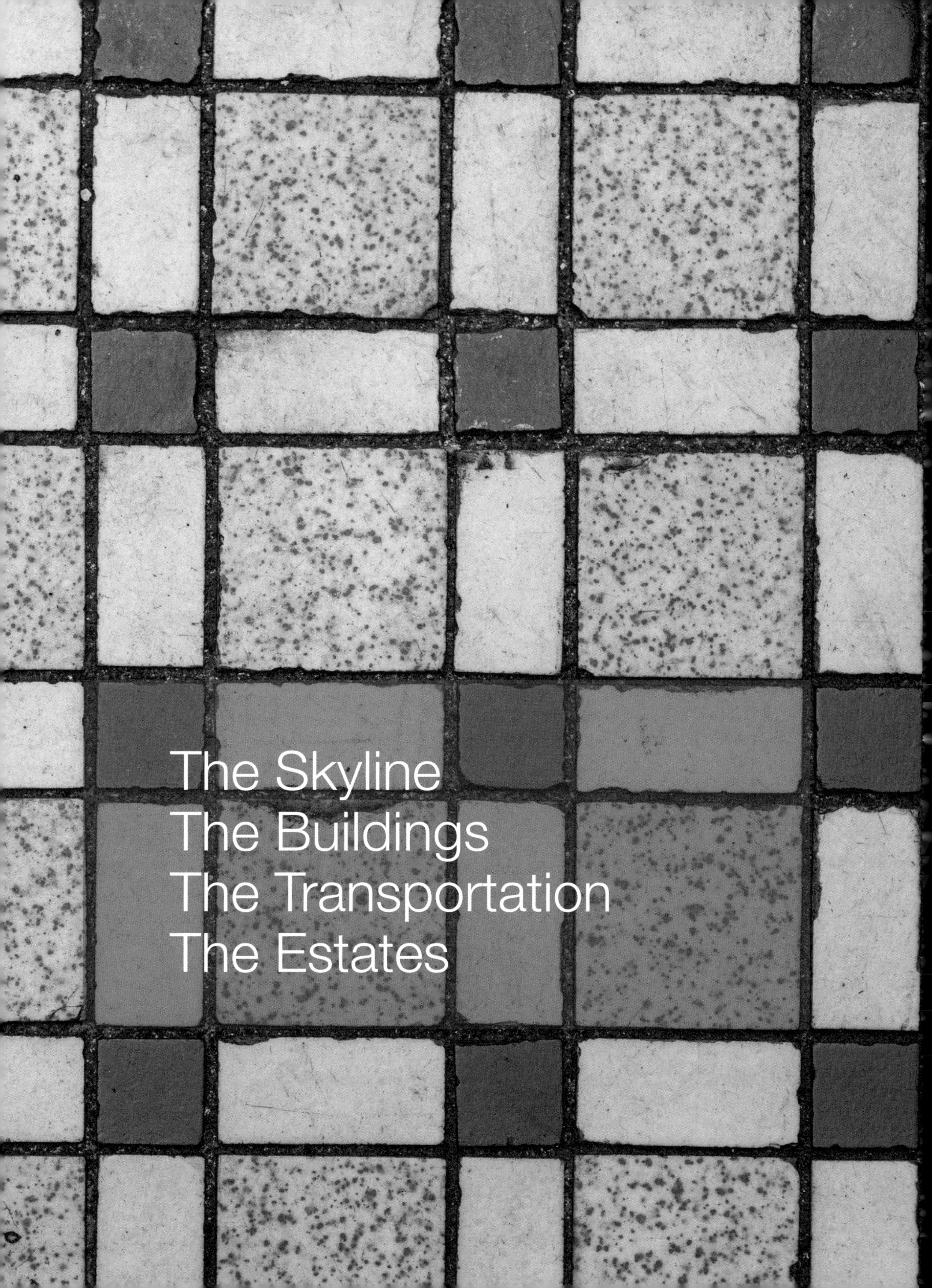

The Skyline
The Buildings
The Transportation
The Estates

URBAN RHYTHMS

THE SKYLINE

Hong Kong is mostly known for its iconic skyline, shimmering against the equally dazzling Victoria Harbour. Over the years, I have taken a lot of images of the city's busy silhouette during different times of the day and under different weather conditions.

The night view is stunning, with the whole city lit up and the reflections of buildings bouncing off the waters. I've even had the pleasure of taking aerial images of Hong Kong on a few helicopter rides, getting to really see the city from a bird's eye perspective.

38. View from The Peak

39. View of Hong Kong Island

40. Aerial view of Victoria Harbour

41. Another aerial view of Victoria Harbour

42. Night view of Hong Kong Island

43. Lion Rock in the distance

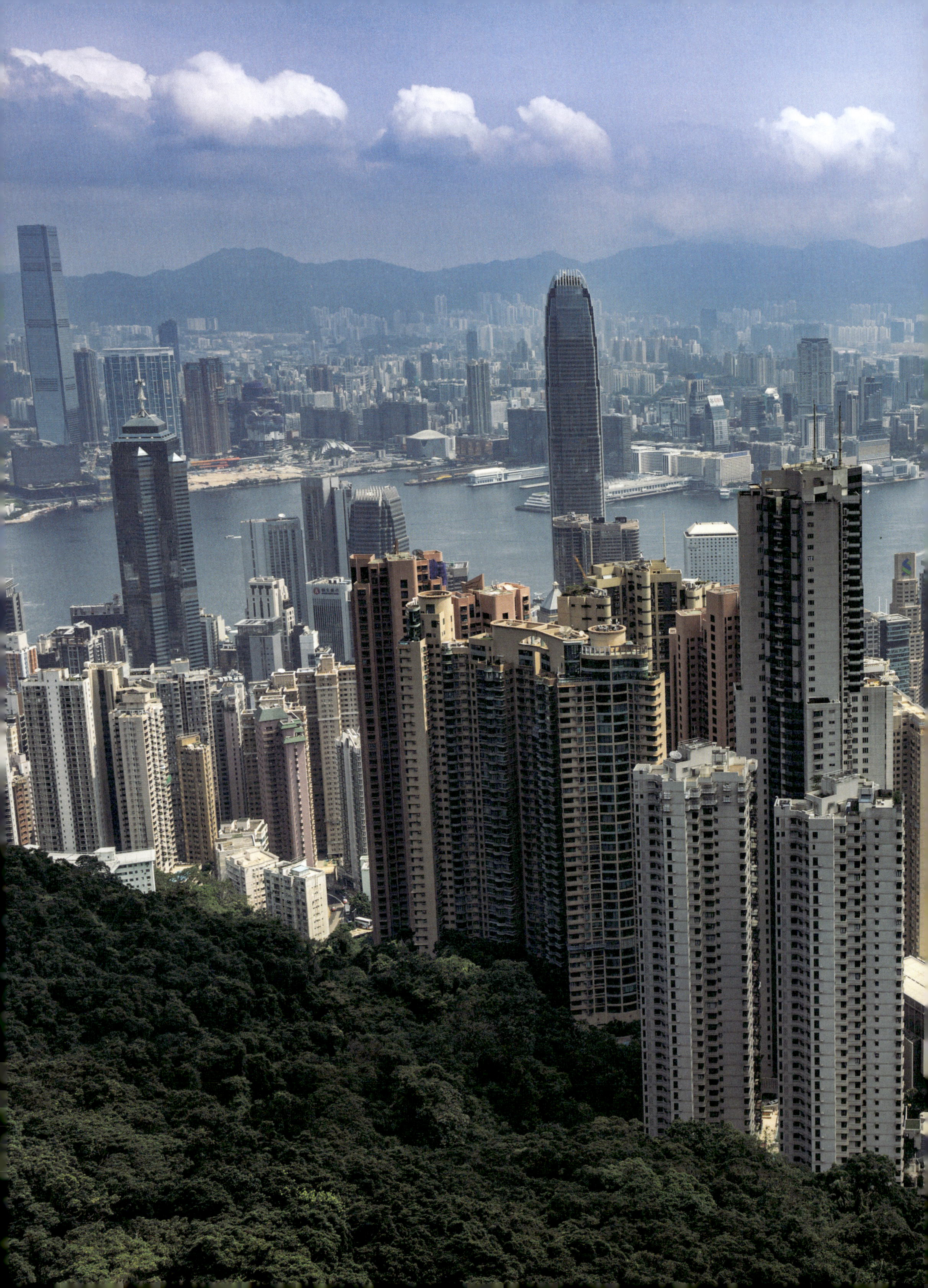

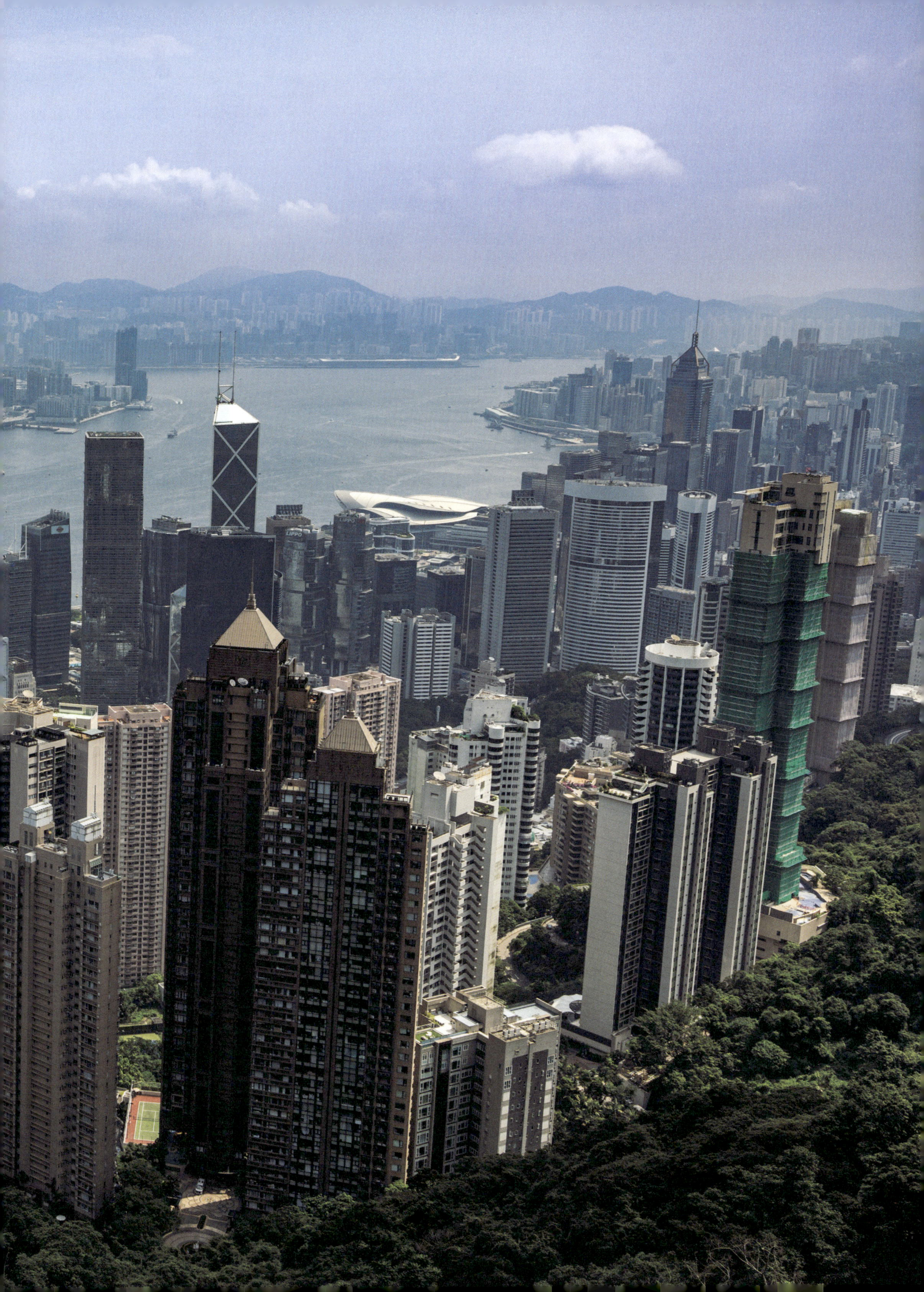

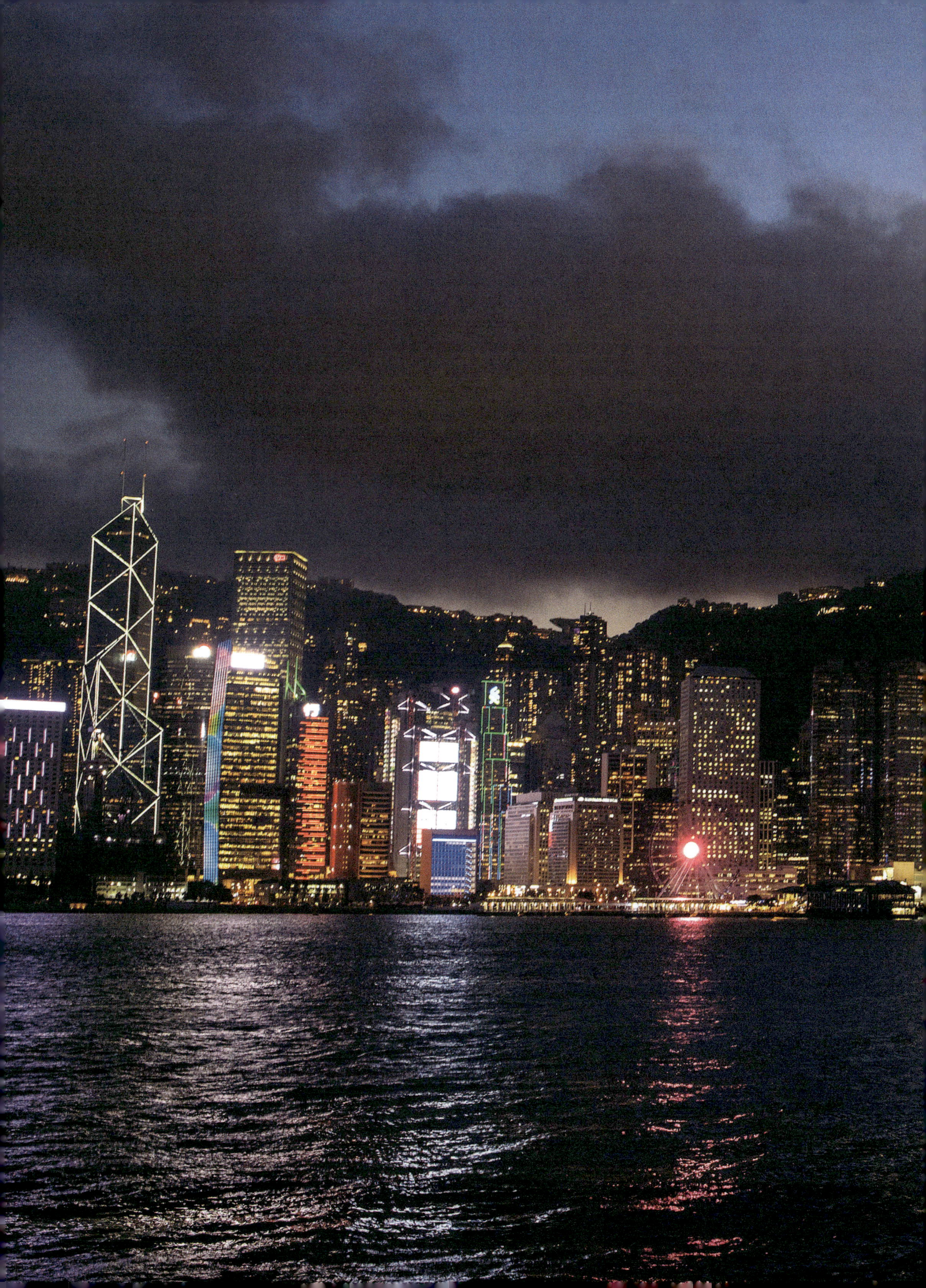

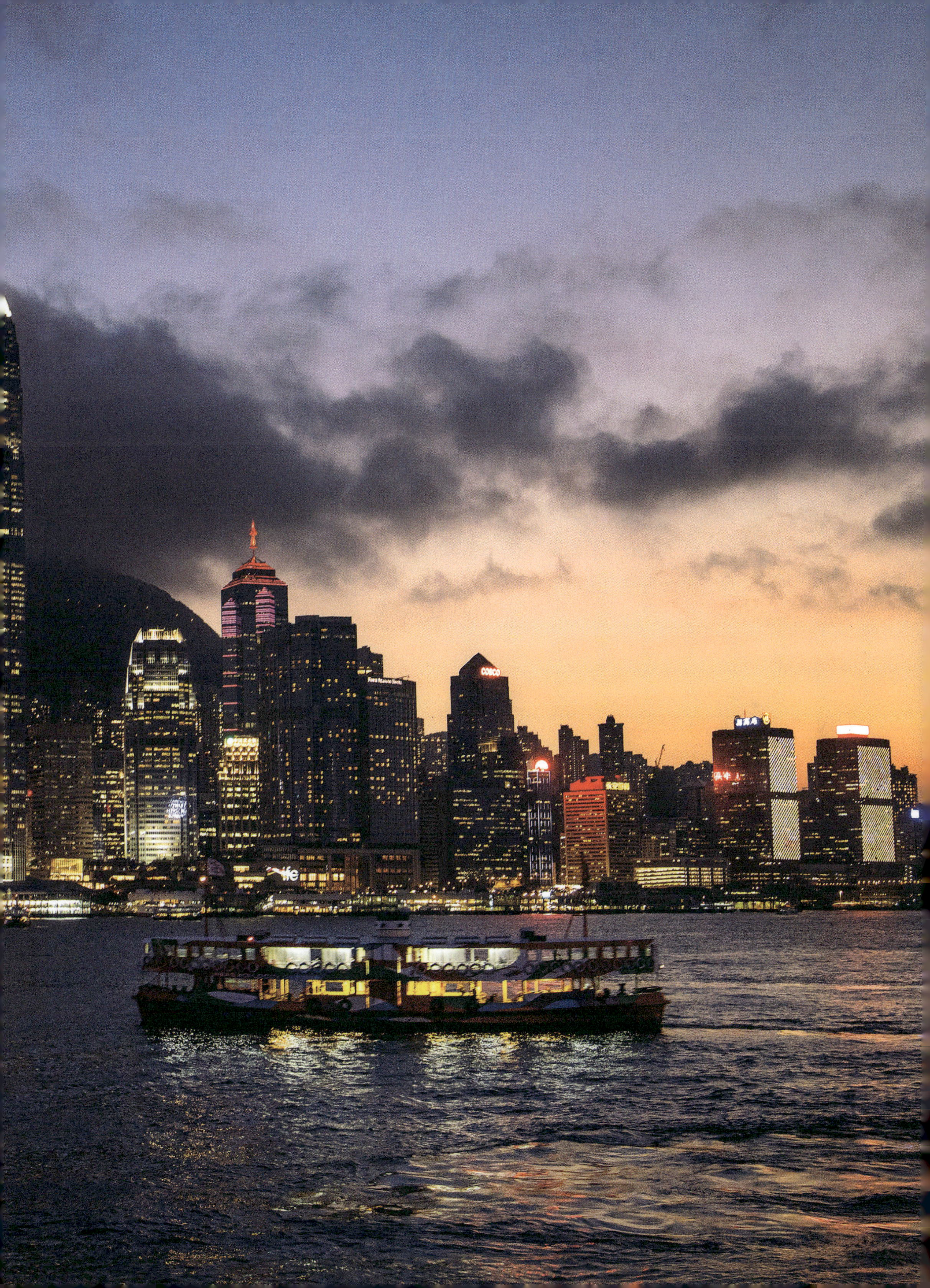
COSCO

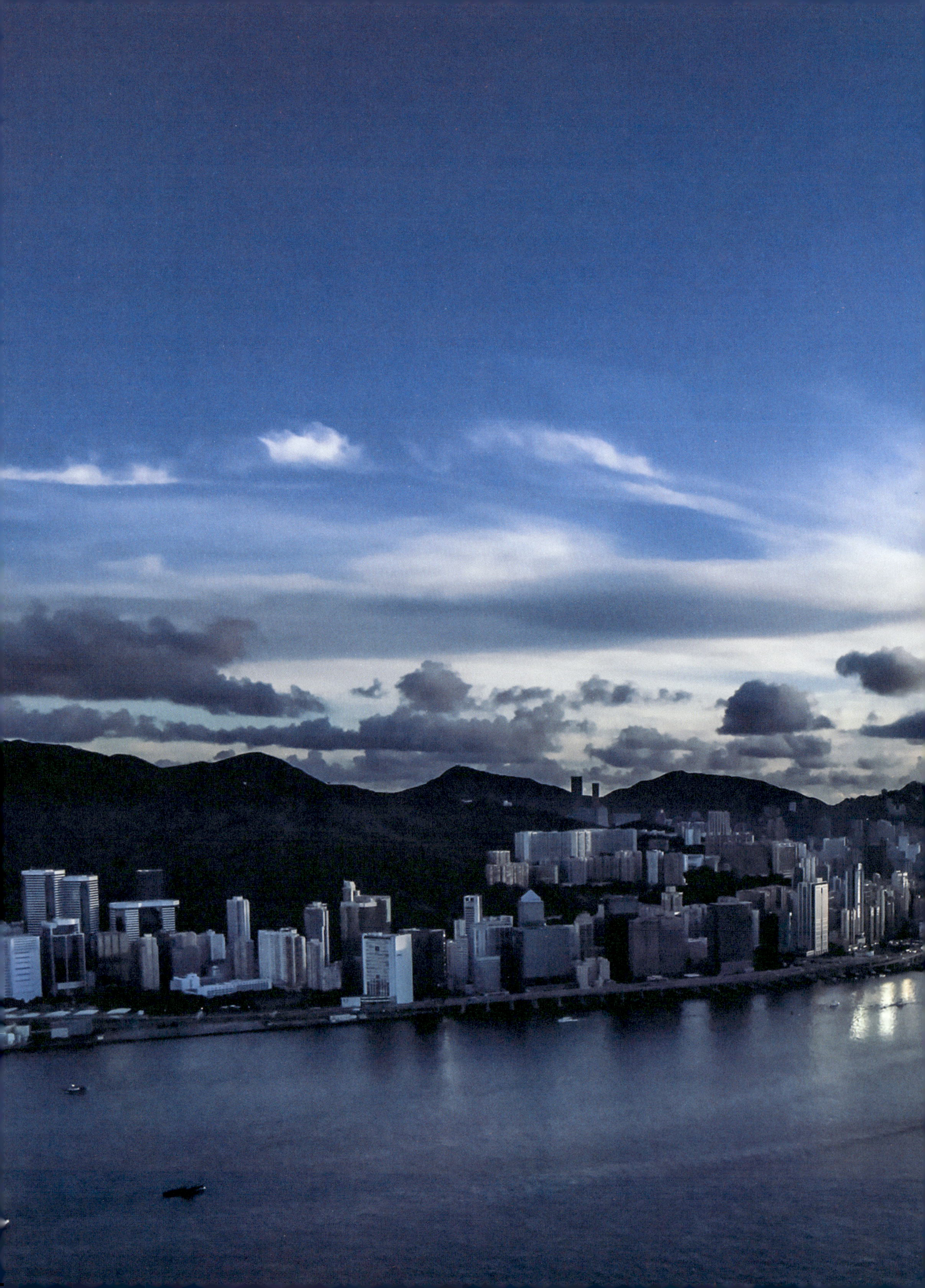

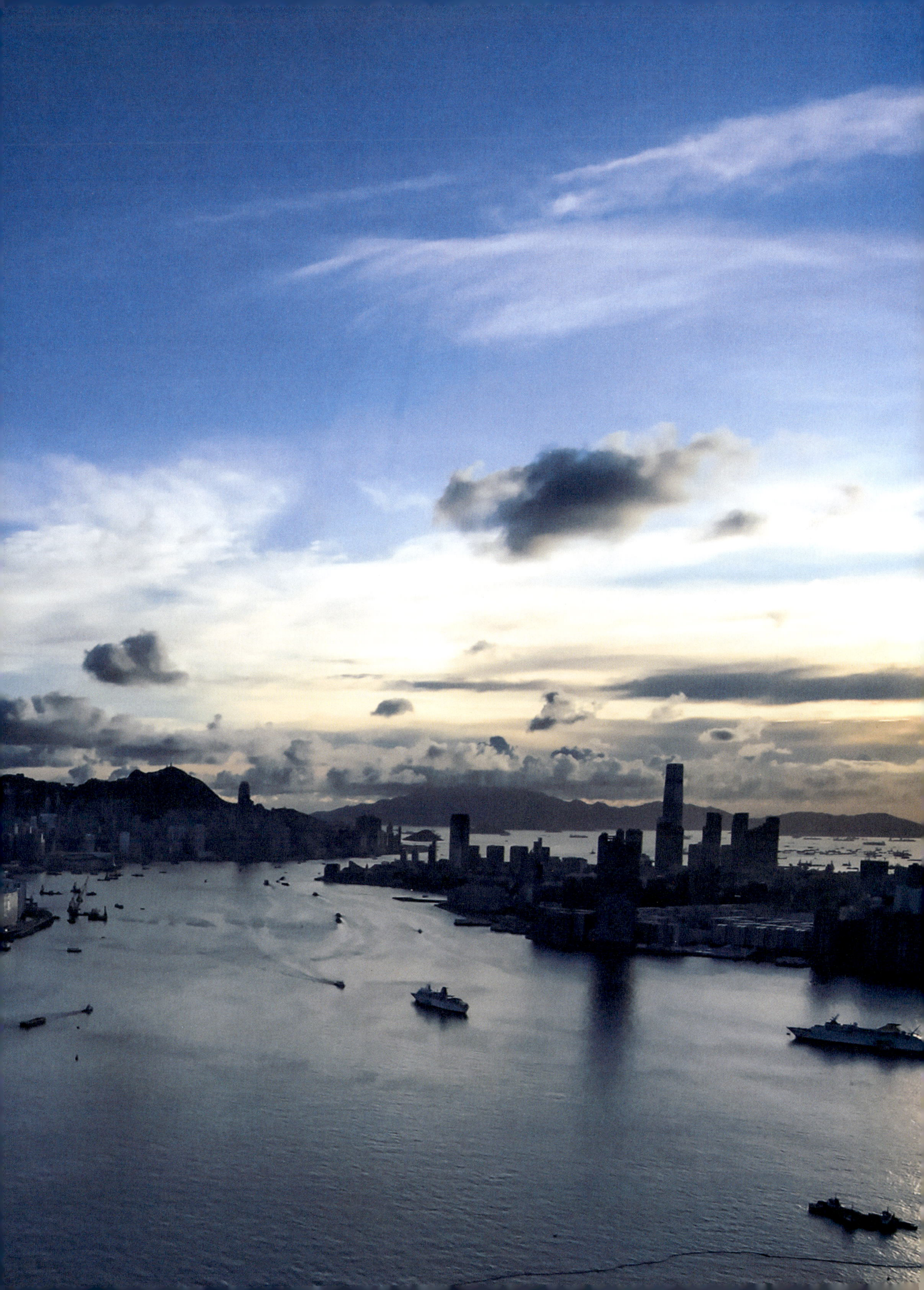

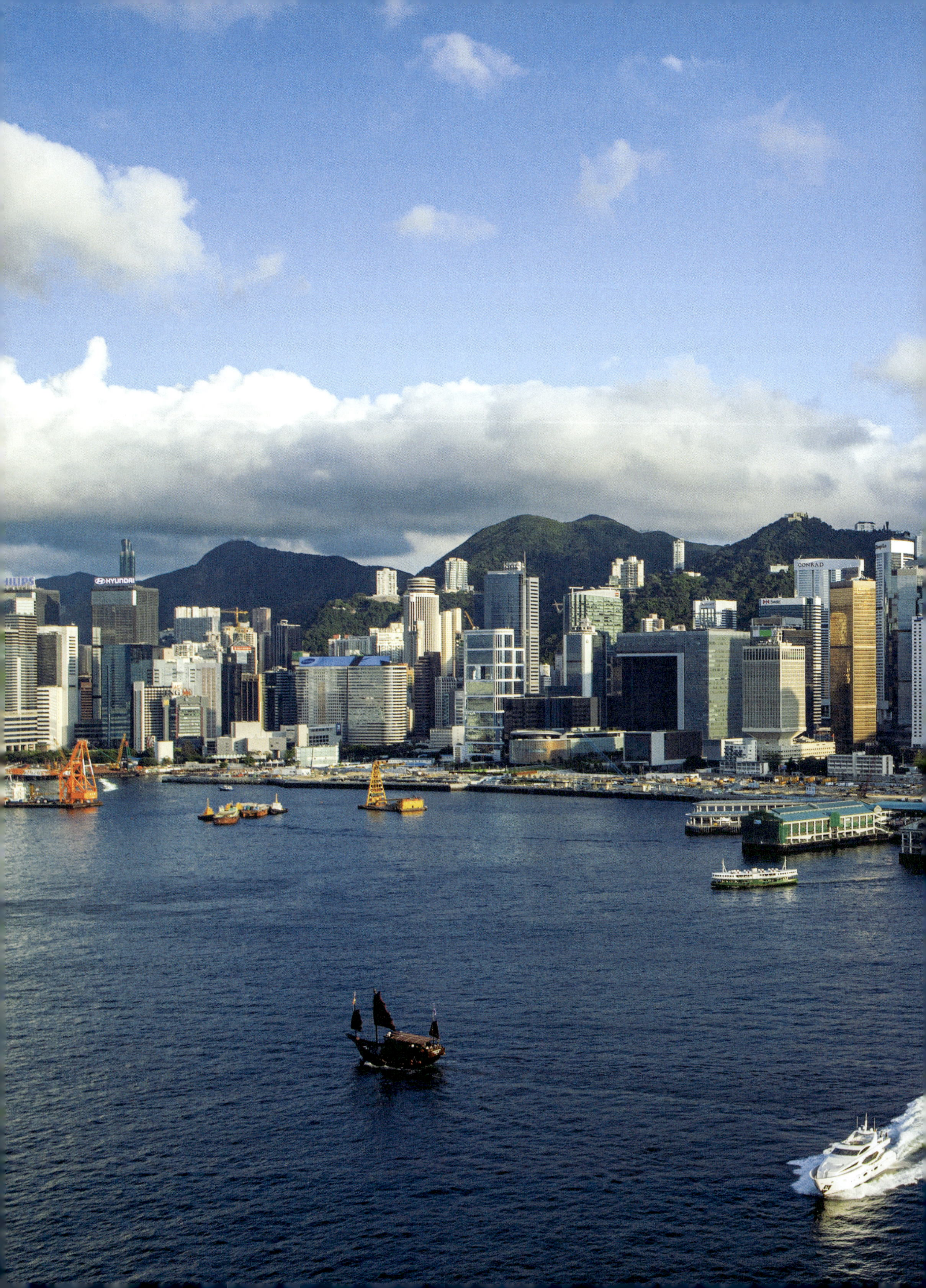
HYUNDAI
CONRAD

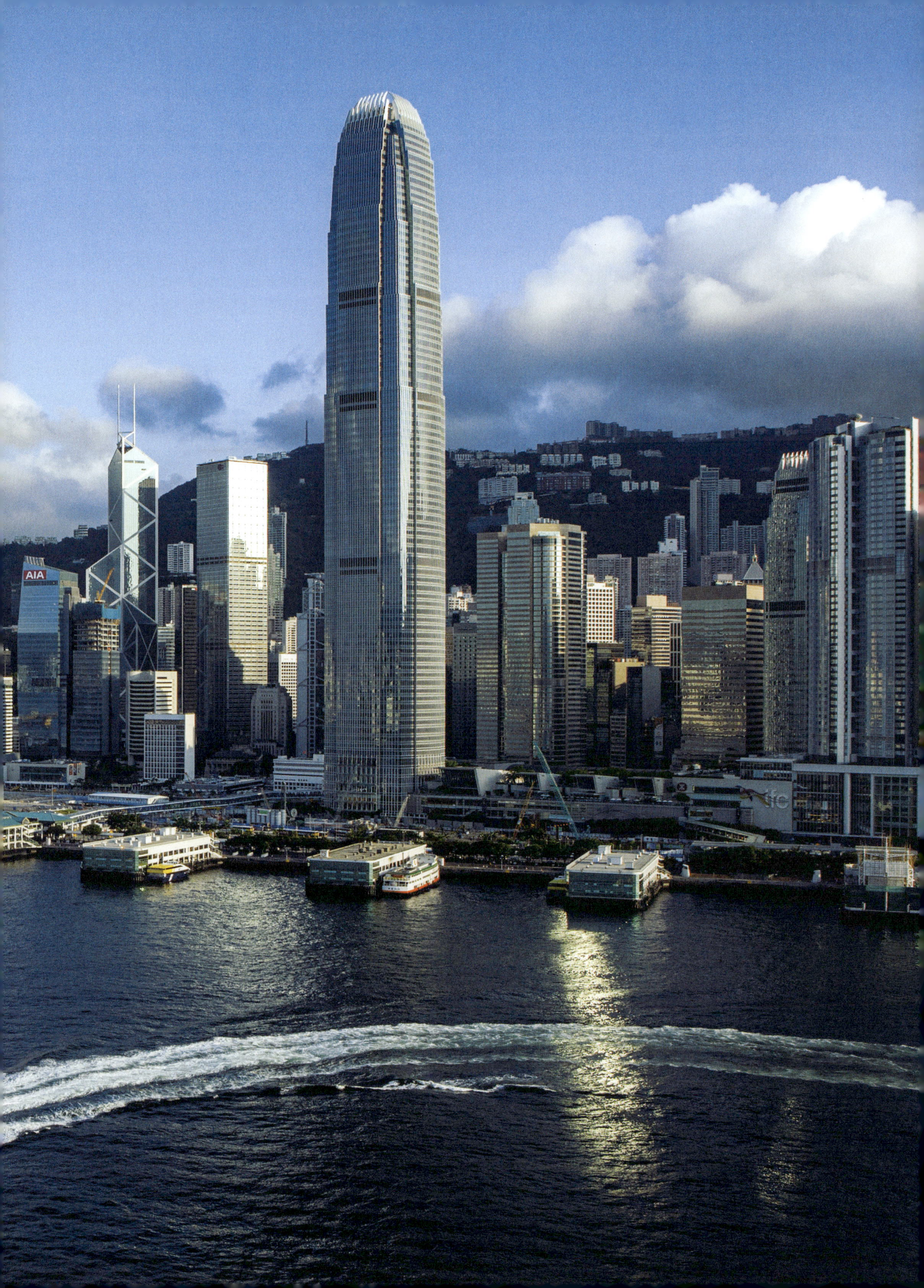
AIA

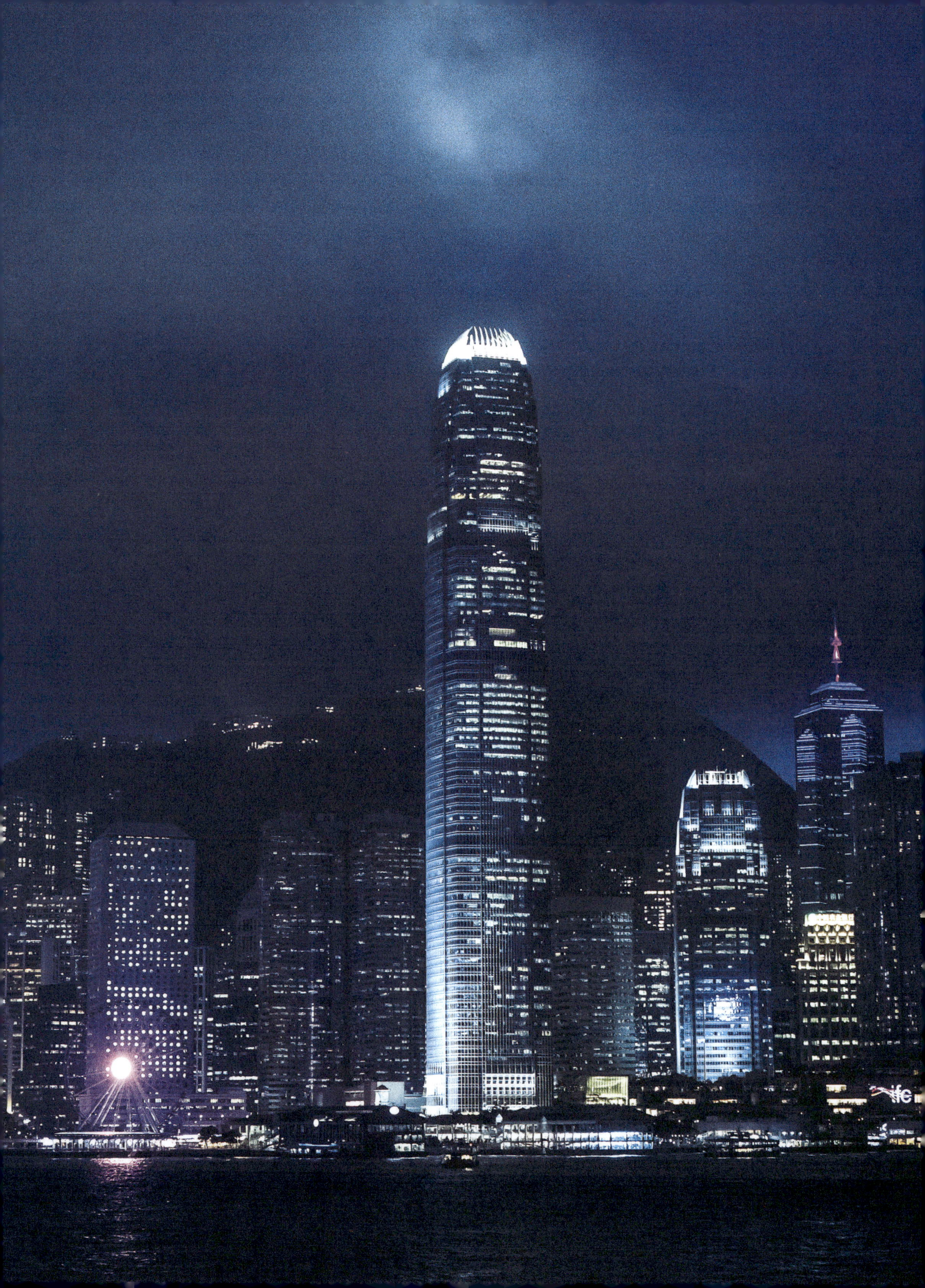

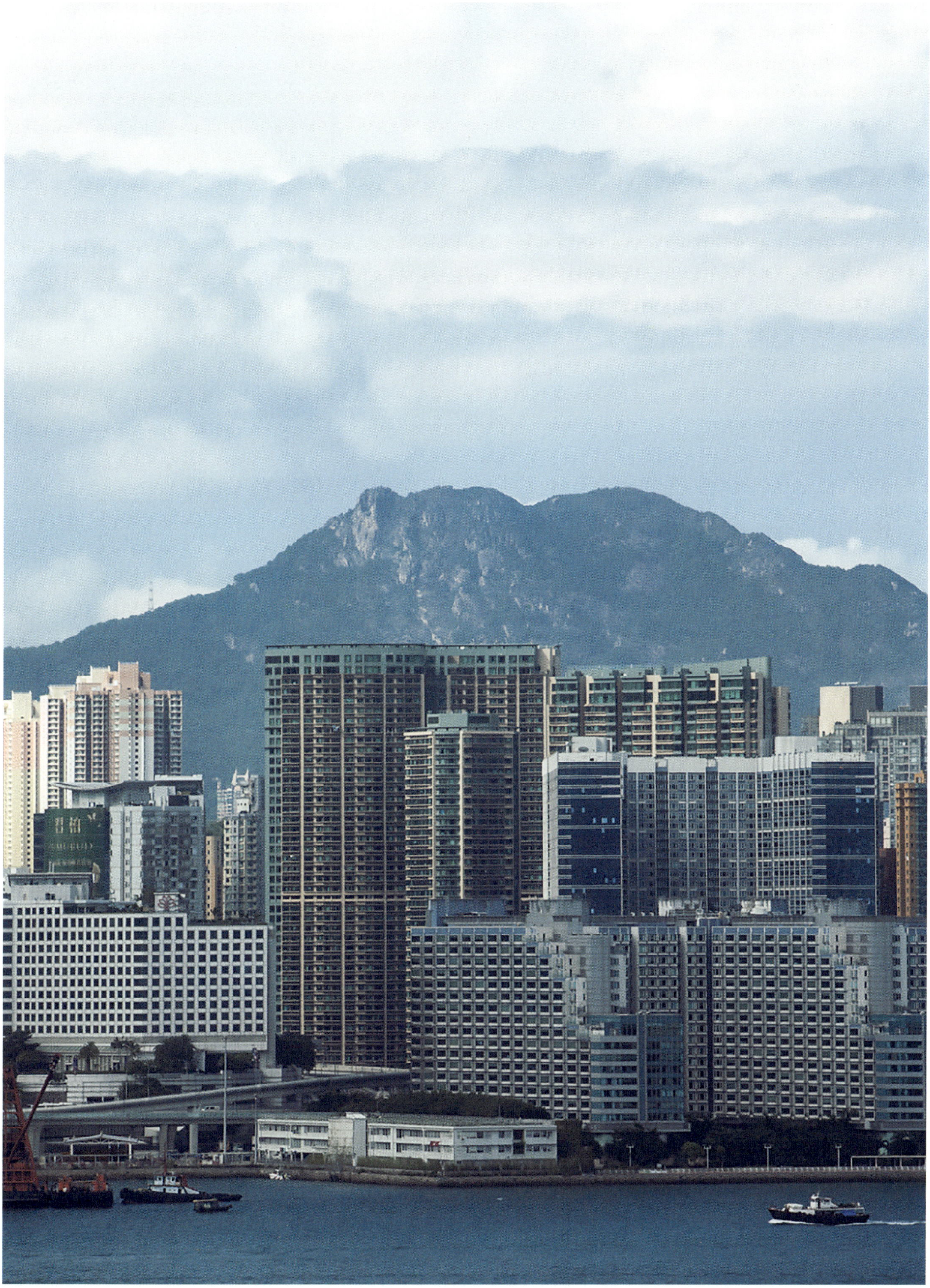

THE BUILDINGS

There are so many spectacular buildings in Hong Kong, many even designed and built by famous architects. The buildings keep getting taller and taller. There are not too many places in the world where the 20th floor is considered relatively low. And it's not just the commercial buildings that are record-breaking tall — residential buildings can also easily reach 70 stories high.

44. Zero Carbon Building in Kowloon Bay
45. St. Regis Hotel in Wan Chai
46. One ifc in Central
47. The Murray Hotel and surrounding buildings, in Central
48. Scaffolding in Sham Shui Po
49. Looking up at Hopewell Centre and its neighbors in Wan Chai

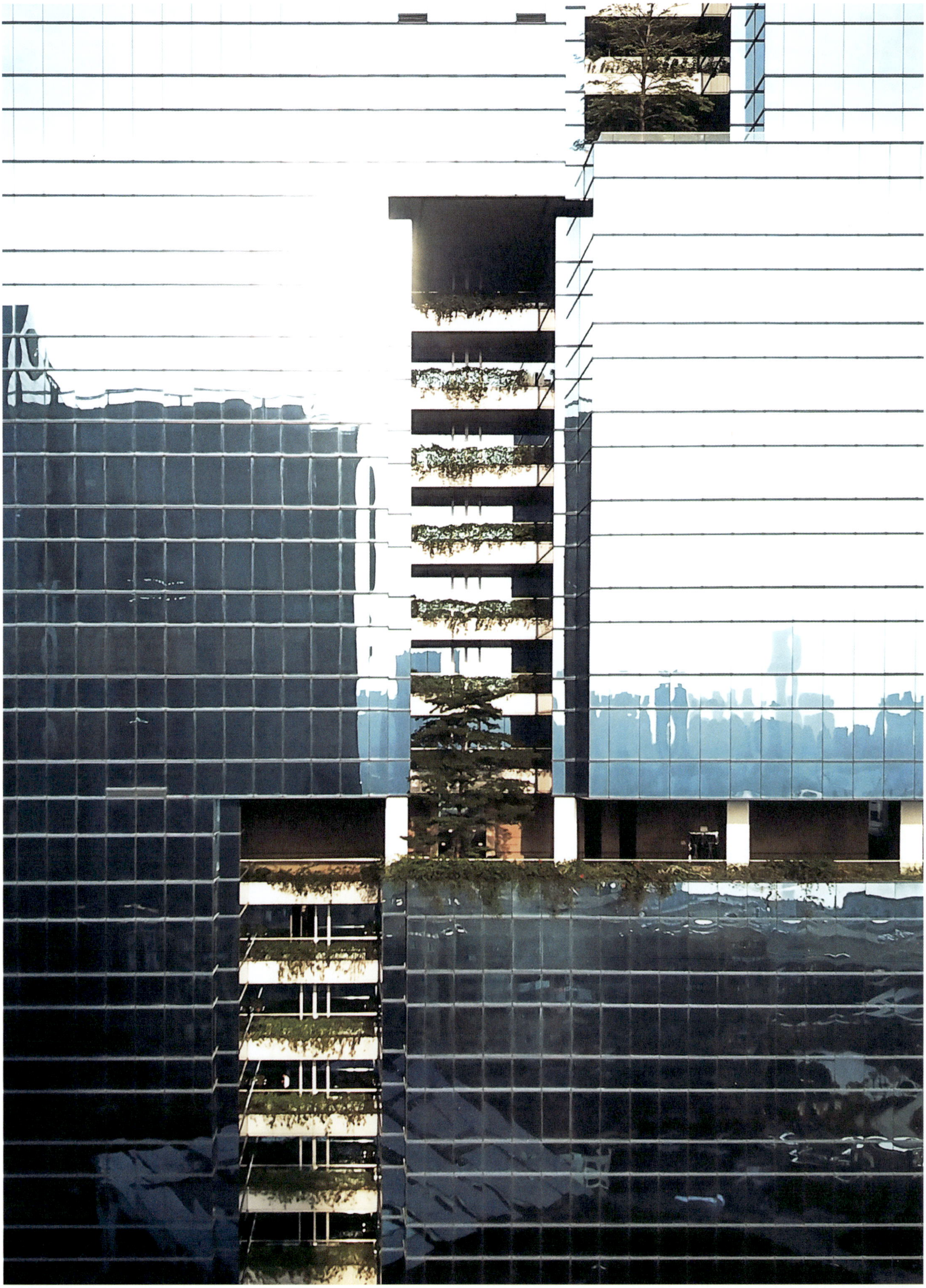

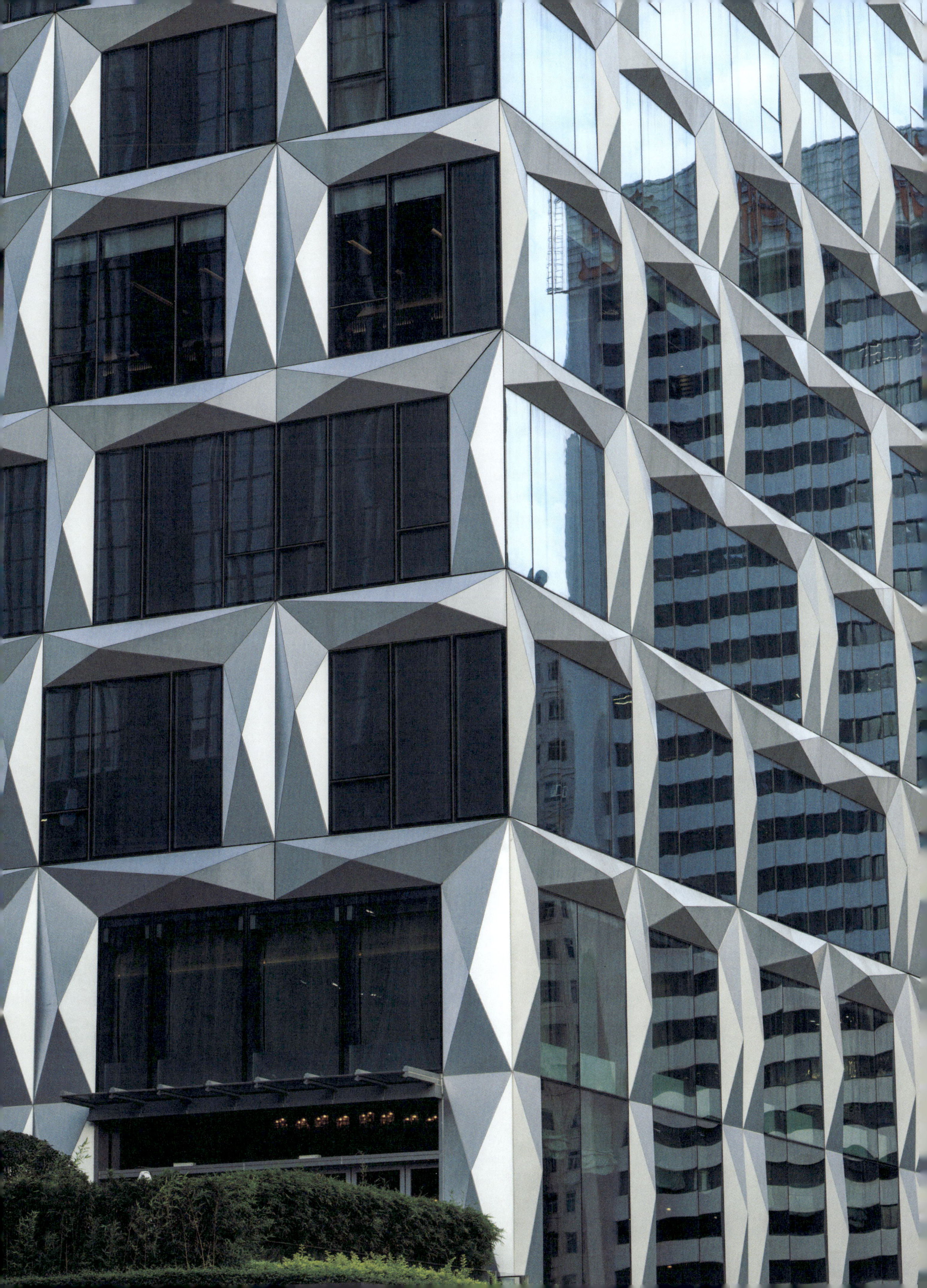

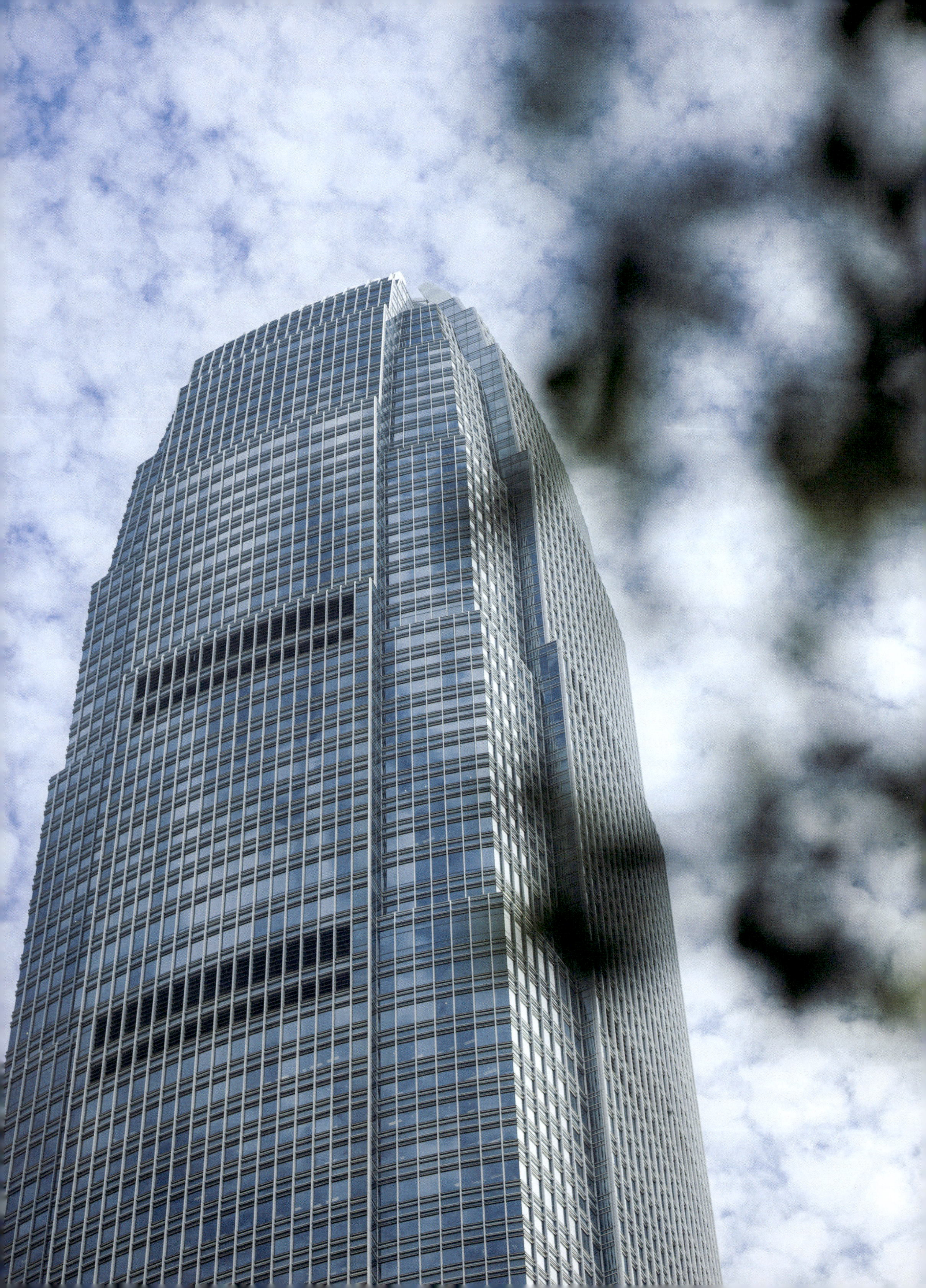

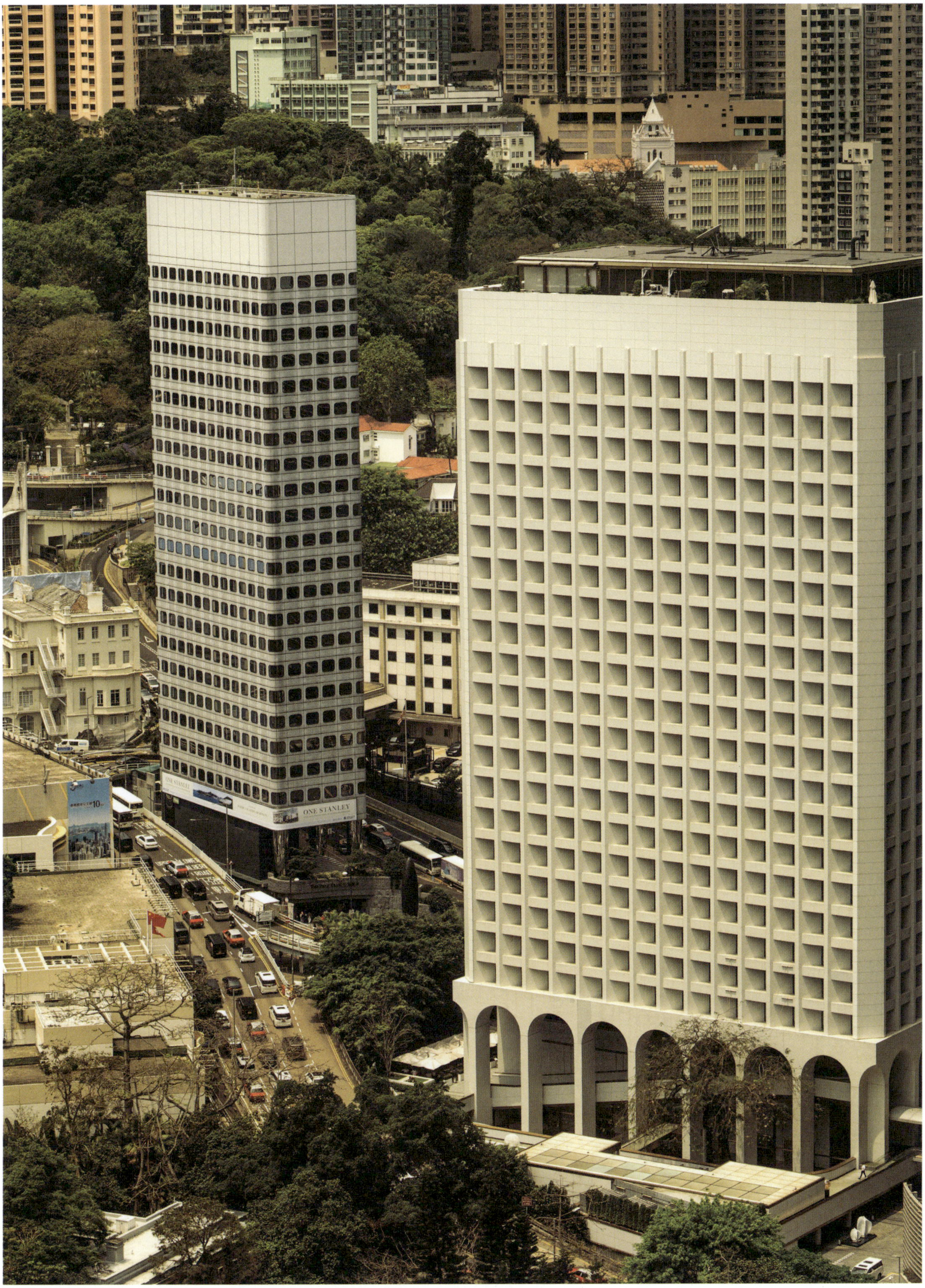
ONE STANLEY

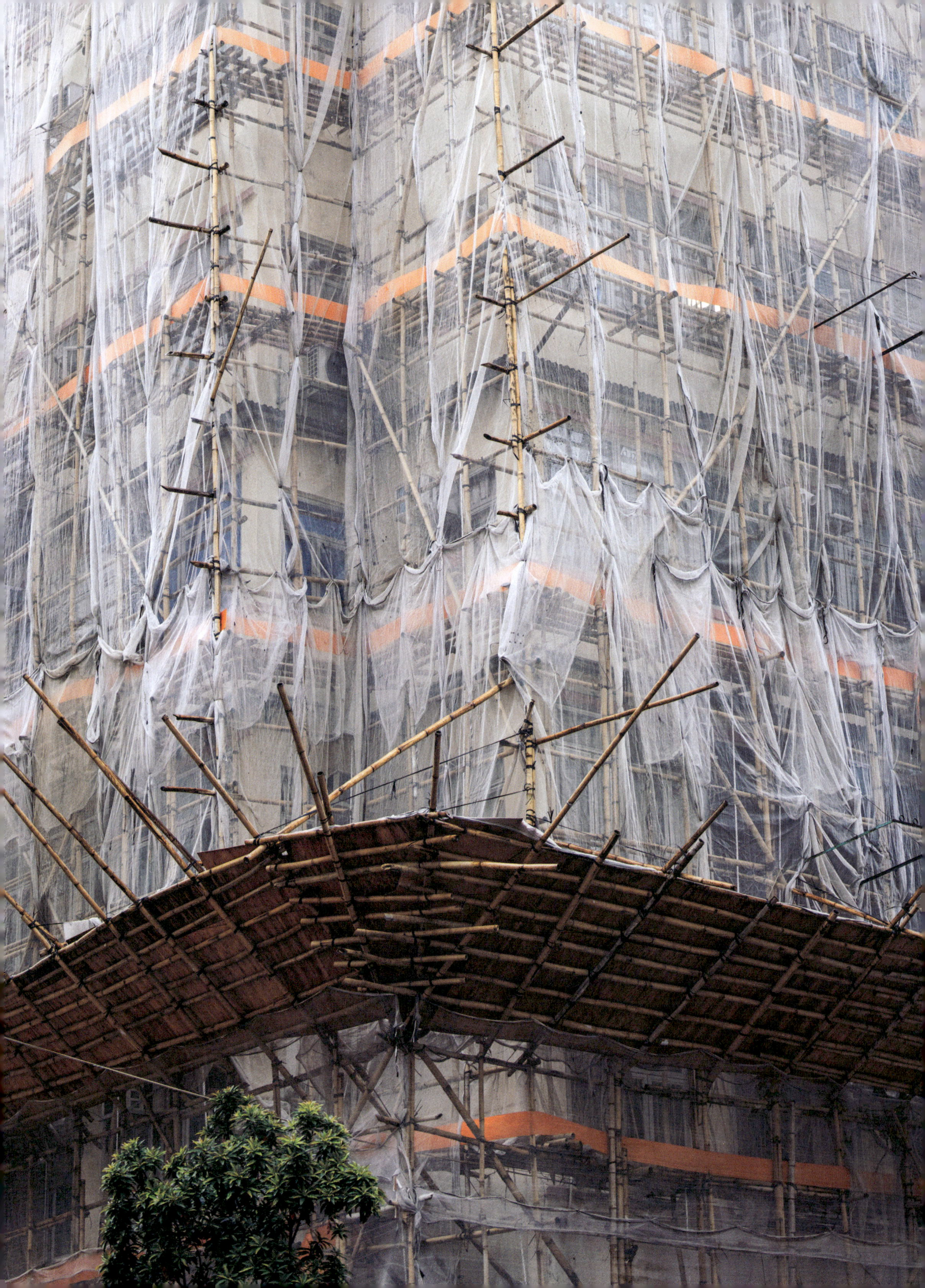

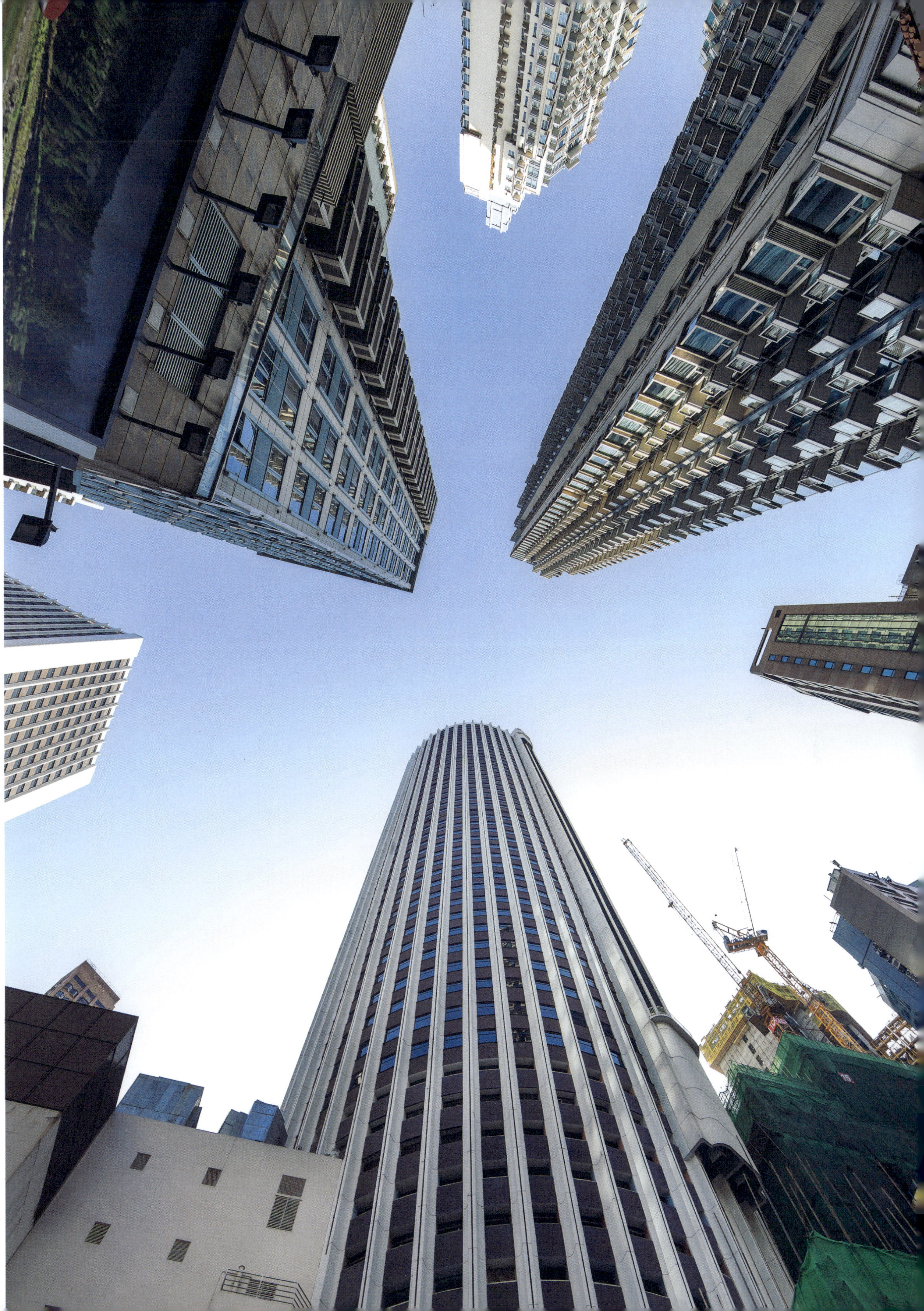

URBAN RHYTHMS

THE TRANS-PORTATION

I love how easy it is to get from one place to another in Hong Kong. I think it makes the city more connected, the people more active and independent. It is also more environmentally sustainable too. The MTR and Light Rail train systems are pretty comprehensive, able to reach all of the major districts. The trains themselves are safe, efficient, reliable, super clean, and frequent.

Then, there are the buses and minibuses to fill in any transport gaps. The minibus is very unique to Hong Kong, with specific routes that go to lesser known areas. There is also the historic tram and the iconic Star Ferry, both of which I love taking. They offer such scenic routes and an enjoyable experience, when you're not in a rush.

50. A plane flying above Ma Wan
51. Cargo ships passing Ap Lei Chau
52. The Star Ferry, docked in Central
53. Sampan off an island in Sai Kung
54. A tram in Sai Ying Pun
55. Transportation options abound on Des Voeux Road Central
56. Hong Kong's iconic red taxi on Hollywood Road
57. MTR train passing through Wu Kai Sha
58. A minibus in Mong Kok
59. A school bus in Ngau Tau Kok

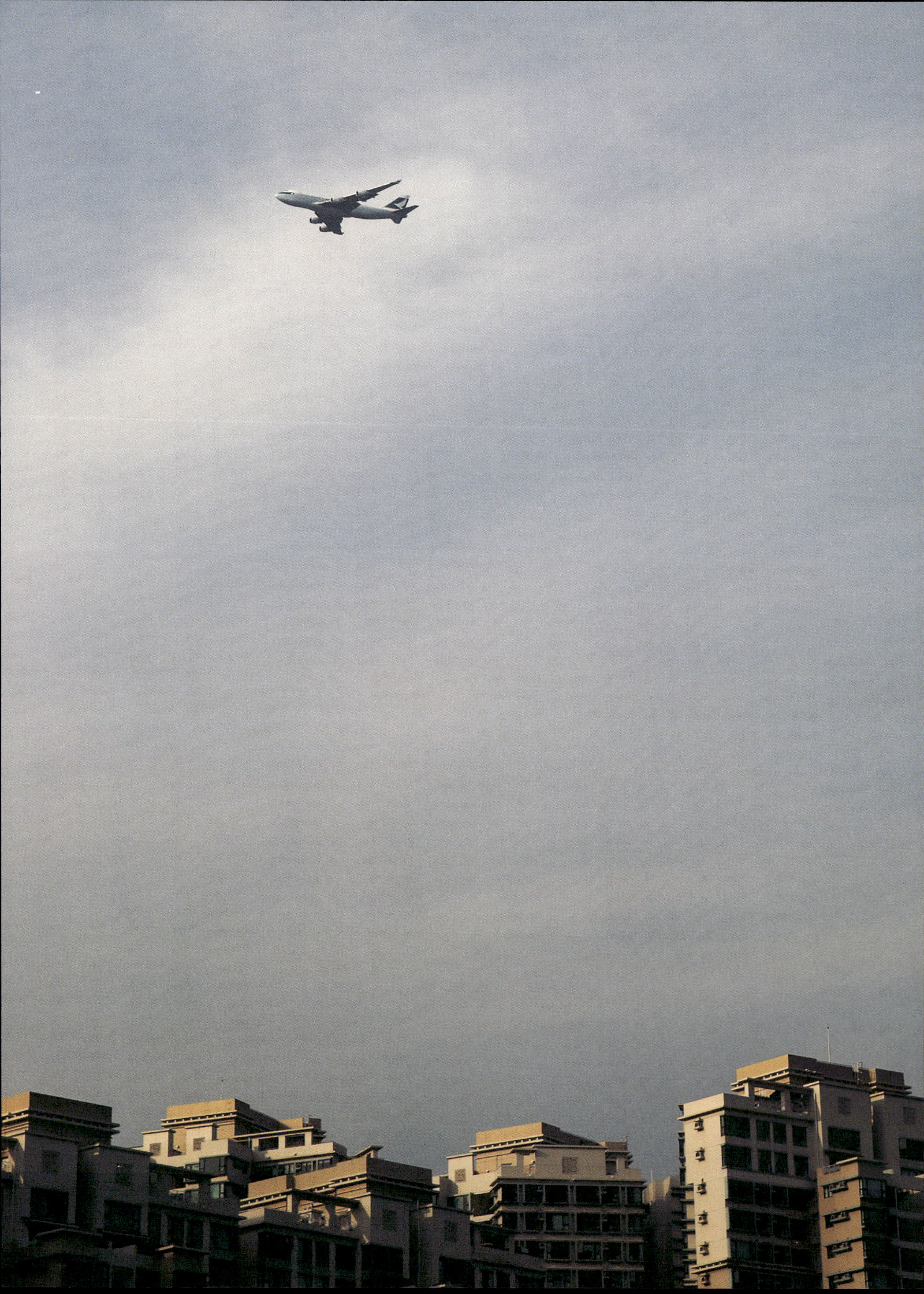

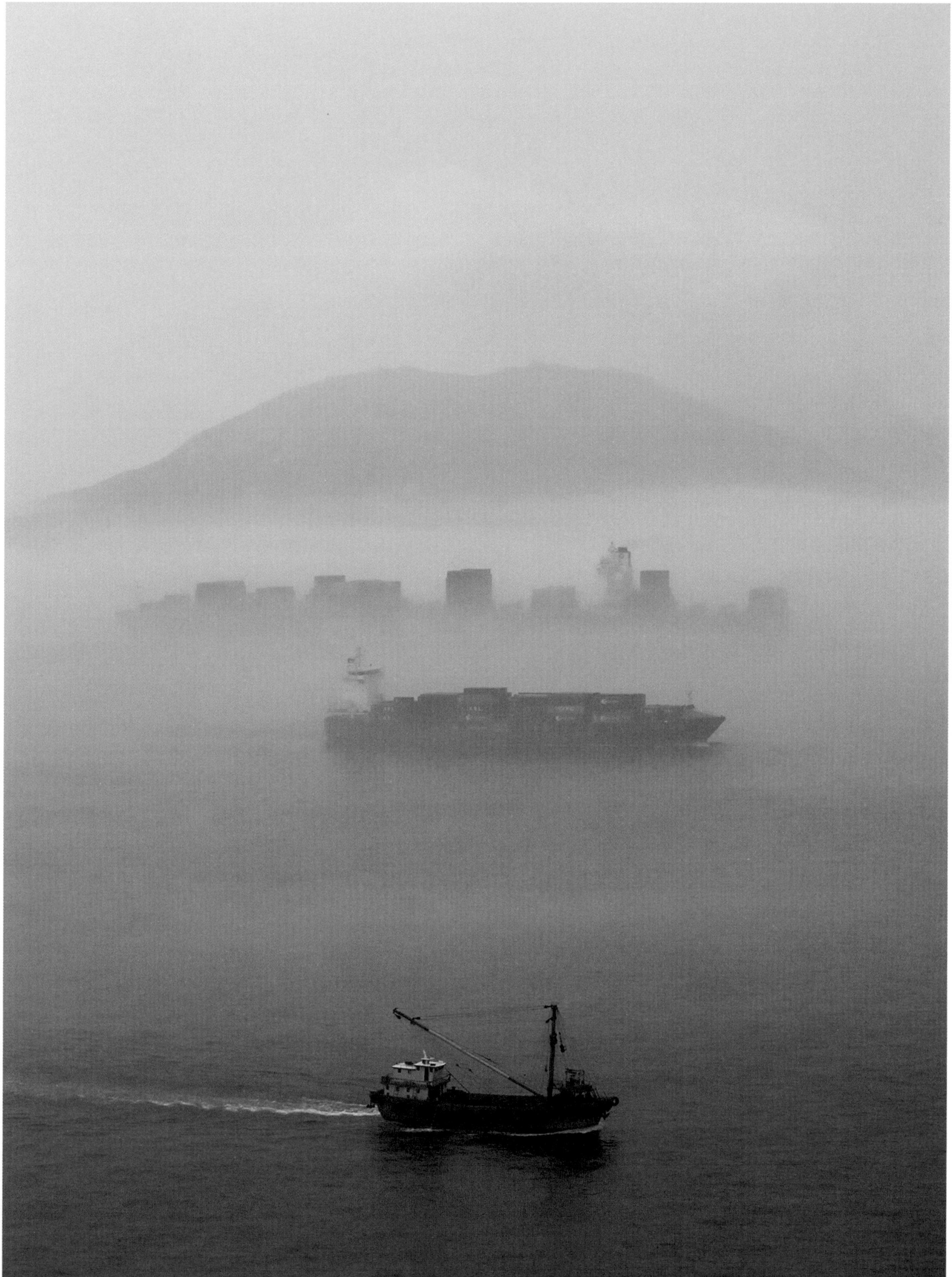

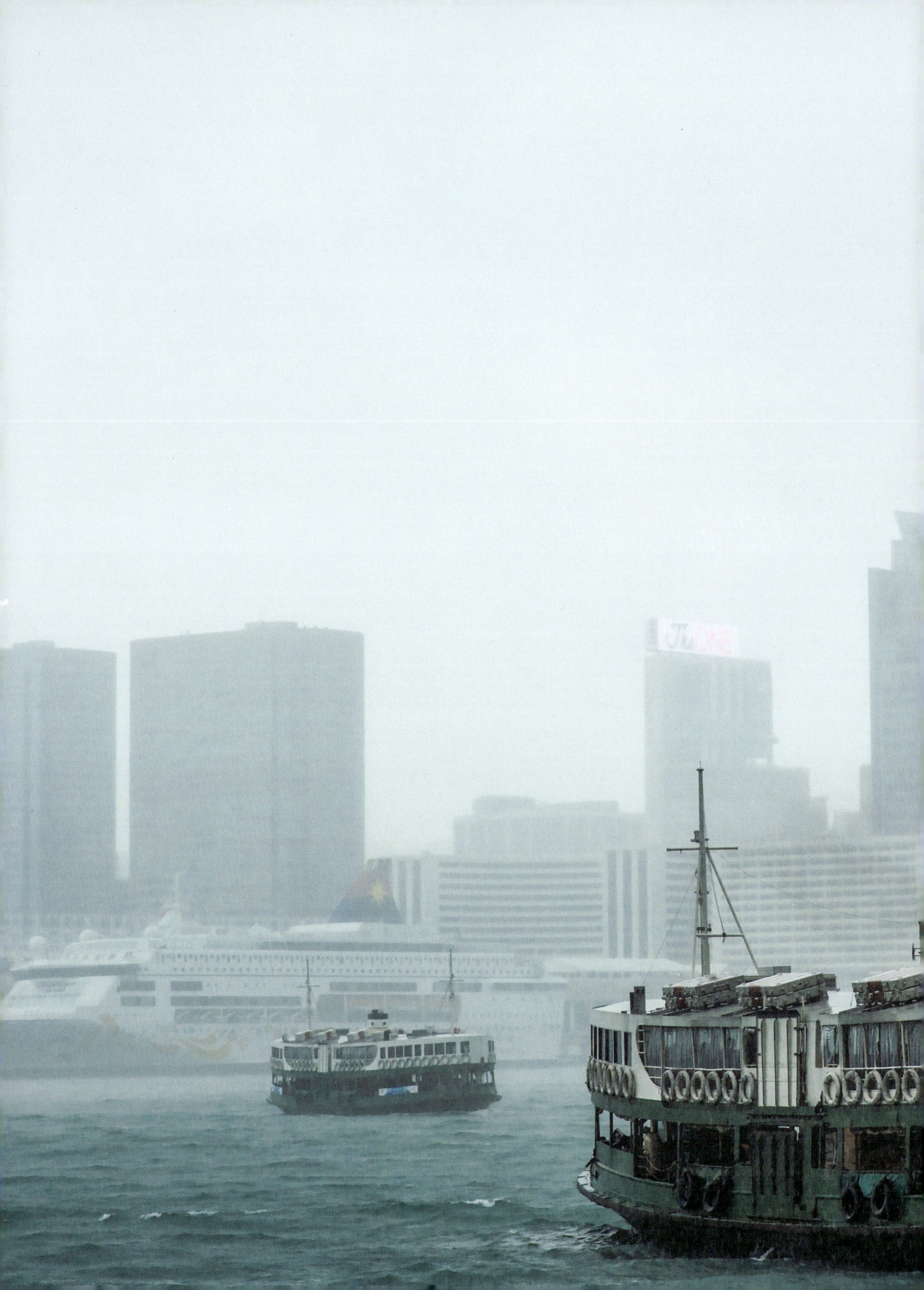
The ONE

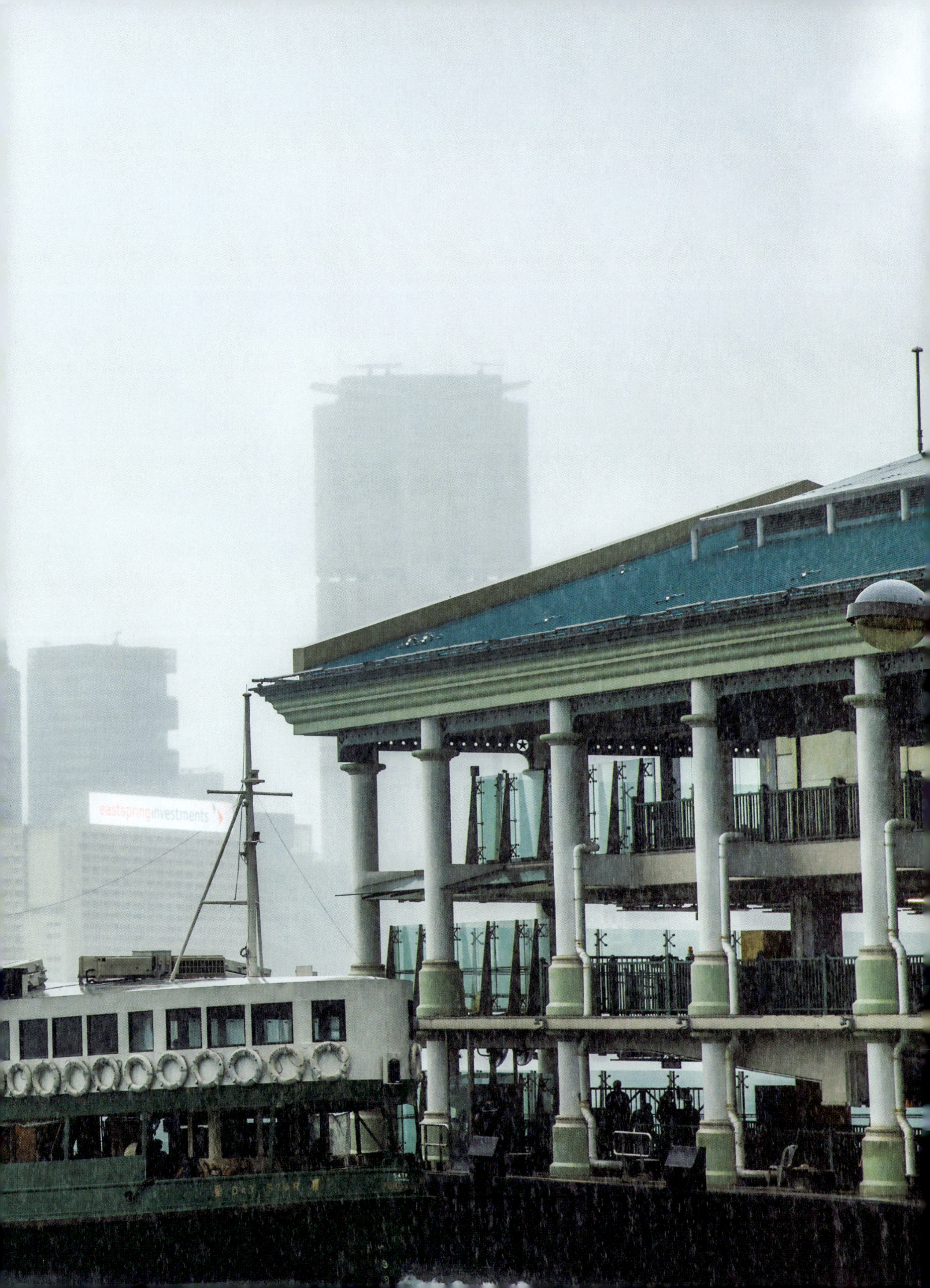
eastspringinvestments

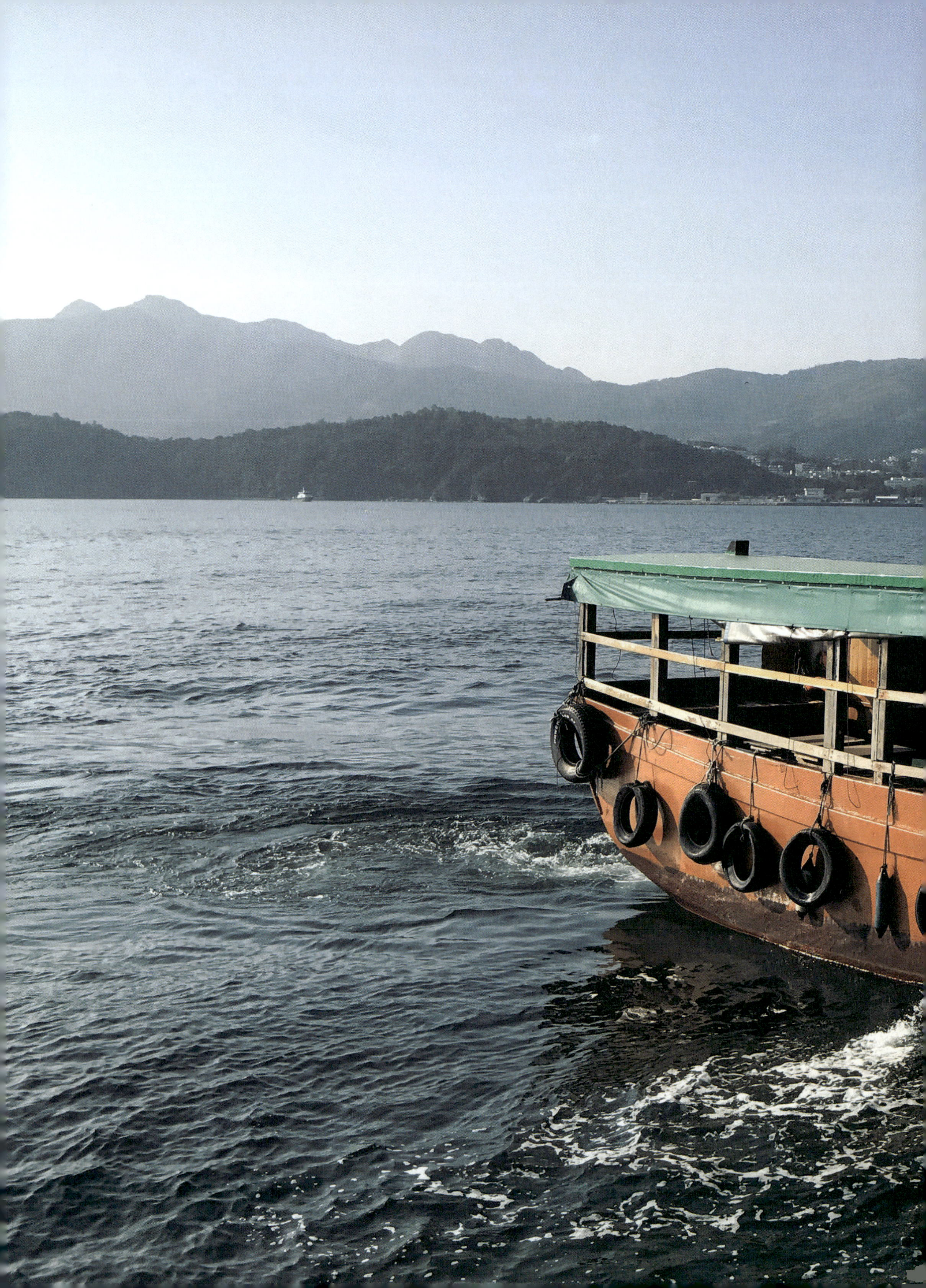

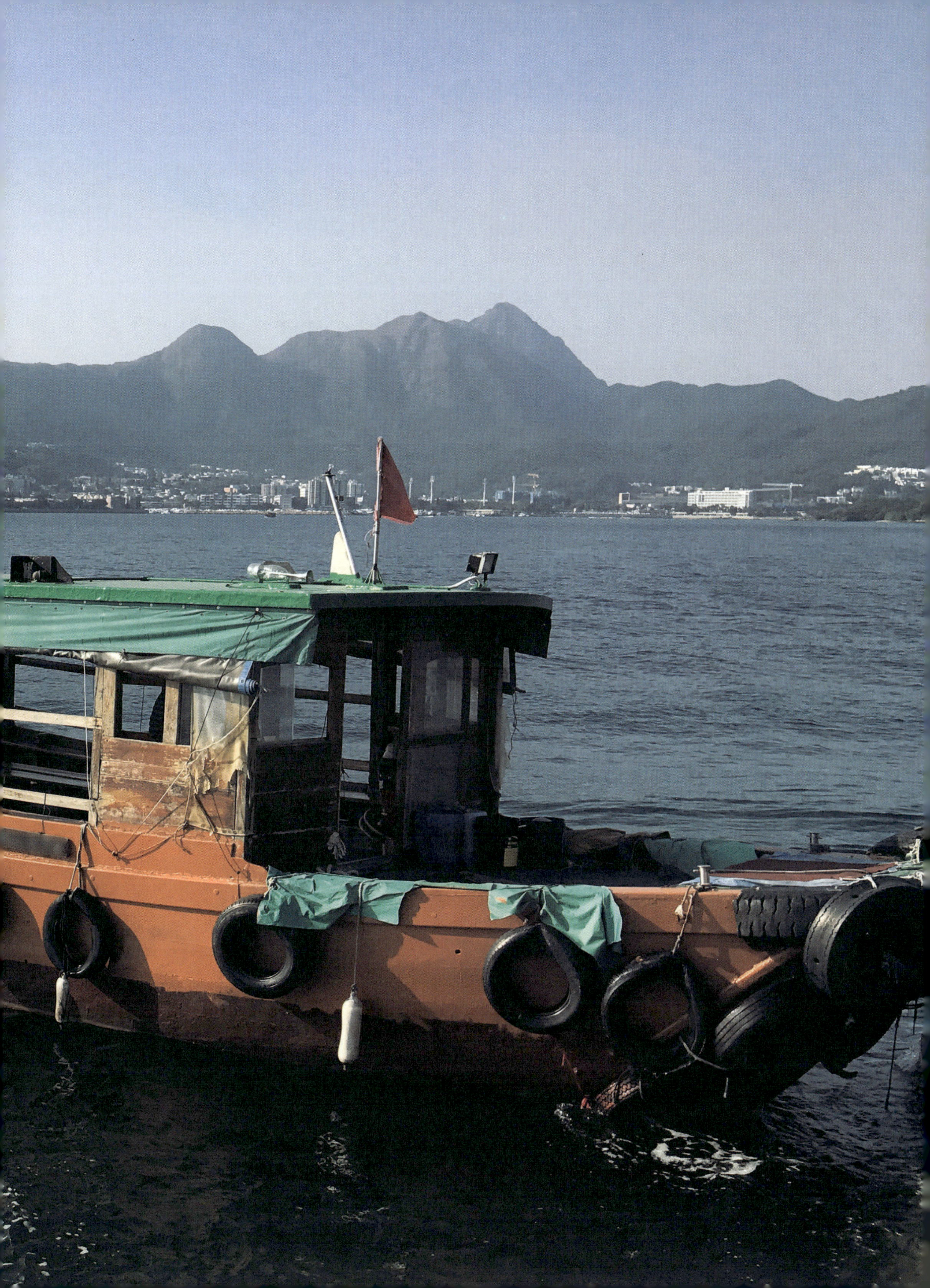

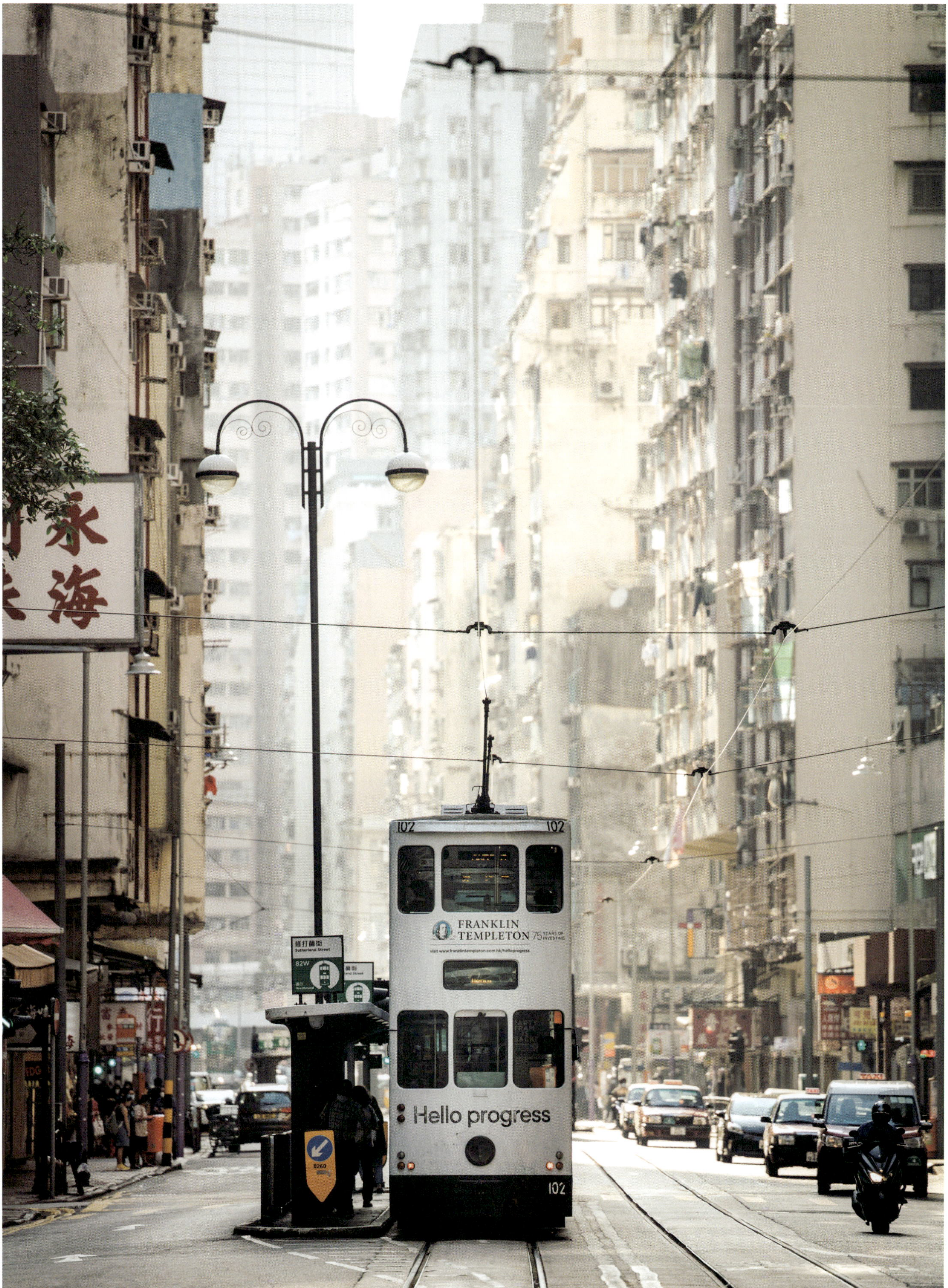
永
海
102
FRANKLIN
TEMPLETON
Hello progress
102

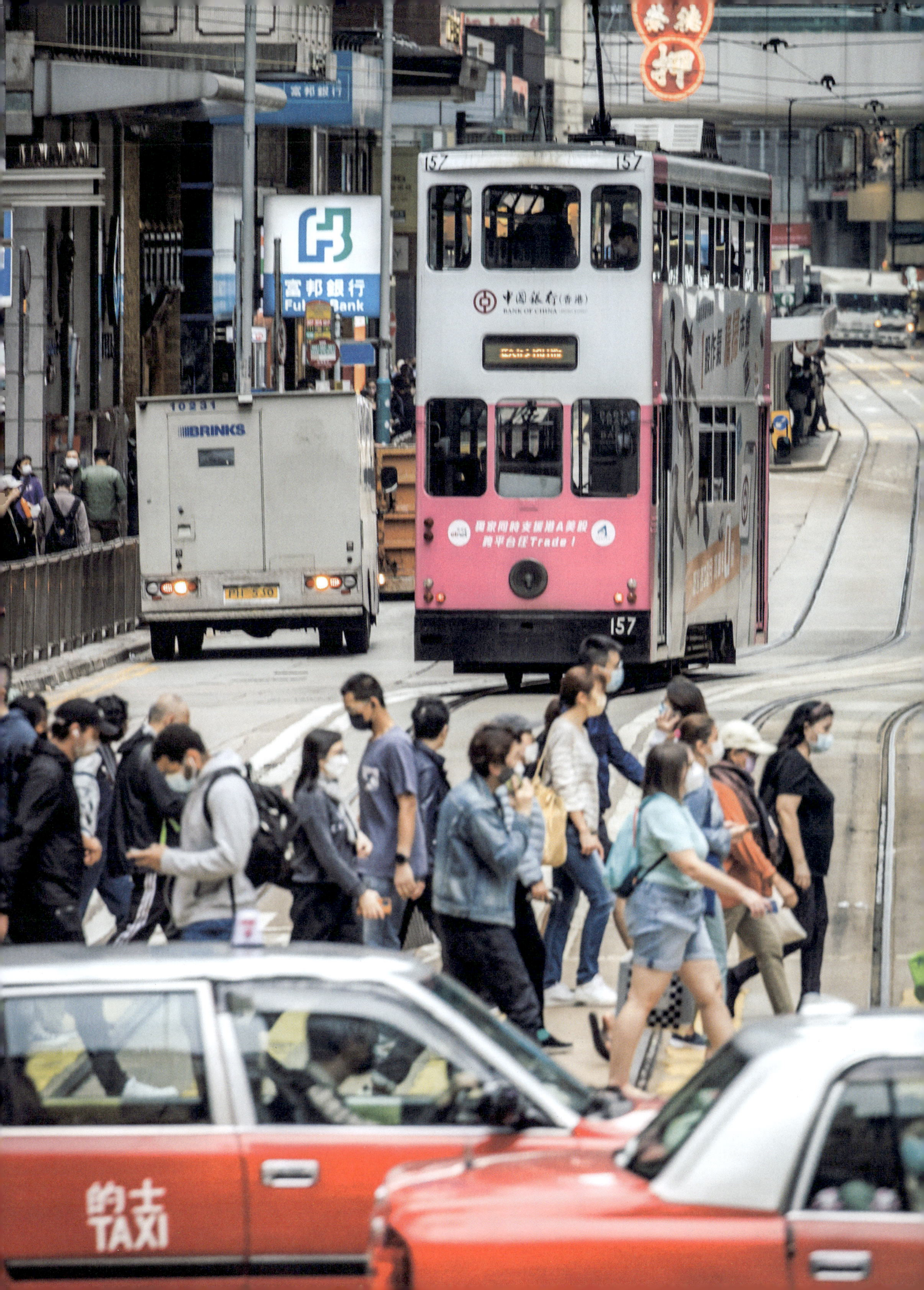

富邦銀行
BRINKS
157
BANK OF CHINA
的士
TAXI

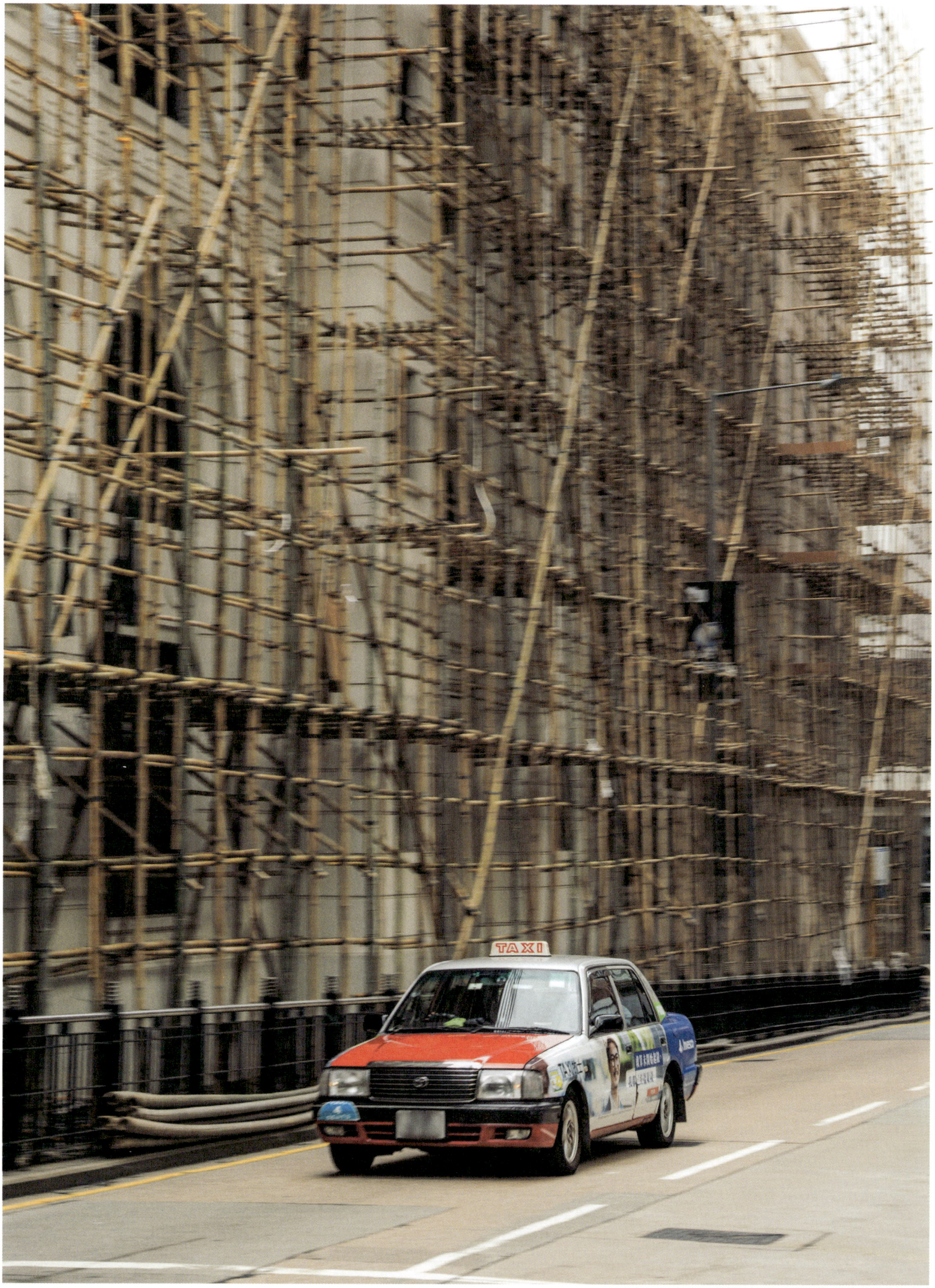
TAXI

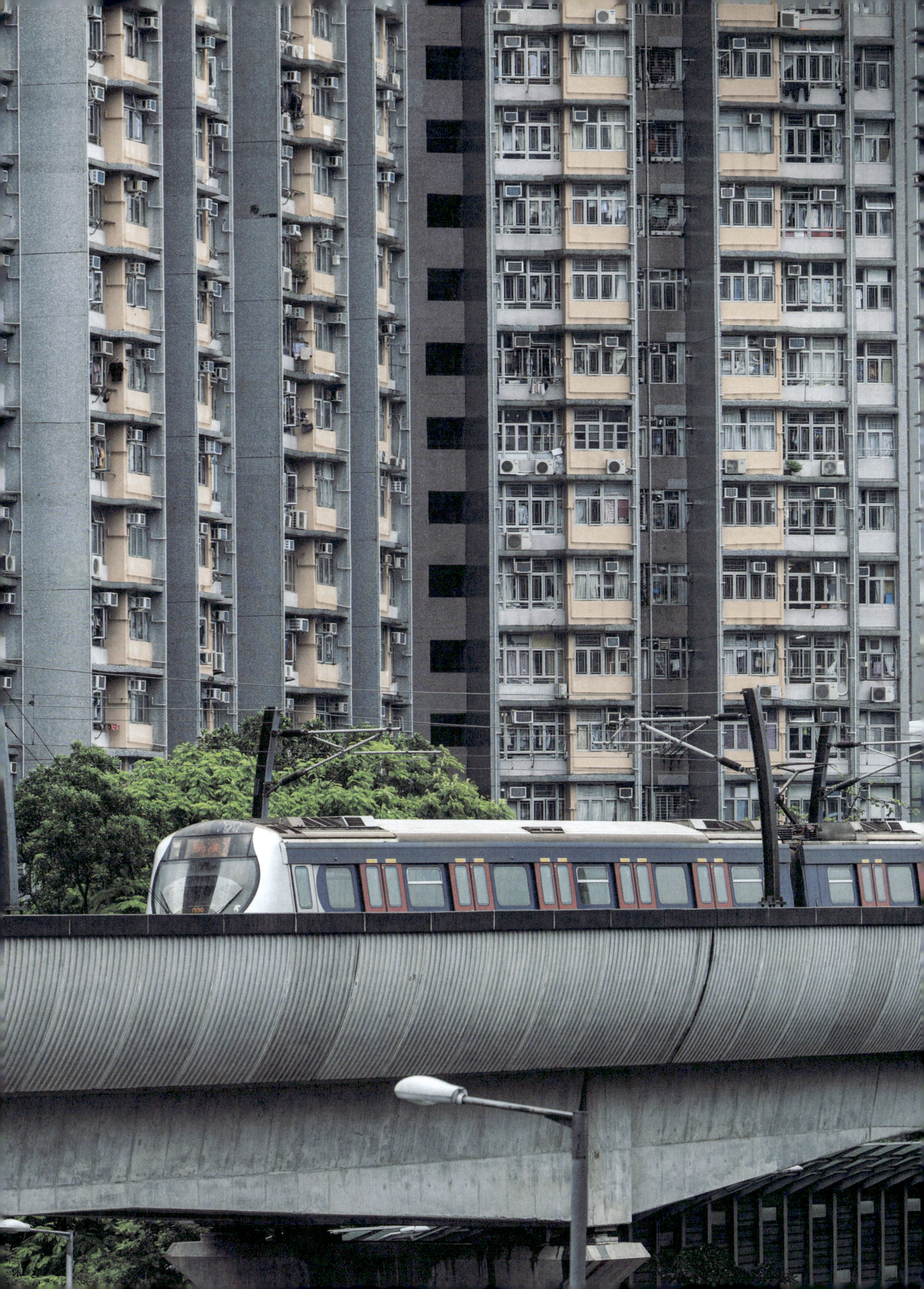

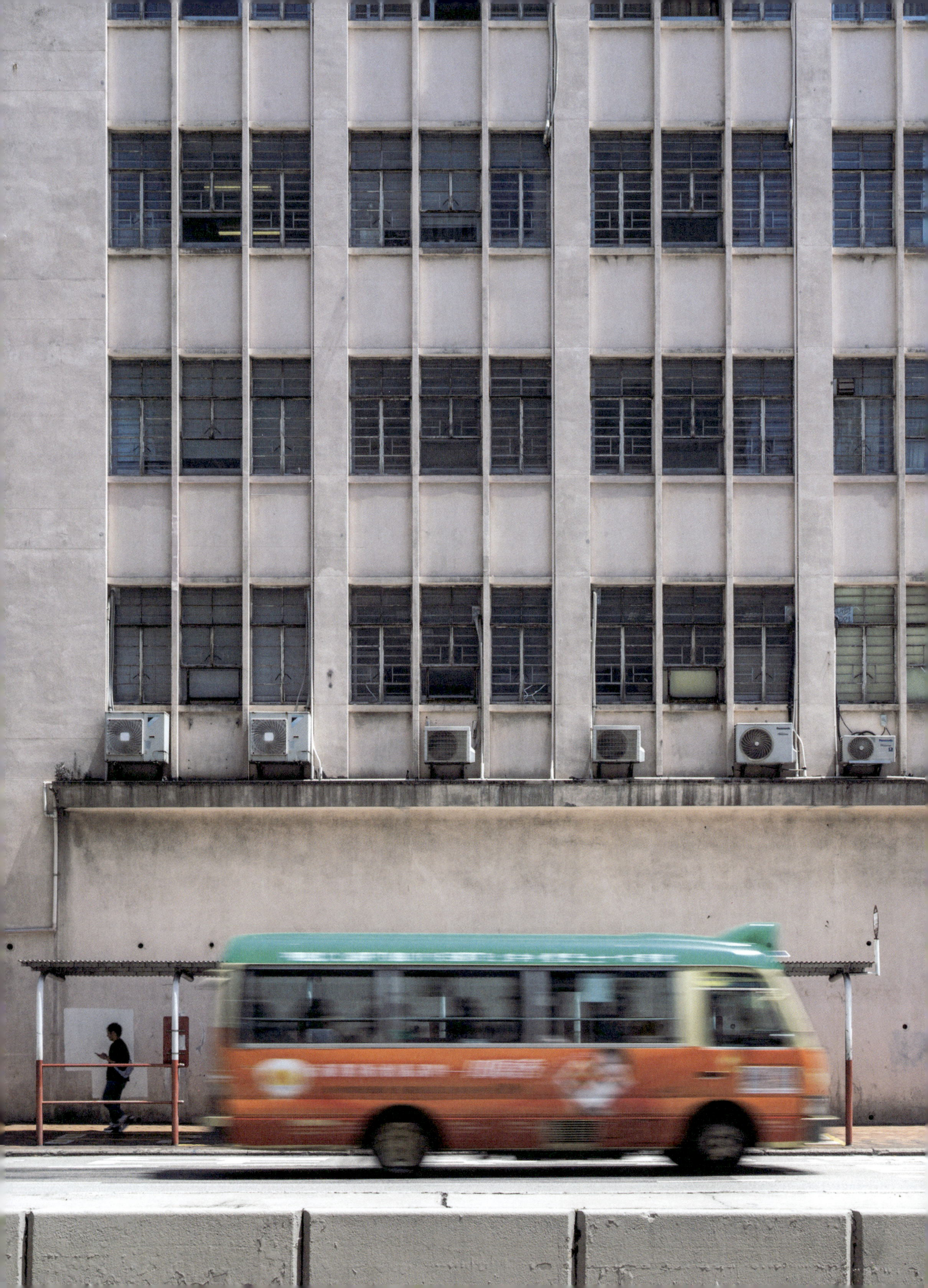

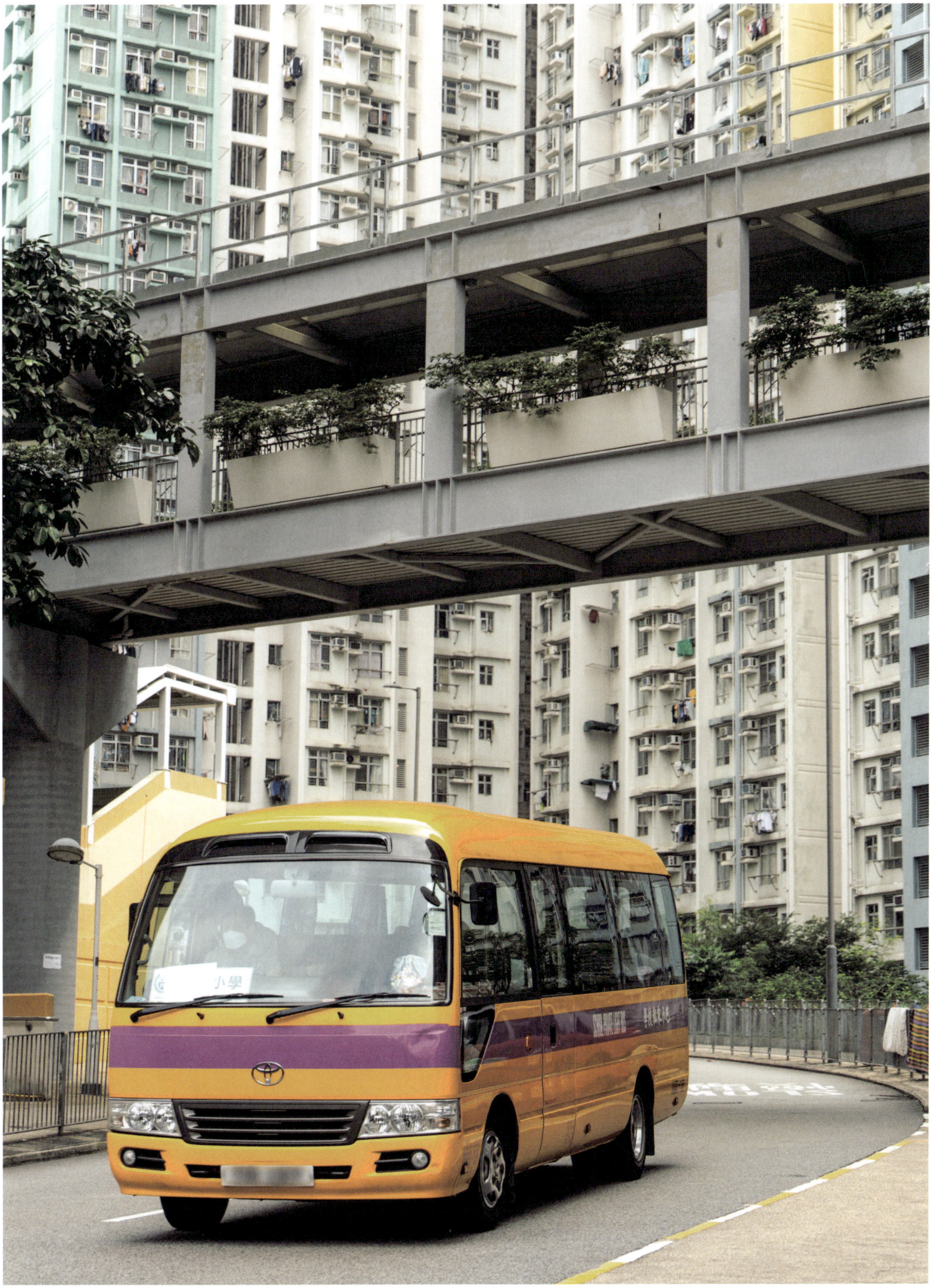
小學

THE ESTATES

In recent years, many public housing estates in Hong Kong have become popular on social media platforms due to their unique structures, colors and looks. The estates are typically quite densely built, and the government tries to make some of them more aesthetically pleasing by adding lots of color to the exteriors and surroundings.

60. Choi Hung Estate

61. A school near Shek Kip Mei Estate

62. Nam Shan Estate in Shek Kip Mei

63. Lok Wah Estate in Ngau Tau Kok

64. Yick Cheong Building, aka Monster Building, in Quarry Bay

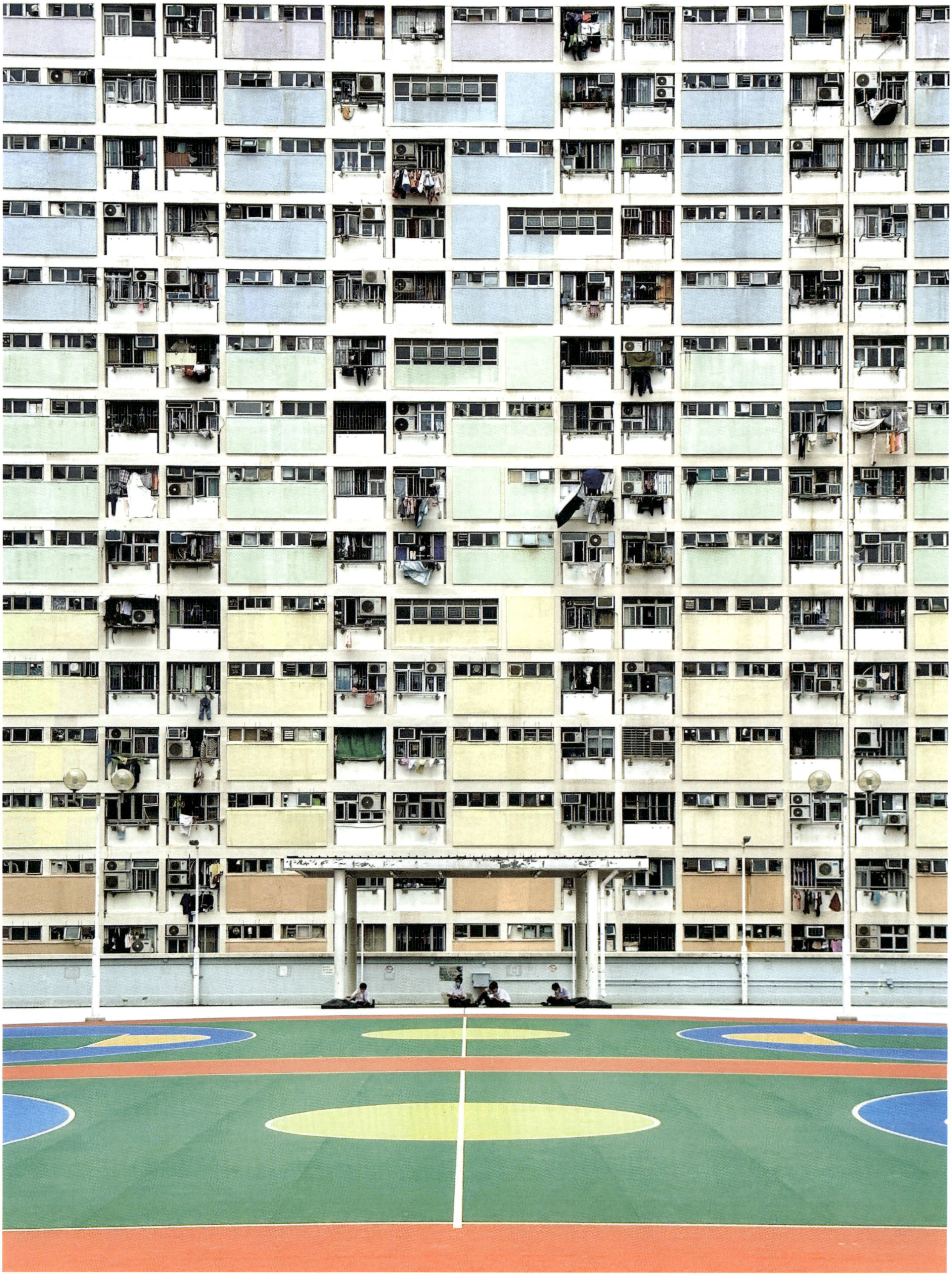

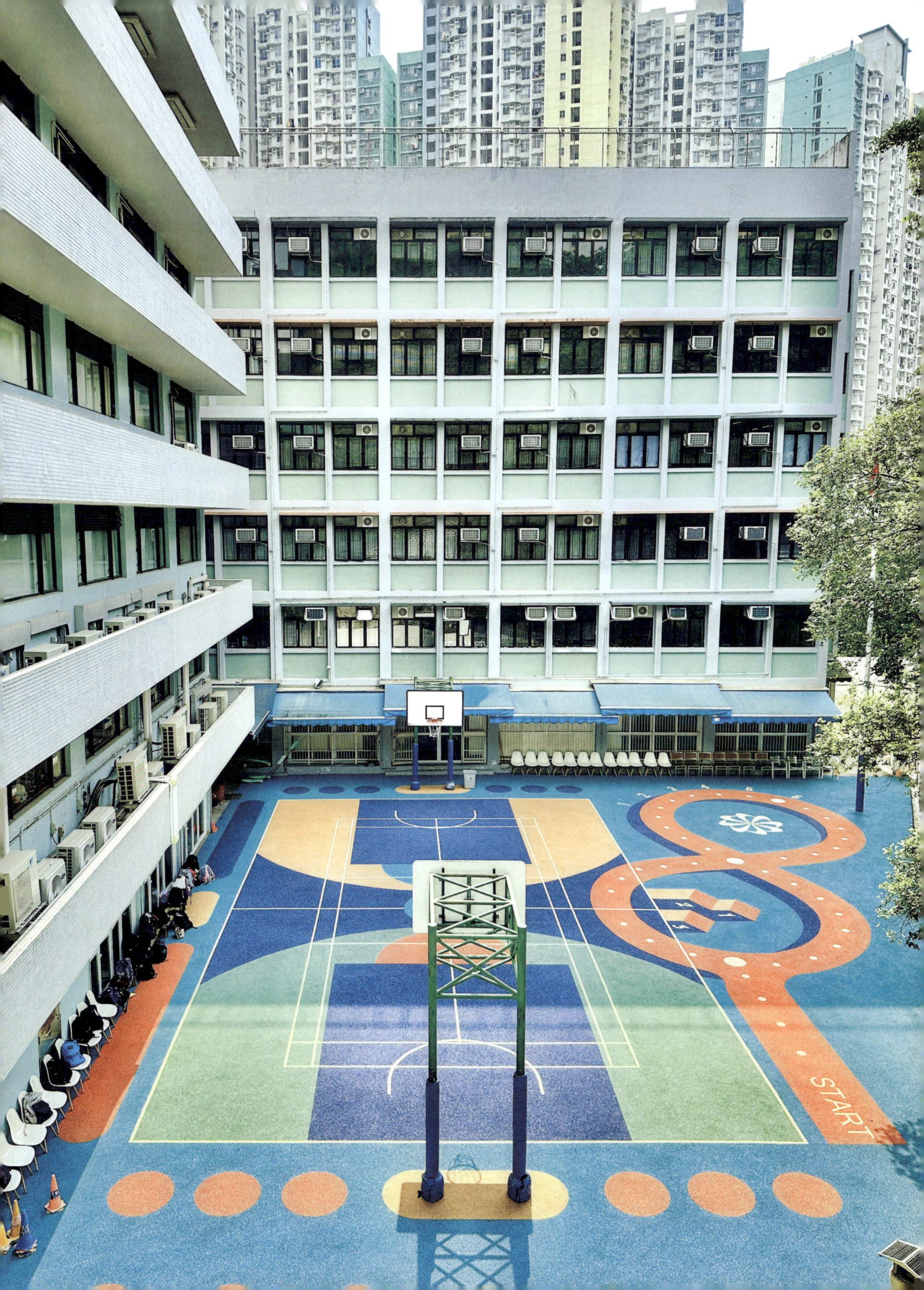
START

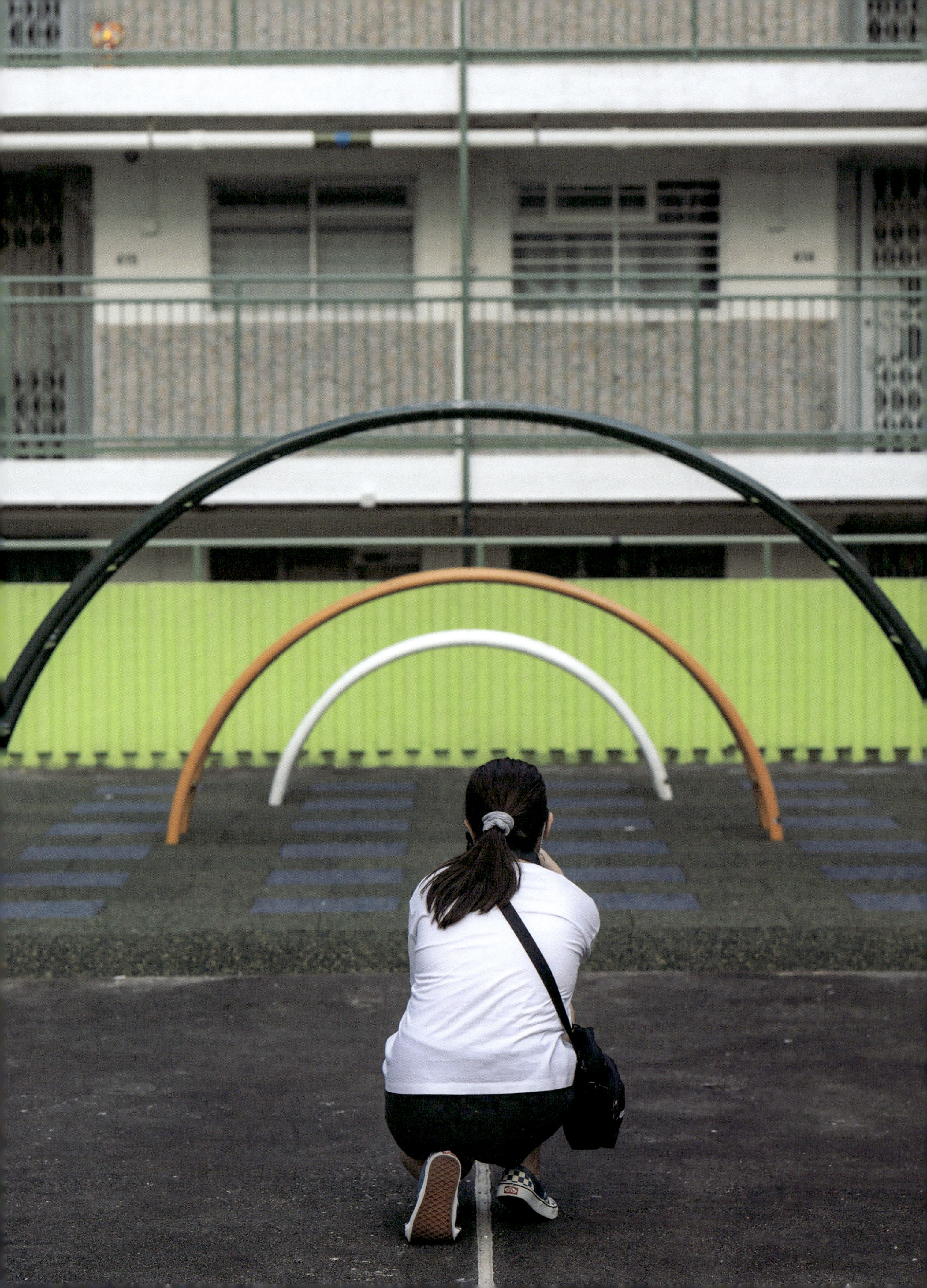

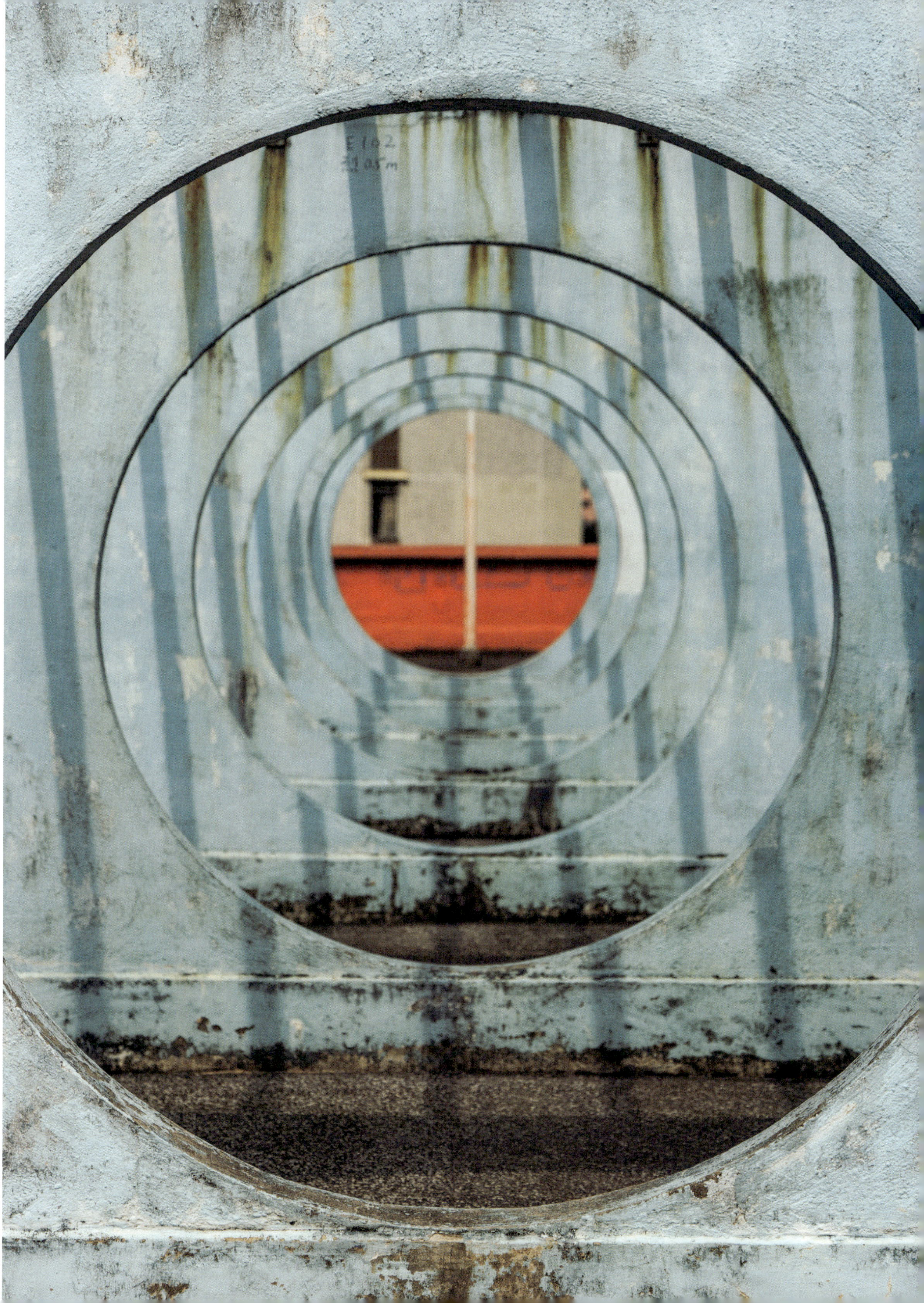

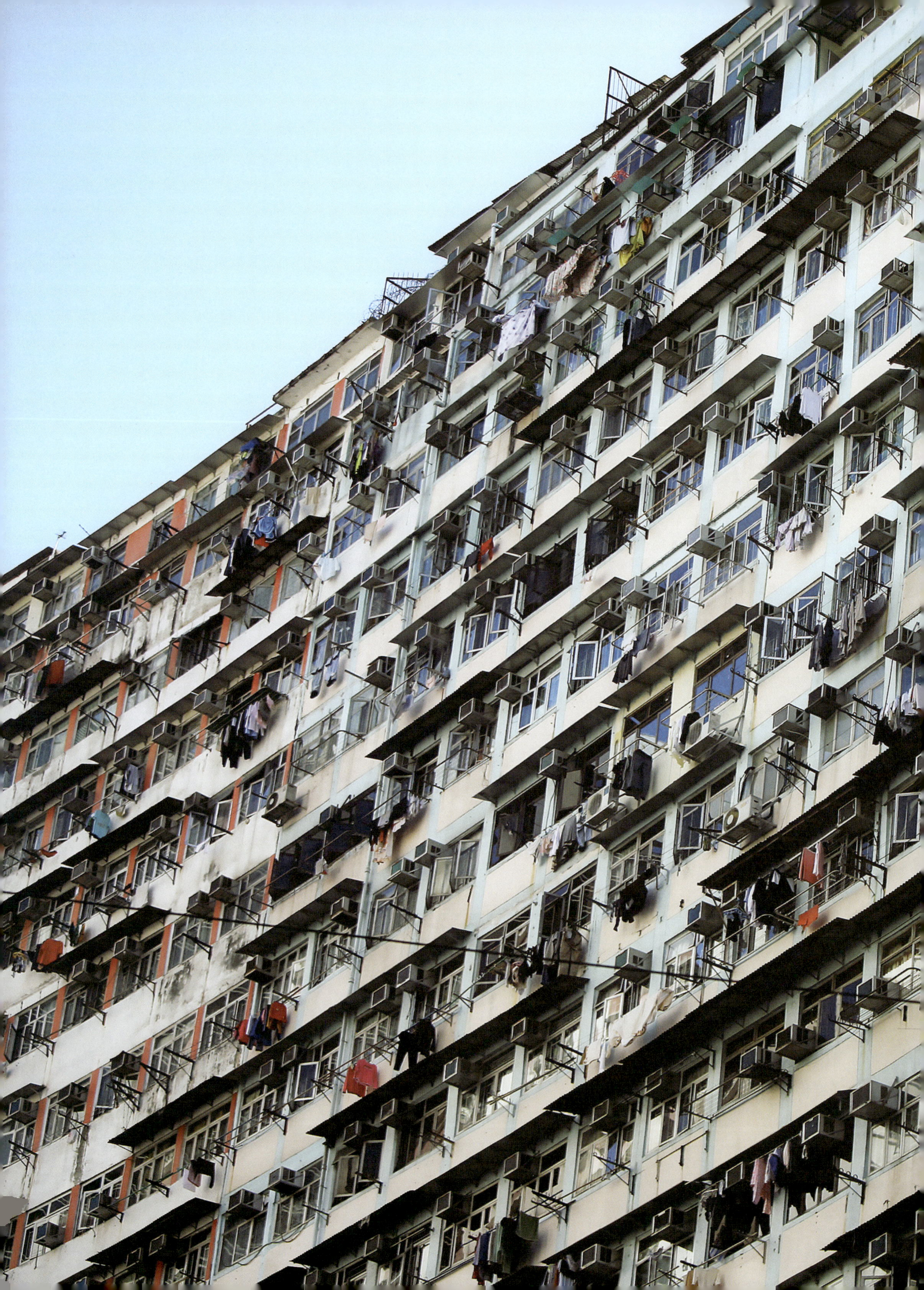

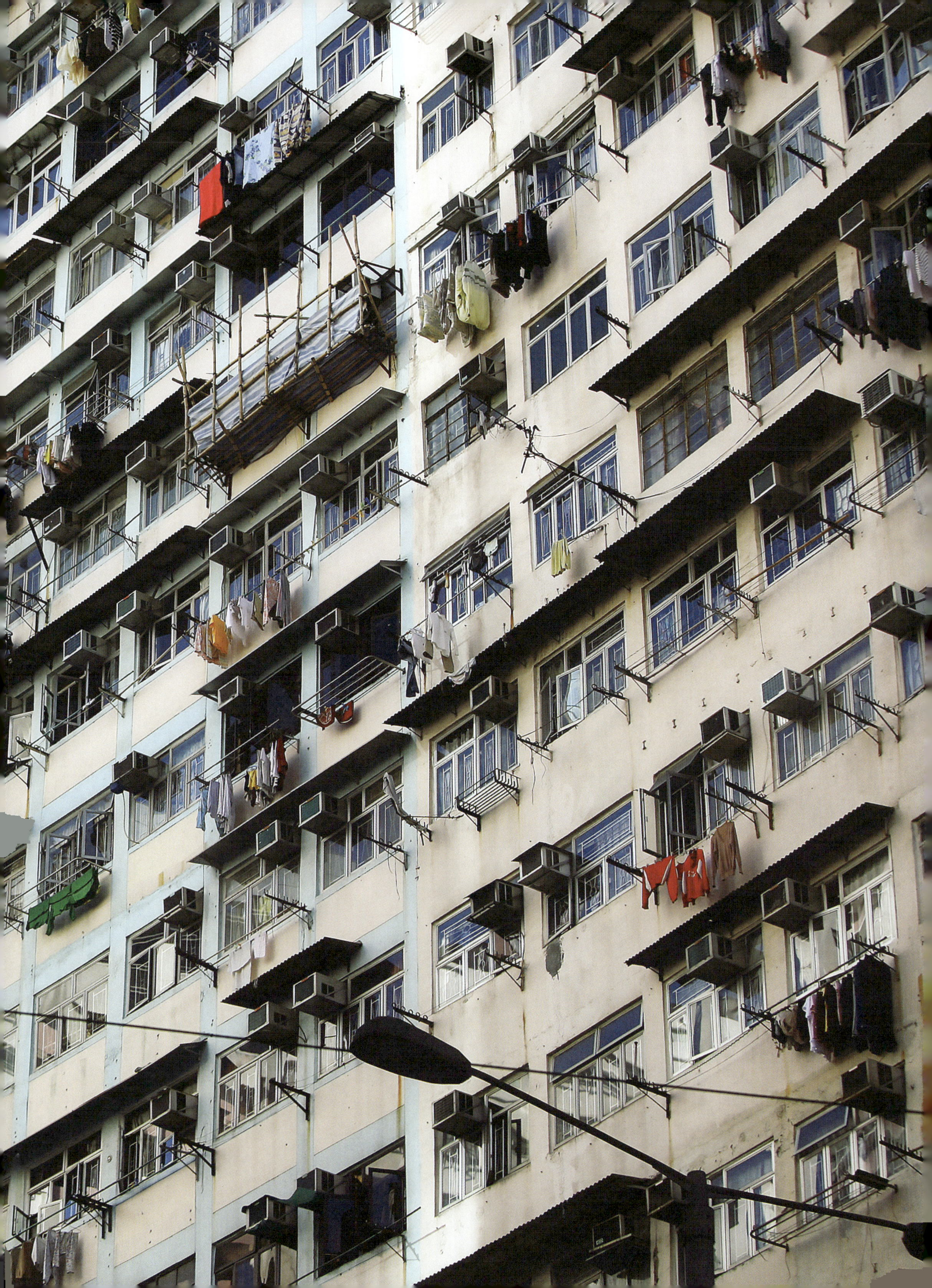

CULTURE & HERITAGE

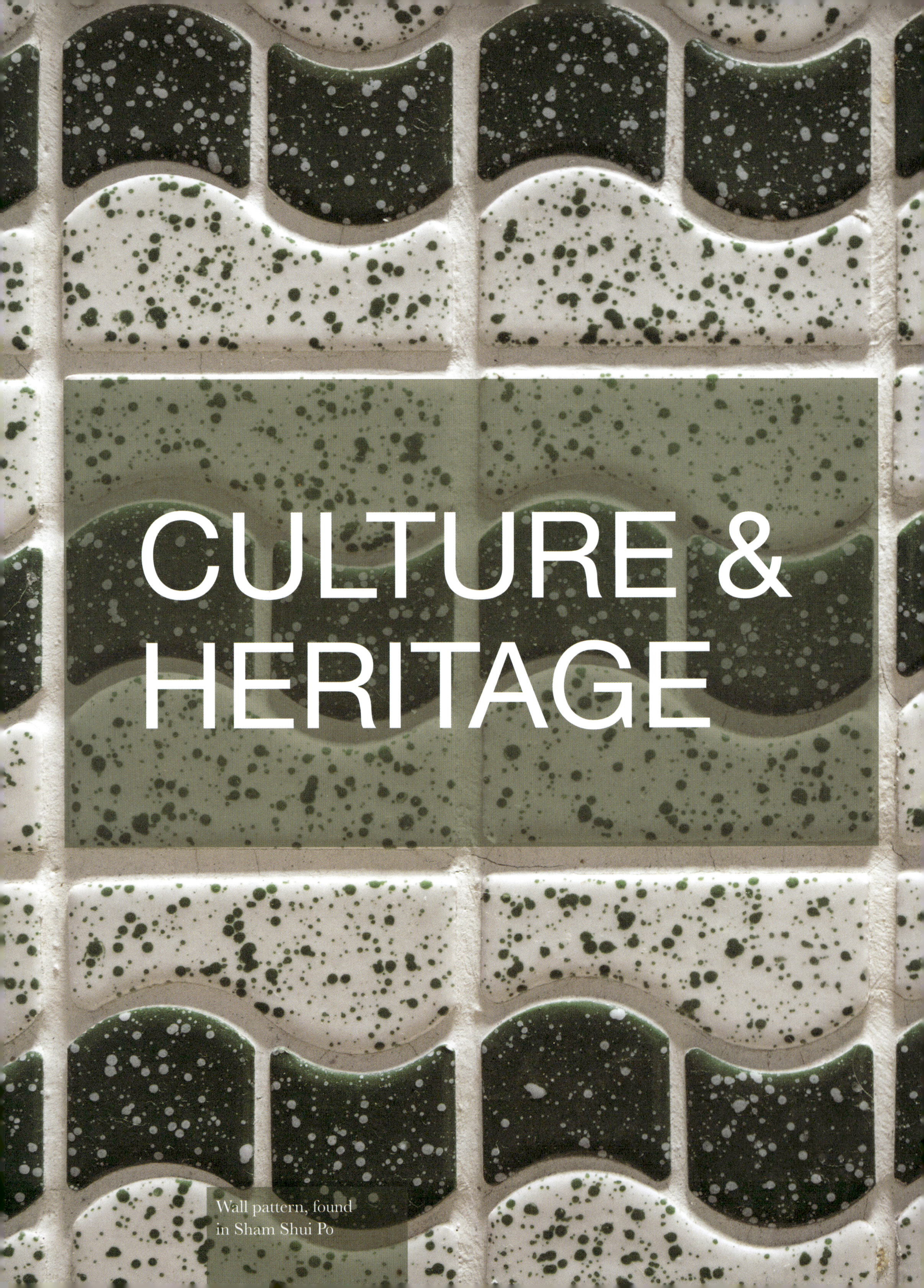

Wall pattern, found in Sham Shui Po

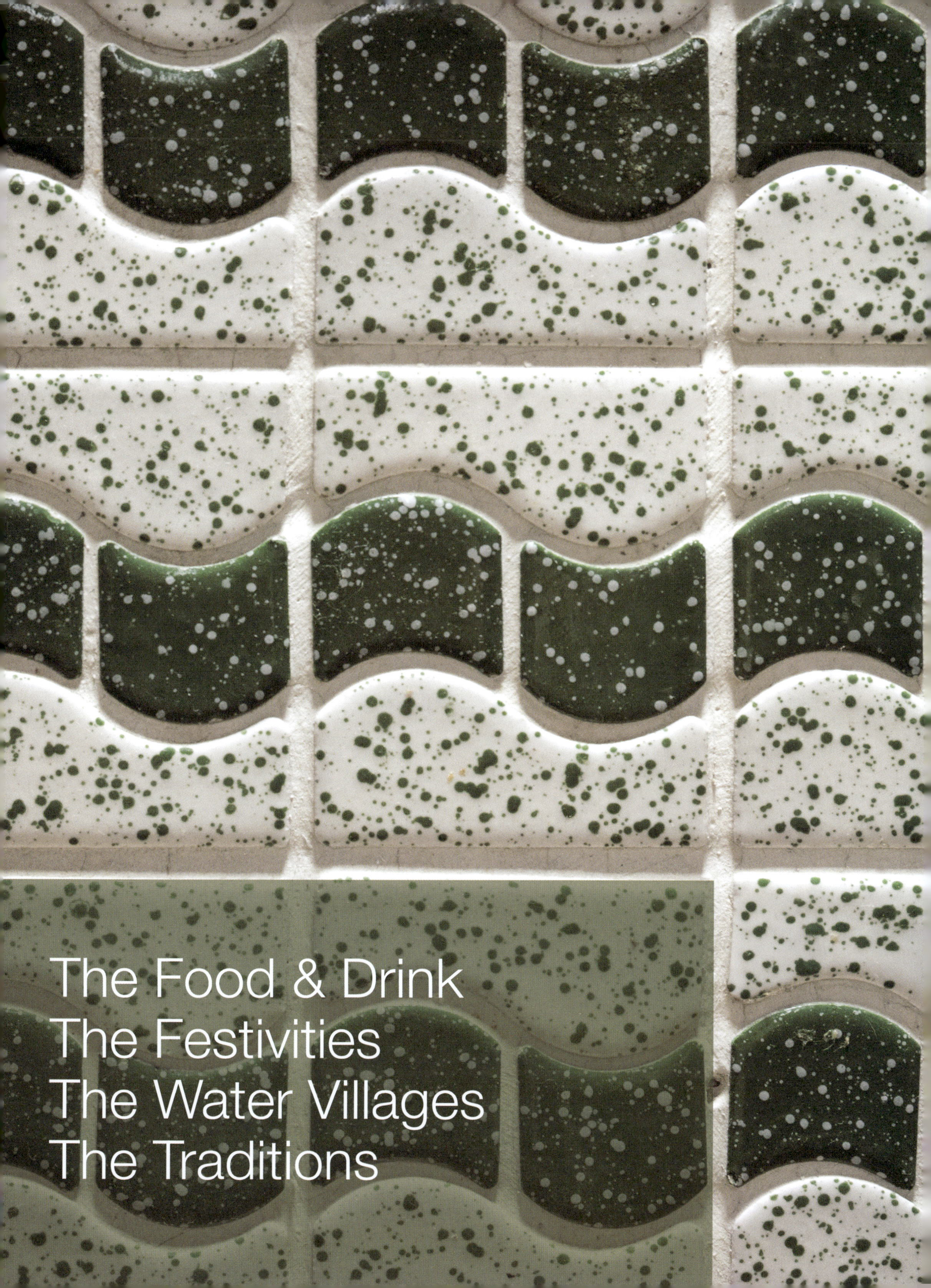

The Food & Drink
The Festivities
The Water Villages
The Traditions

THE FOOD & DRINK

Hong Kong is a city full of Michelin-starred restaurants as well as tradition-rich, uniquely Hong Kong diners. The spectrum is vast, the options diverse. Food-wise, we've also got many treats and delicacies that we can proudly call our own.

Dim sum, a Hong Kong export, is my personal favorite — not to mention every other Hongkonger's. I remember frequently going dim-summing as a child, either spending quality time with my grandparents, celebrating an occasion, or getting together for a family gathering. My mom said I had been eating chicken feet, a popular dim sum dish, ever since I was one. I do remember really loving it — until I found out that it was actually chicken feet!

65. A streetside restaurant in Wan Chai
66. A street vendor in Mong Kok
67. A restaurant in Shek Kip Mei
68. Filling kettles at a traditional dim sum eatery in Sai Ying Pun
69. Ordering dishes at a traditional dim sum eatery in Sai Ying Pun
70. Dessert soups at a traditional dessert house in Mong Kok
71. A dessert display case in Wan Chai
72. Street food in Sham Shui Po
73. Condiments galore at a street food stall in Sham Shui Po

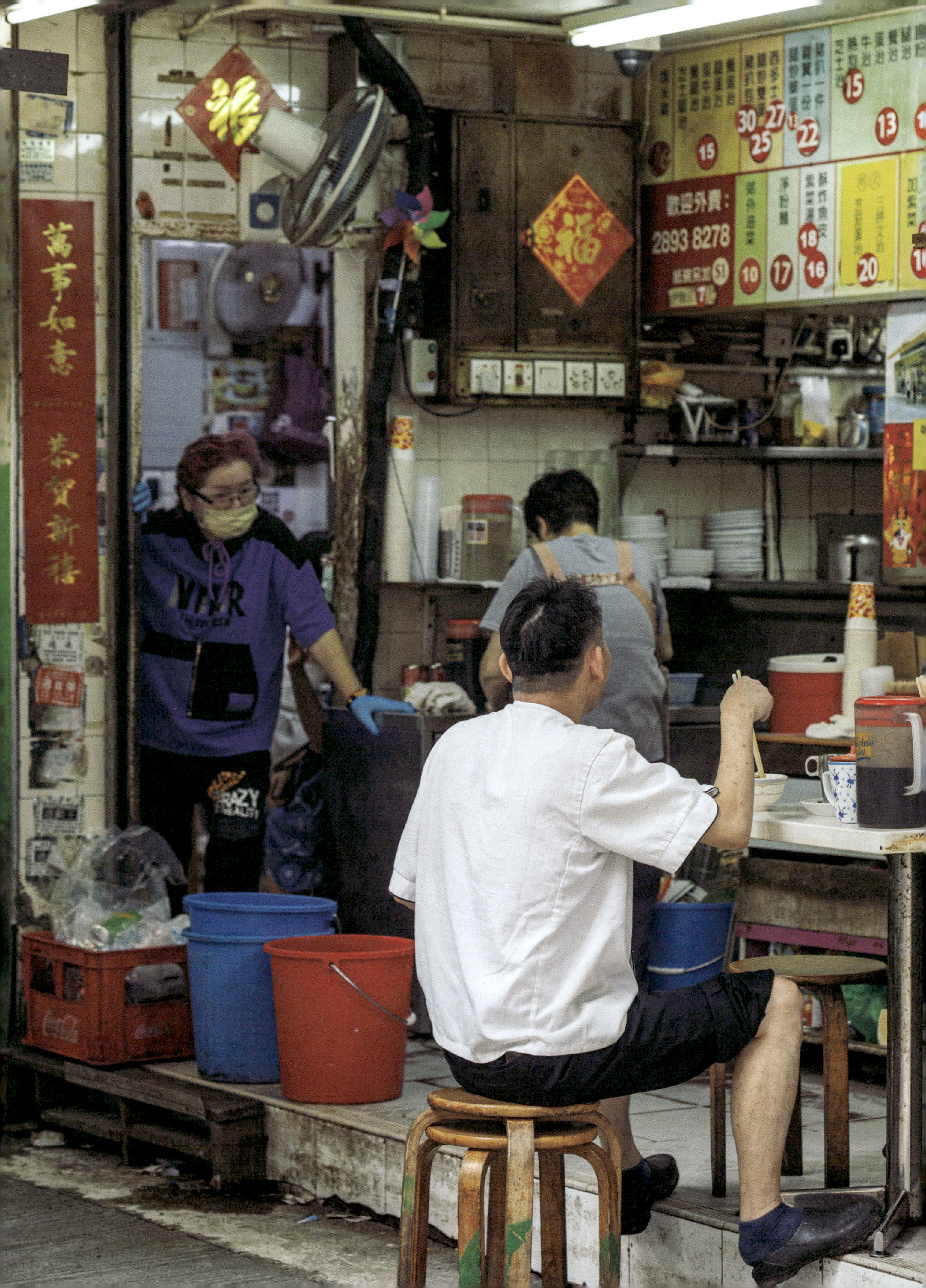
萬事如意
恭賀新禧
福
歡迎外賣：
2893 8278

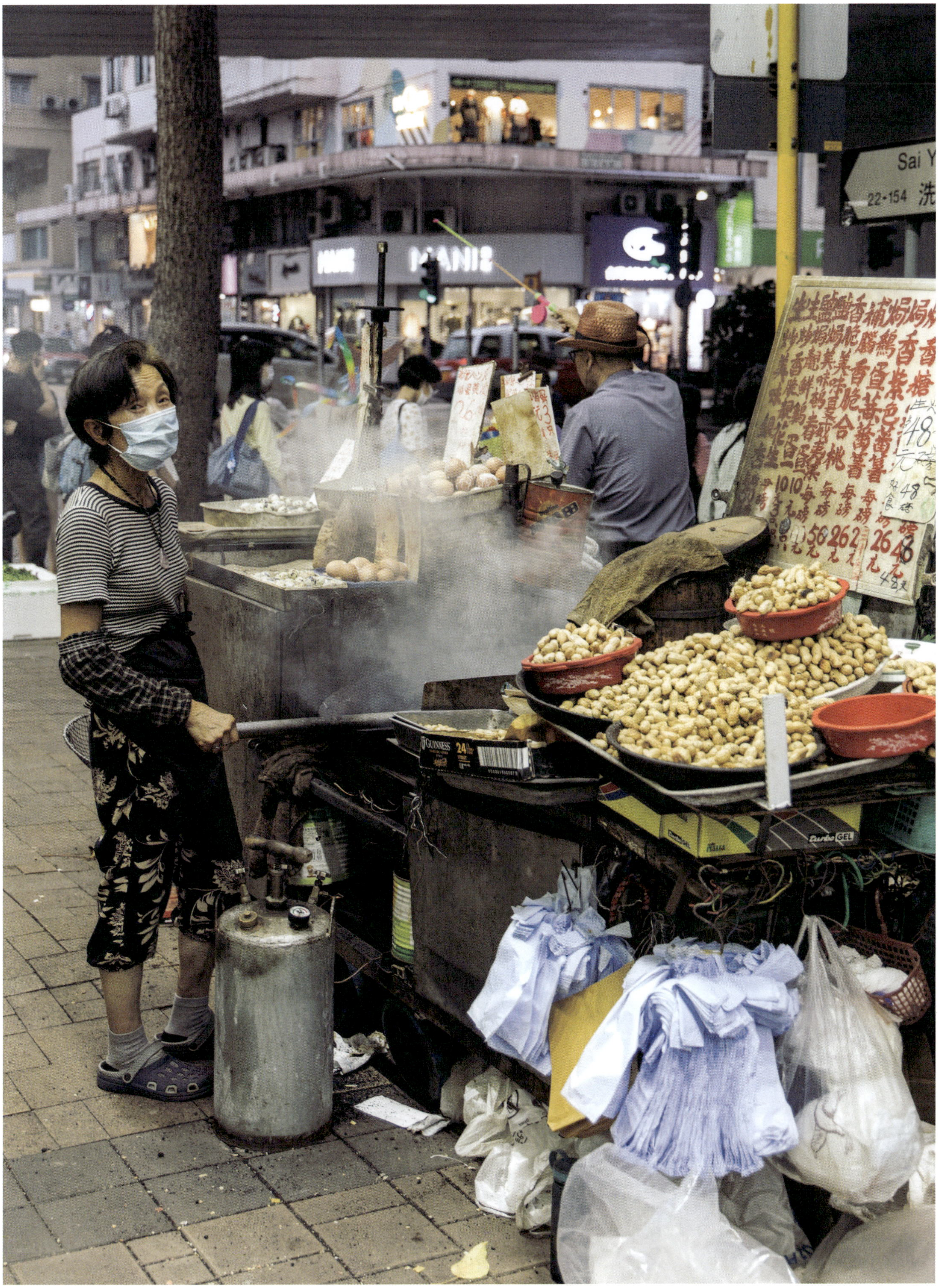
22-154
GUINNESS

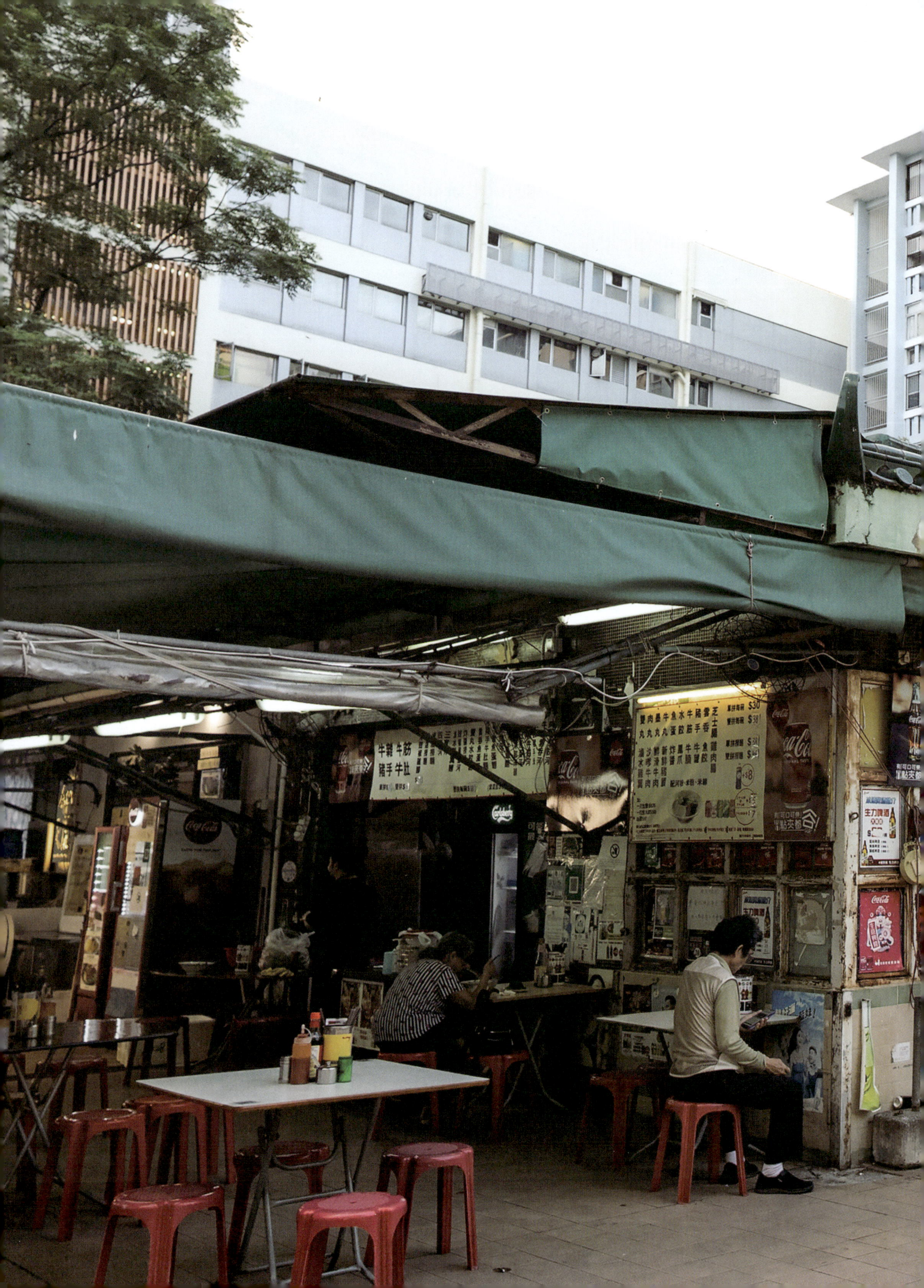

牛腩 牛筋
豬手 牛肚
Carlsberg
$30

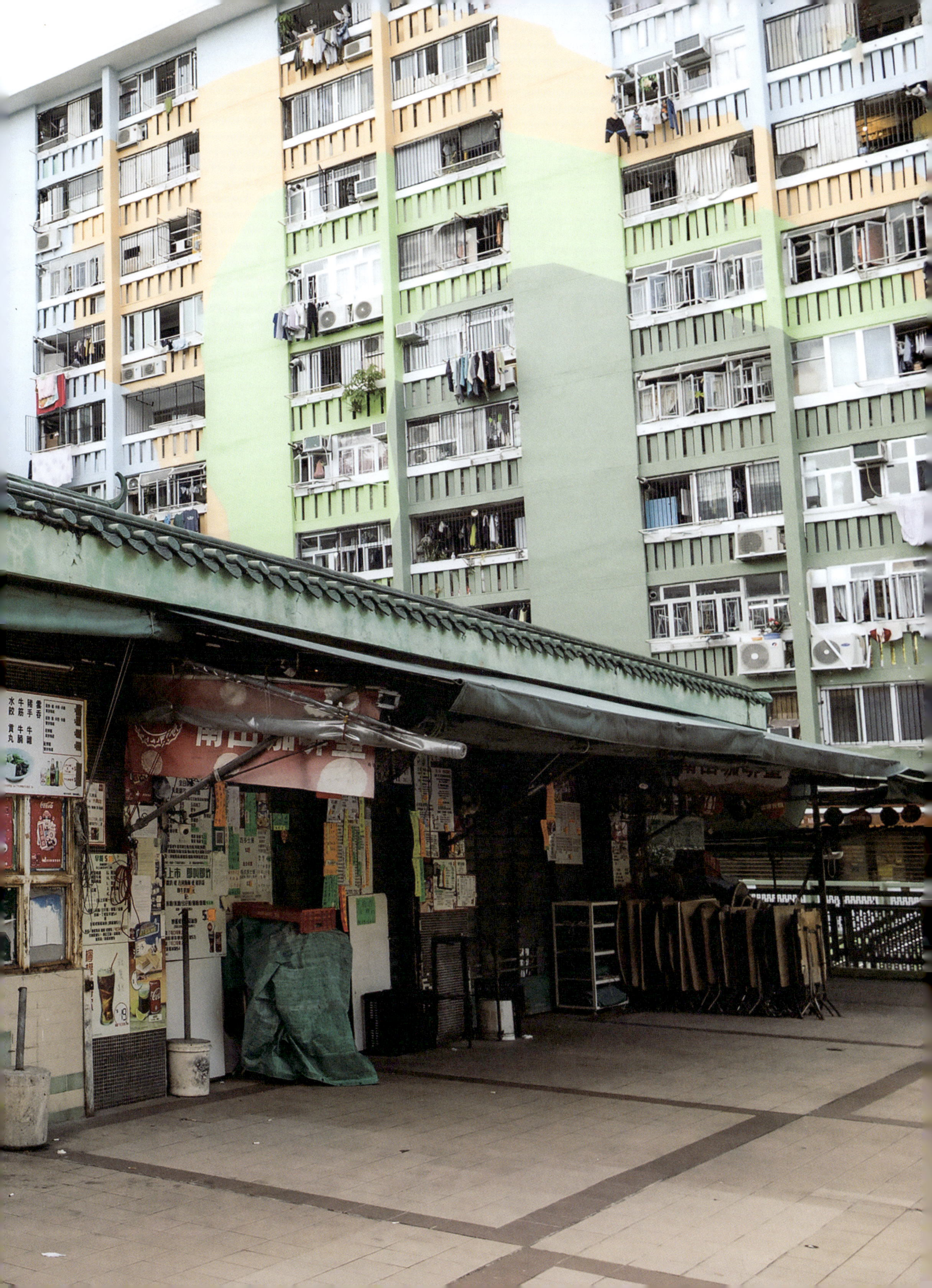

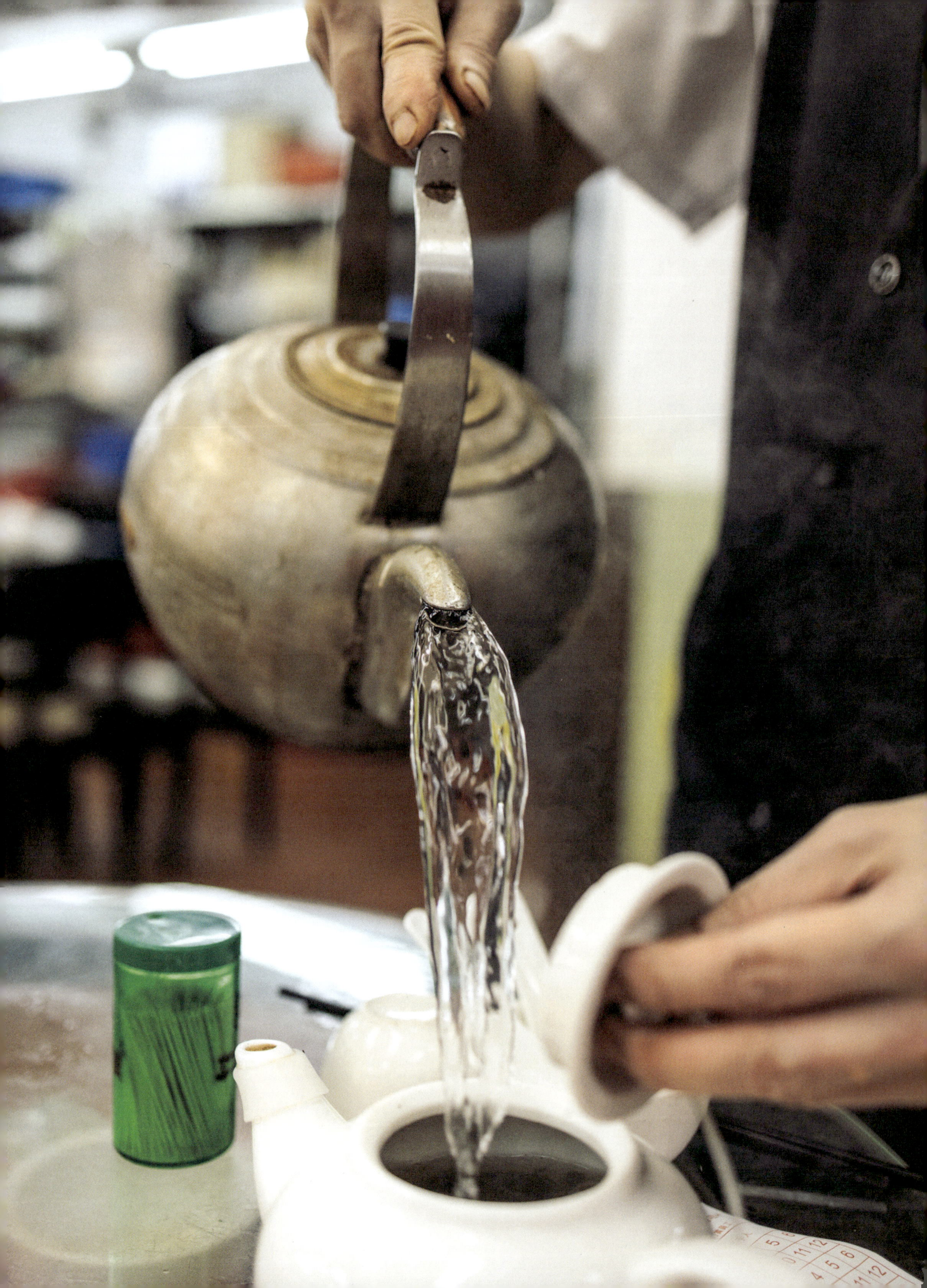

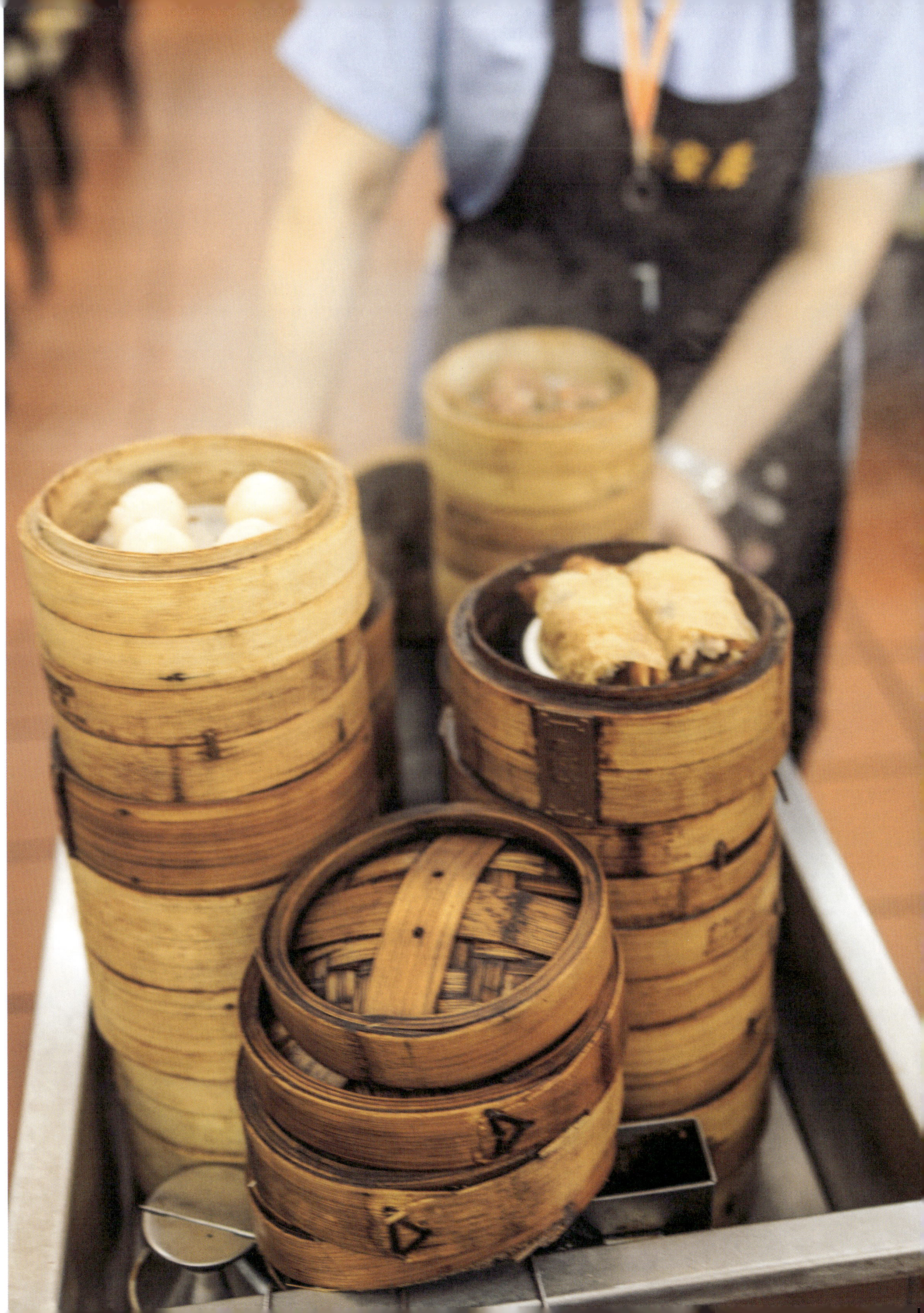

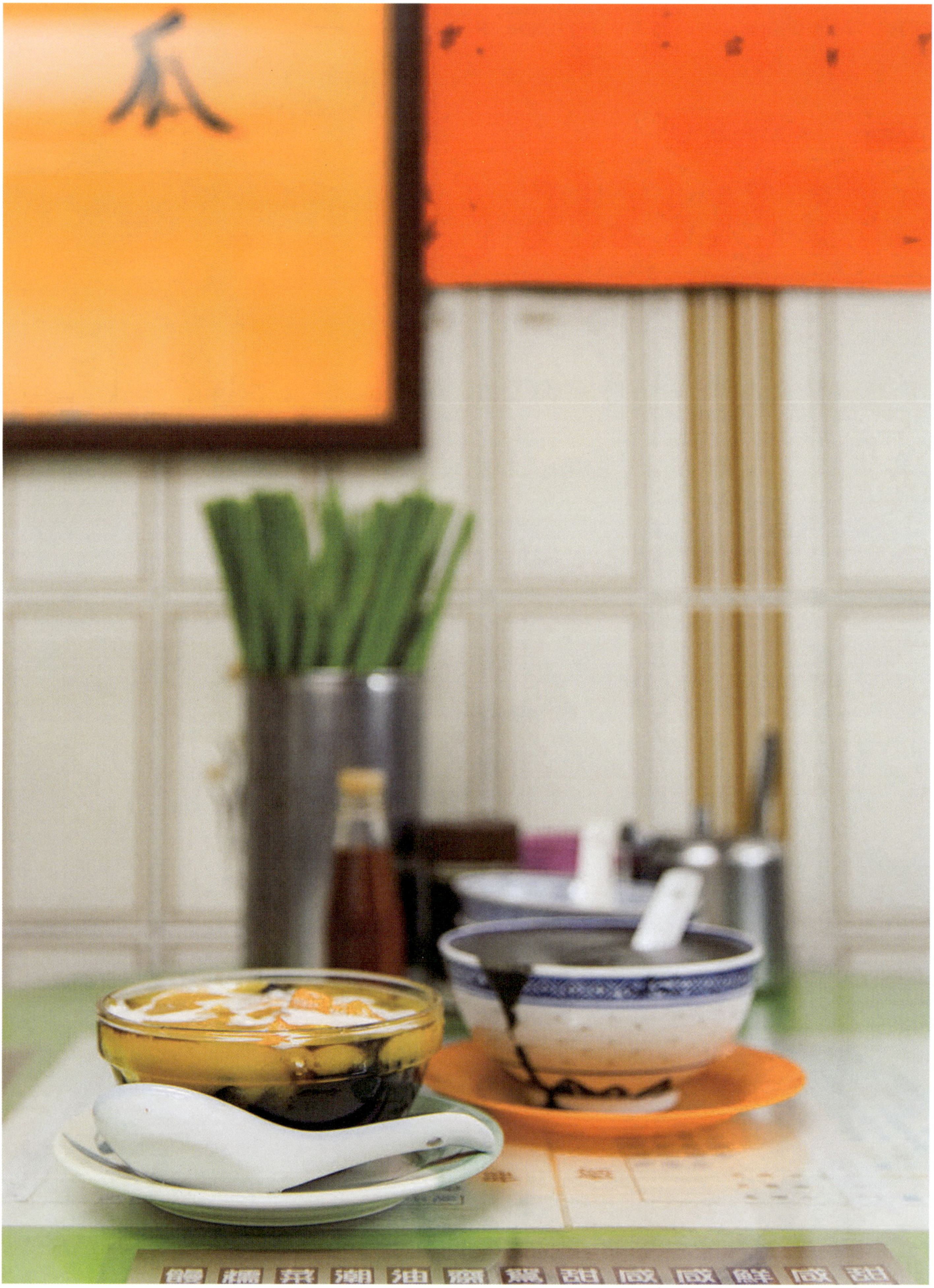

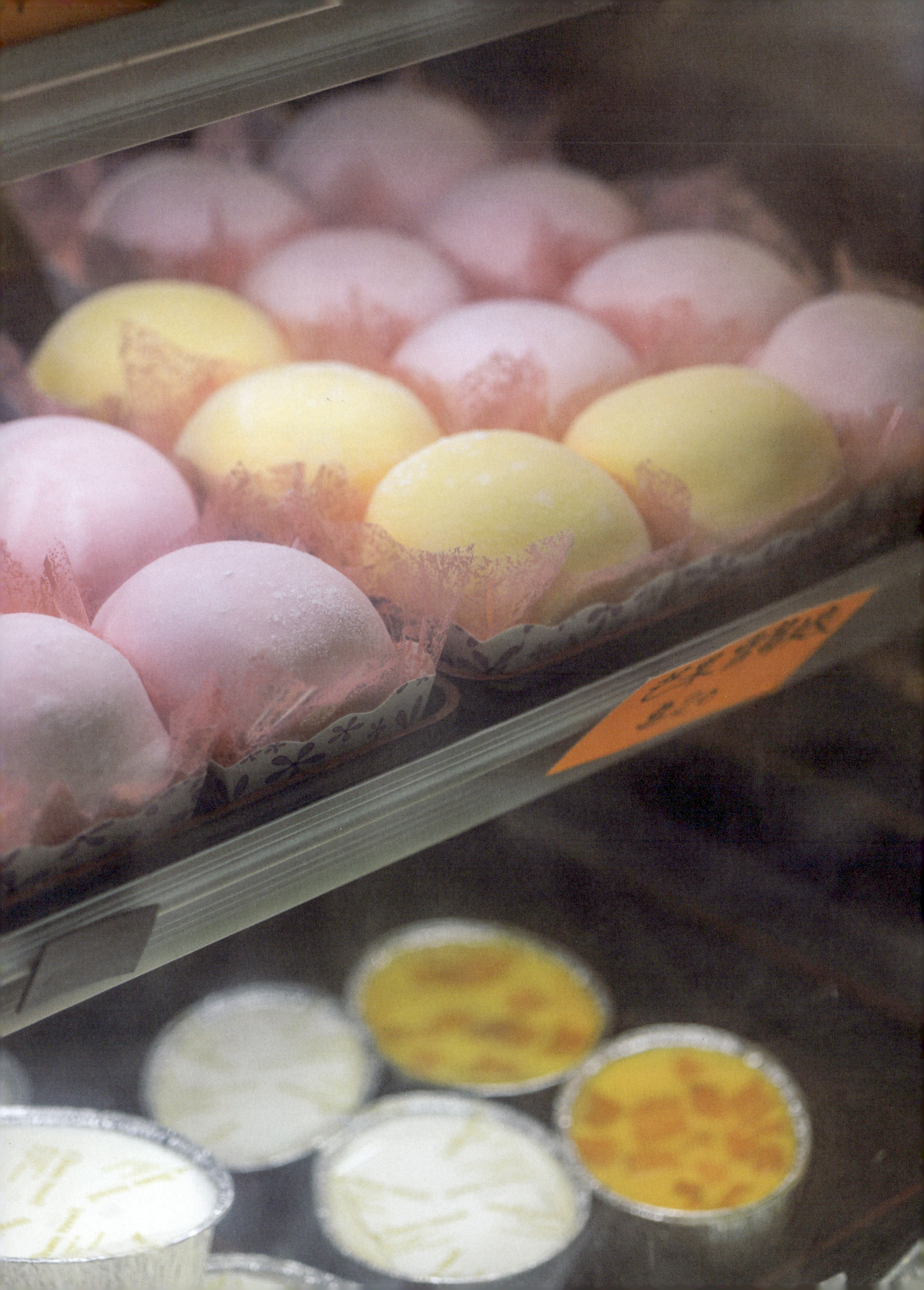

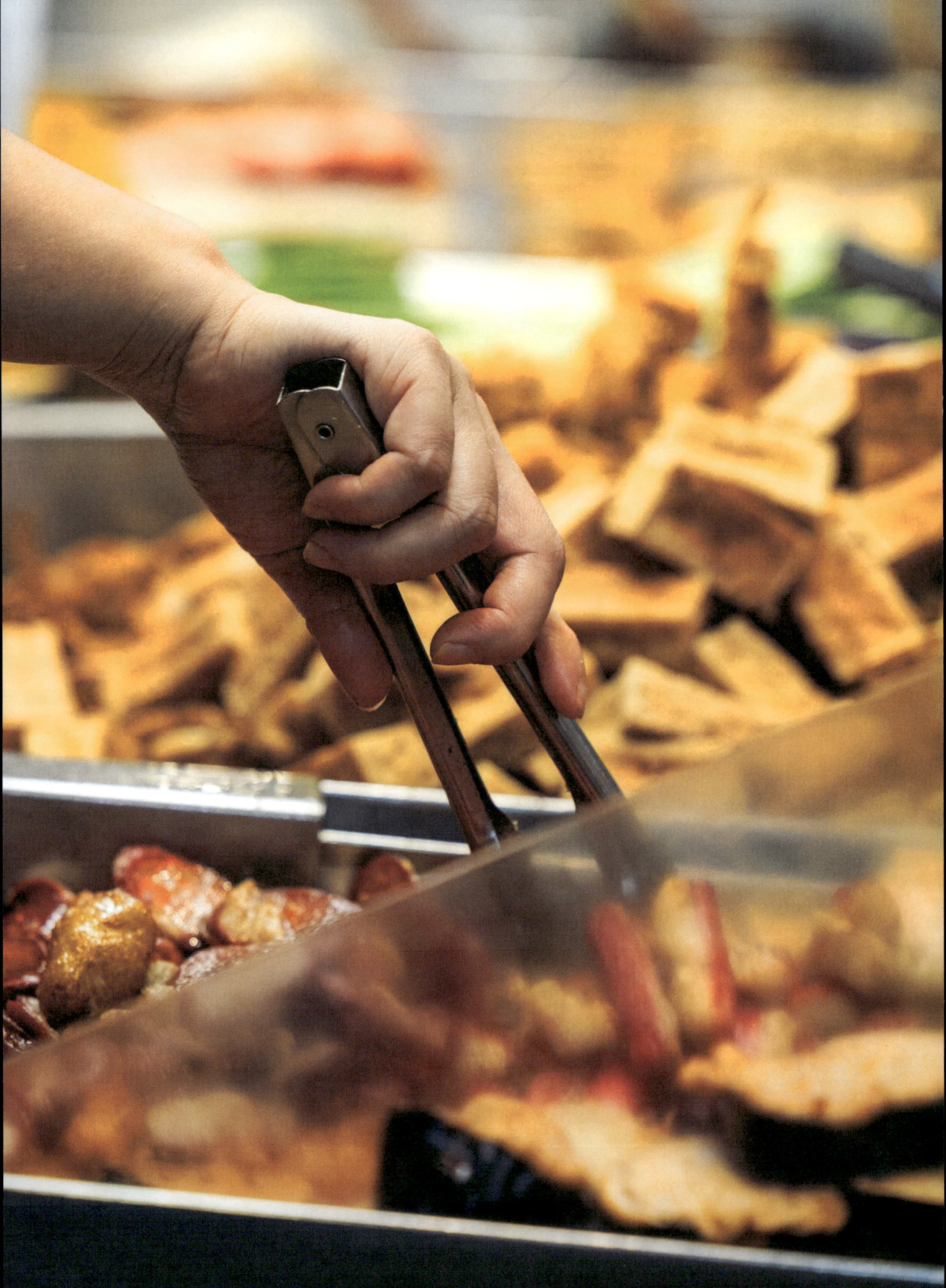

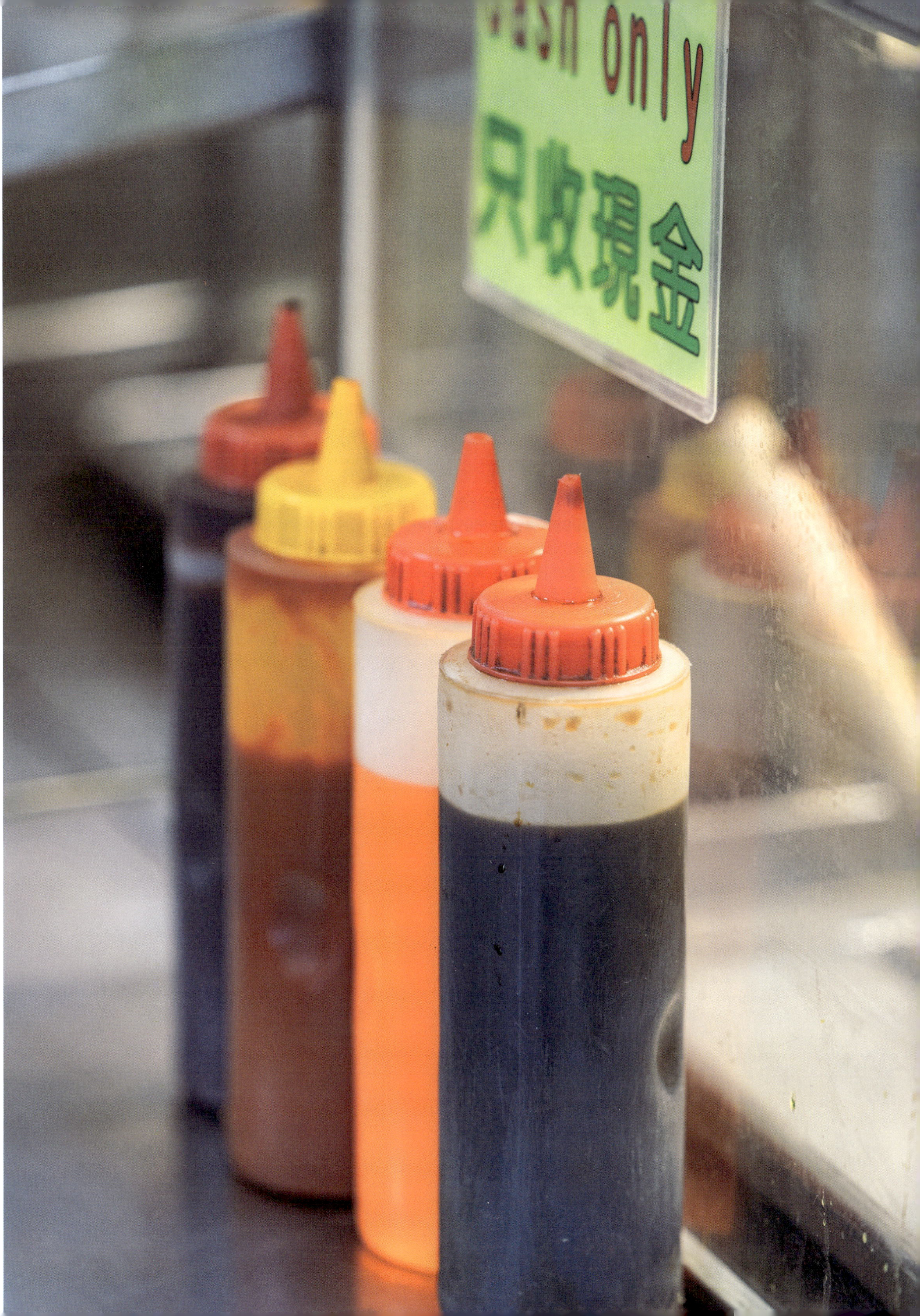
only
只收現金

THE FESTIVITIES

There are so many festive celebrations in Hong Kong, both from a traditional and commercial perspective. Even though we Hongkongers like to celebrate everything, the most important occasion is definitely Lunar New Year, when the city gets covered in red and gold.

I particularly like the Dragon Boat Festival, which also happens around the same time as the really fun Cheung Chau Bun Festival on Cheung Chau island.

My mom would prepare elaborately festive meals for these special occasions. She would cook everyone's favorite dishes, like steamed crab, shrimp, sauteed scallops, sea cucumber, abalone, and stir-fried rice cake, for the whole family to enjoy.

74. Red lantern decorations during Mid-Autumn Festival
75. Festive ornaments for the Lunar New Year, sold in Mong Kok
76. A bamboo theater for the Cheung Chau Bun Festival
77. "Tai Ping Ching Chiu" decor for the Cheung Chau Bun Festival
78. Cheung Chau Bun Festival street mural
79. Dragon Boat Festival races at Victoria Harbour

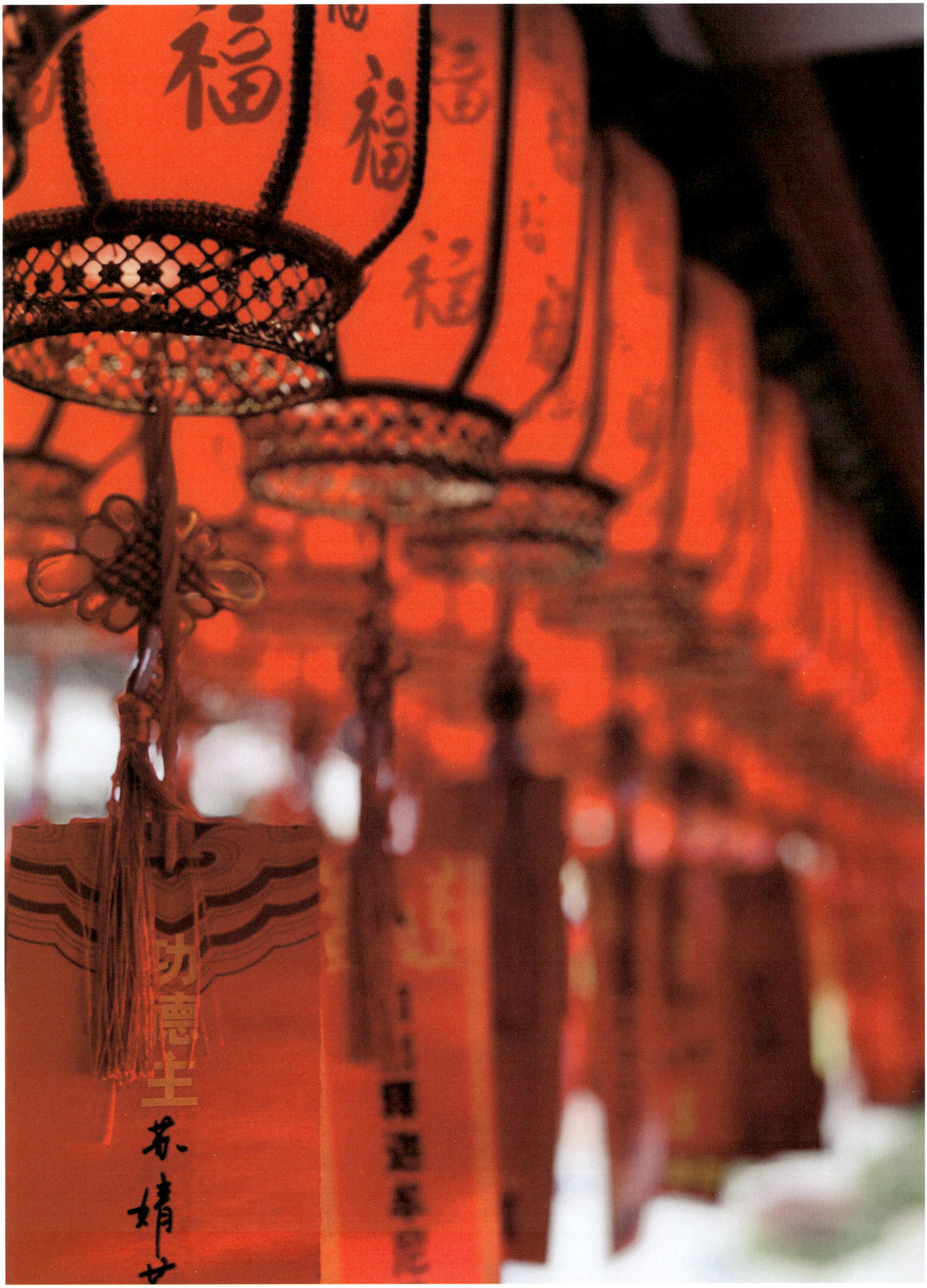
福
福
福
功德主

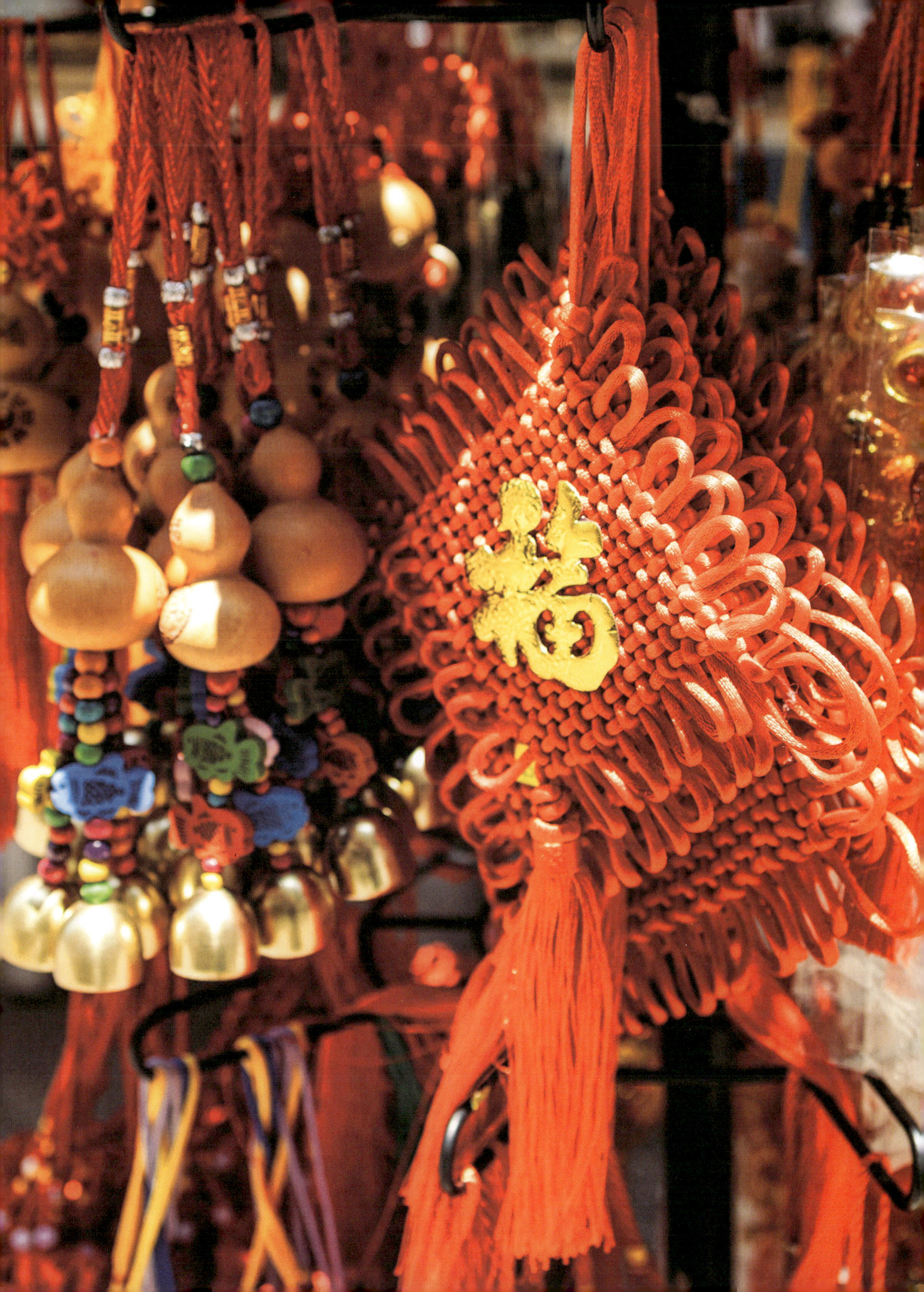
福

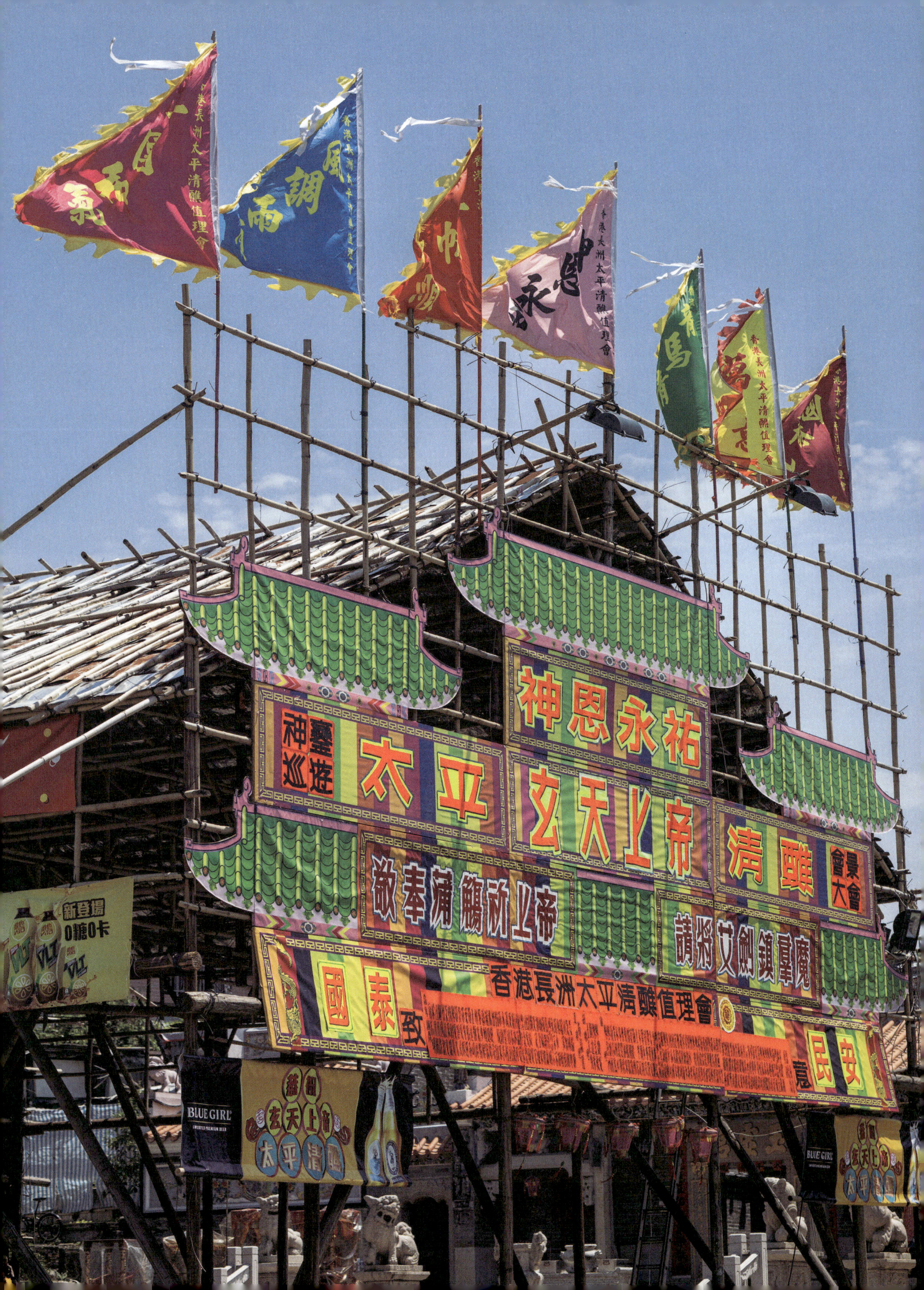
神恩永祐
神鑾巡遊
太平
玄天上帝
清醮
會景大會
請將艾劍鎮羣魔
香港長洲太平清醮值理會
國泰
民安
新登場
0糖0卡
BLUE GIRL

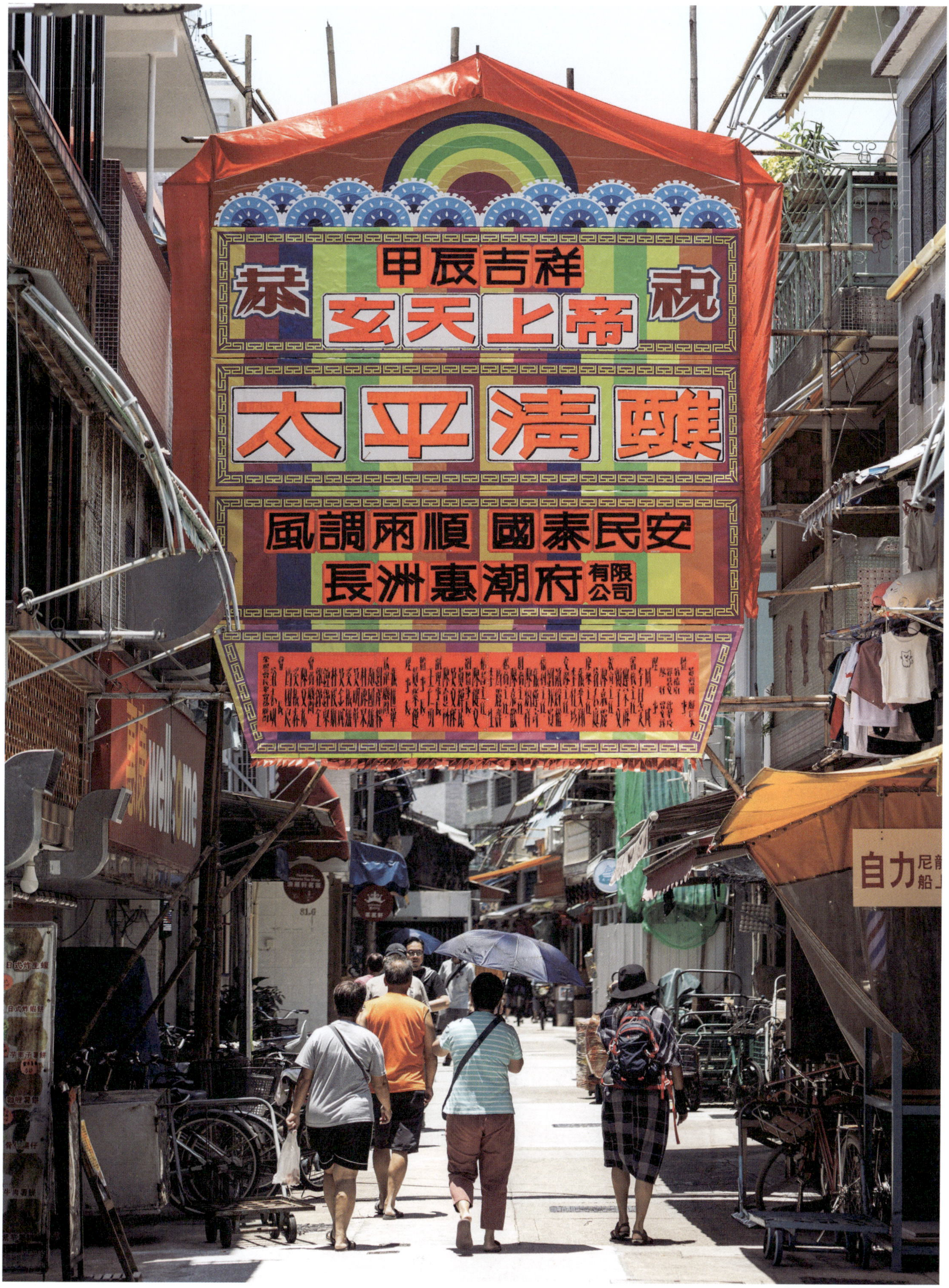
甲辰吉祥
恭
祝
玄天上帝
太平清醮
風調雨順 國泰民安
長洲惠潮府有限公司
自力

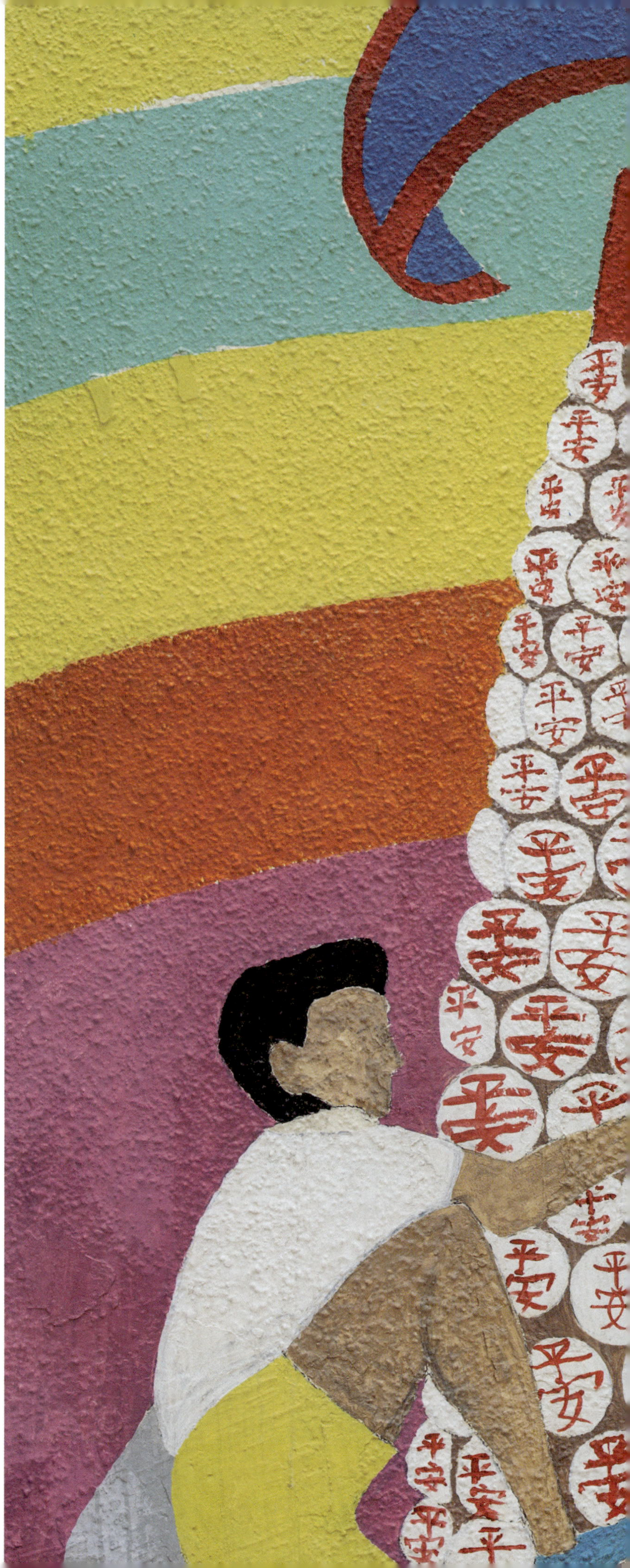
平安

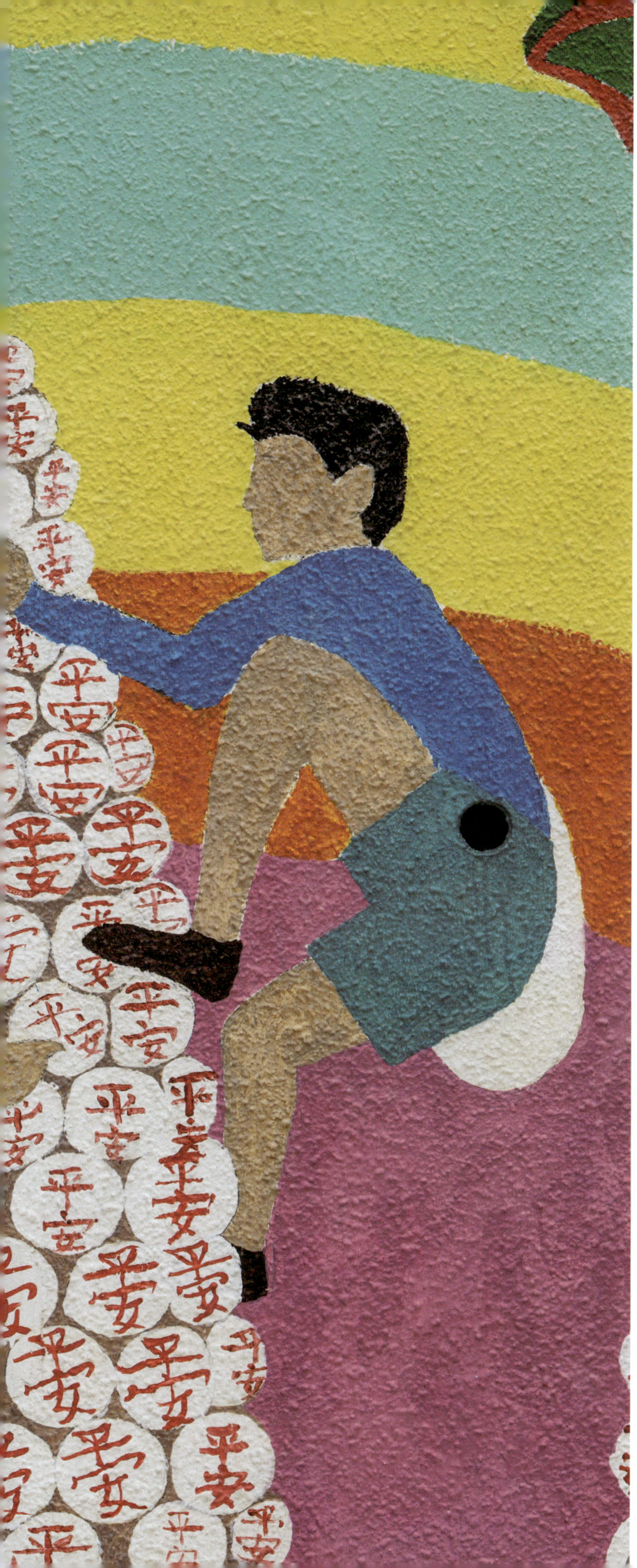
平安

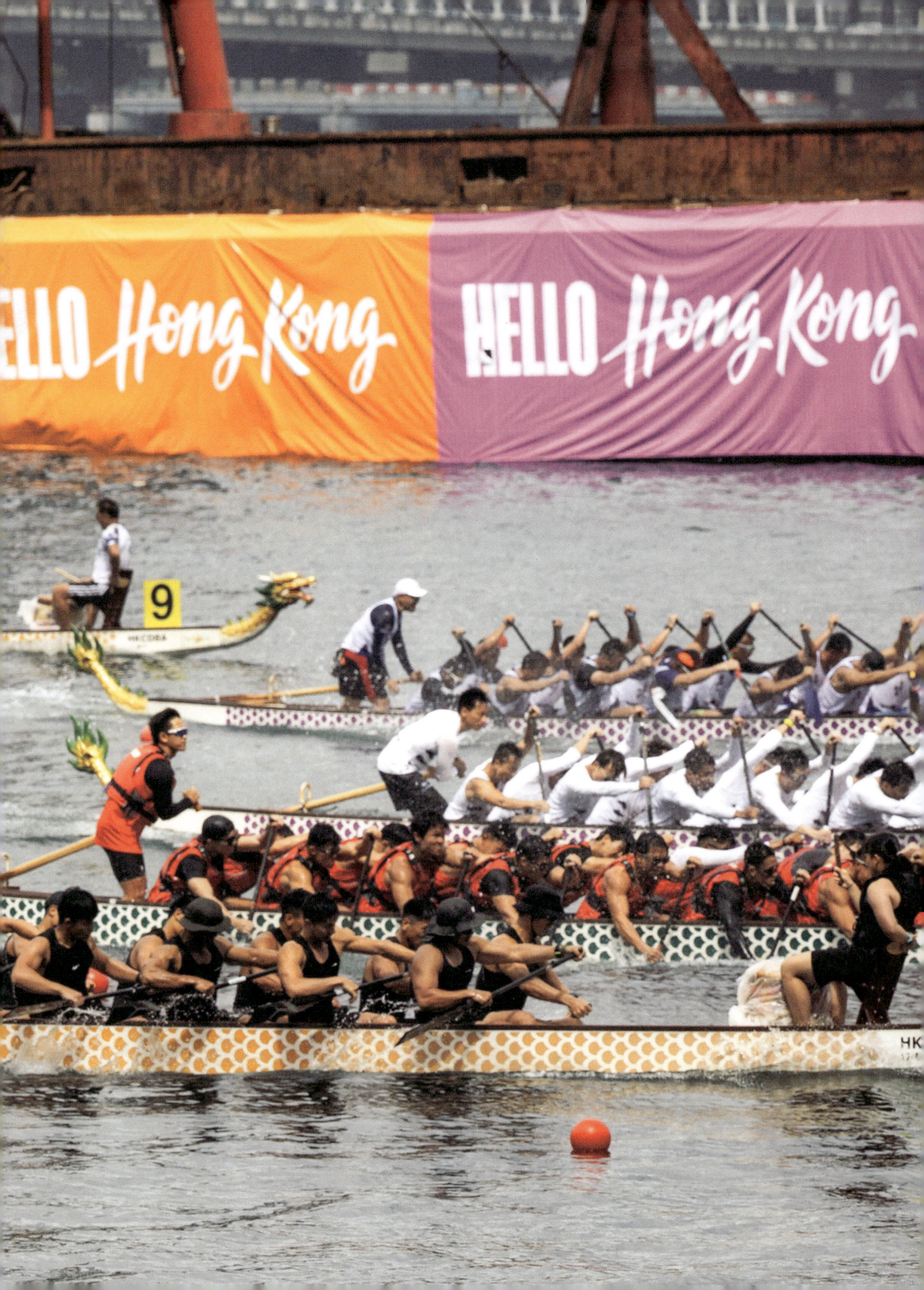
HELLO Hong Kong
HELLO Hong Kong
9

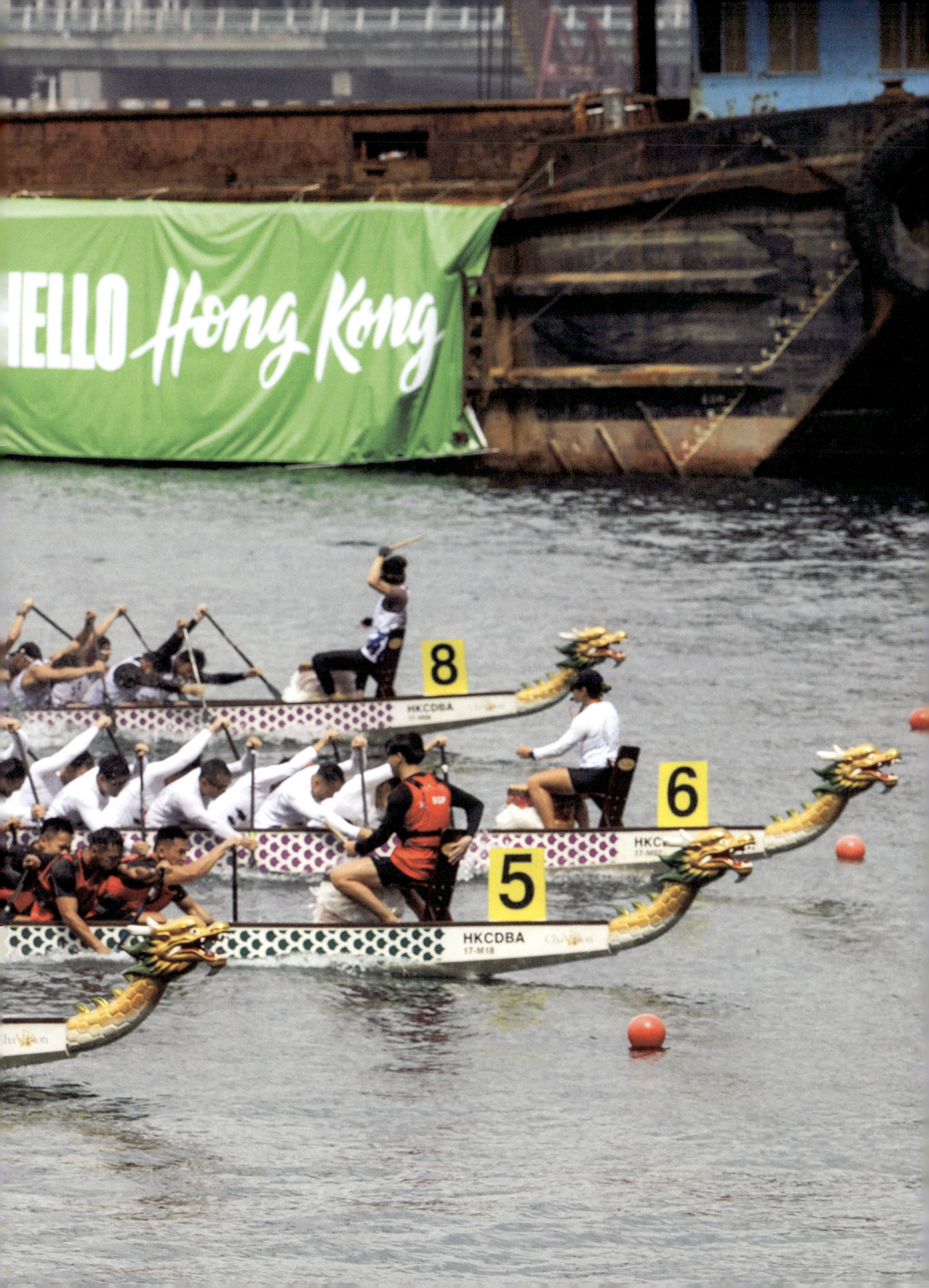
HELLO Hong Kong
8
6
5
HKCDBA
HKCDBA
17-M18

CULTURE & HERITAGE

THE WATER VILLAGES

Not too far from the hustle and bustle of our city, there are those living a more simple life on the coastlines and outlying islands. Although there are 260-plus islands that make up Hong Kong, one of my favorites is the idyllic Cheung Chau.

80. Small boats docked in Cheung Chau
81. Waterfront village houses in Cheung Chau
82. Shops by the water on Lamma Island
83. Houses by the beach in Cheung Chau

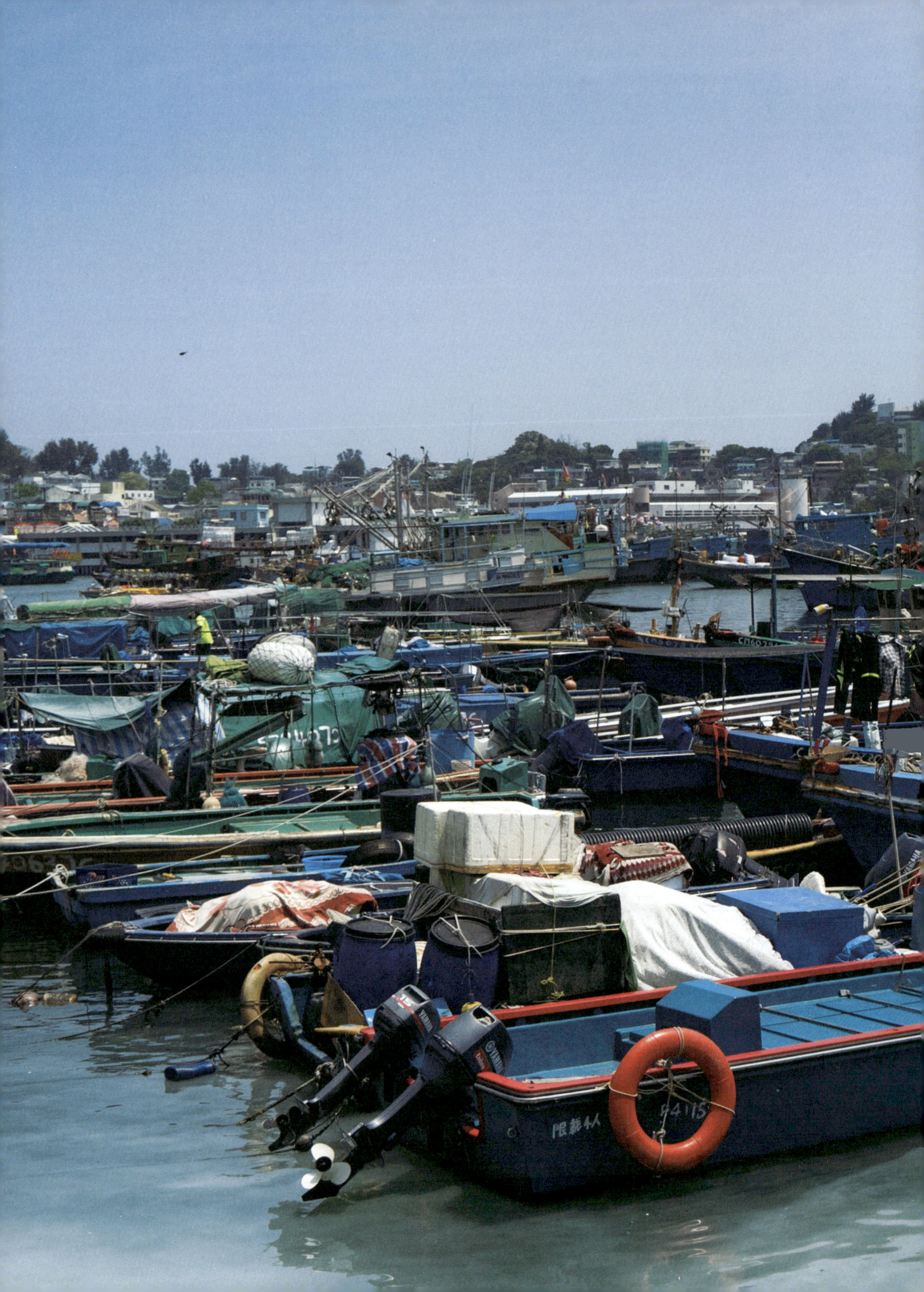

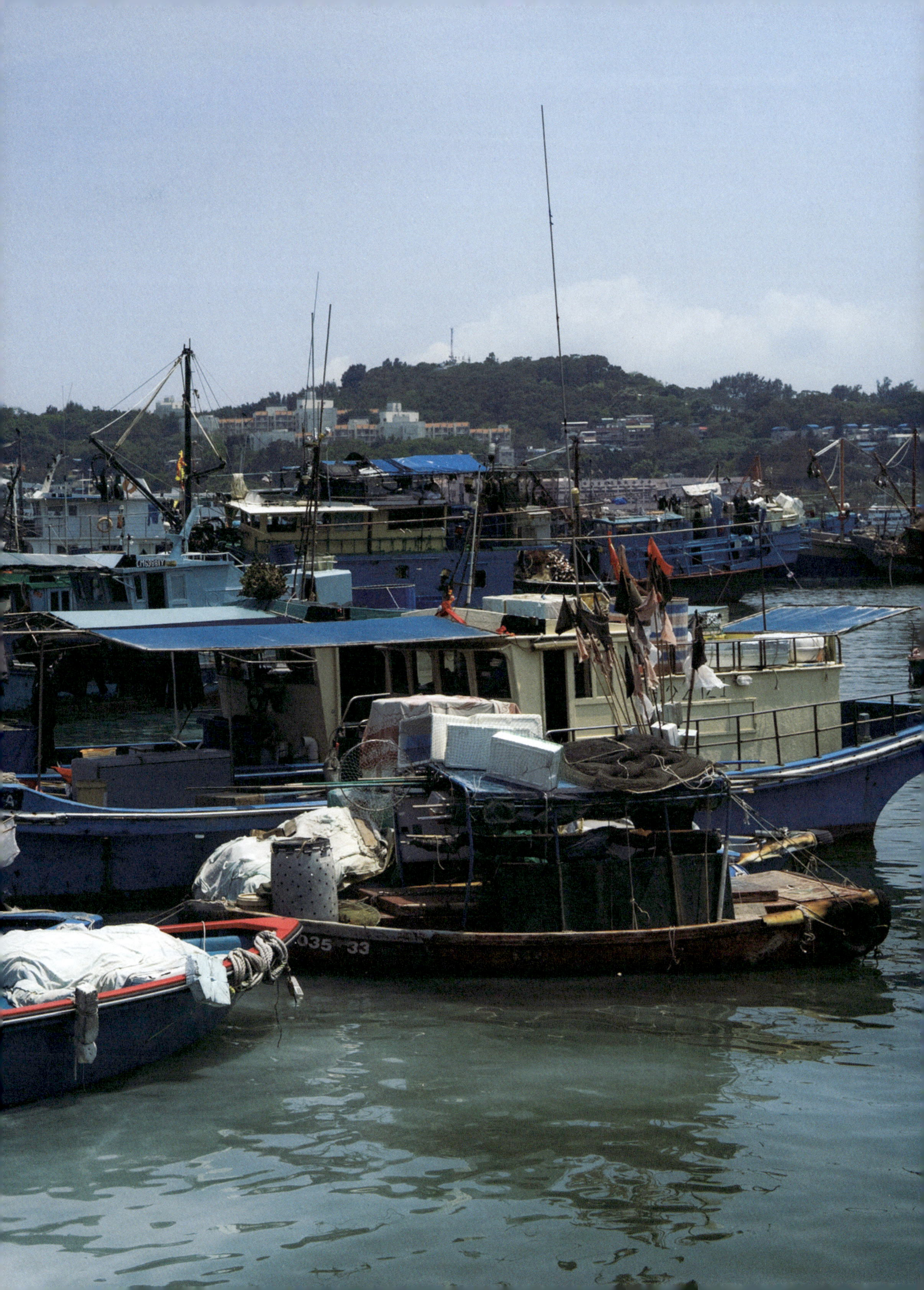
035 33

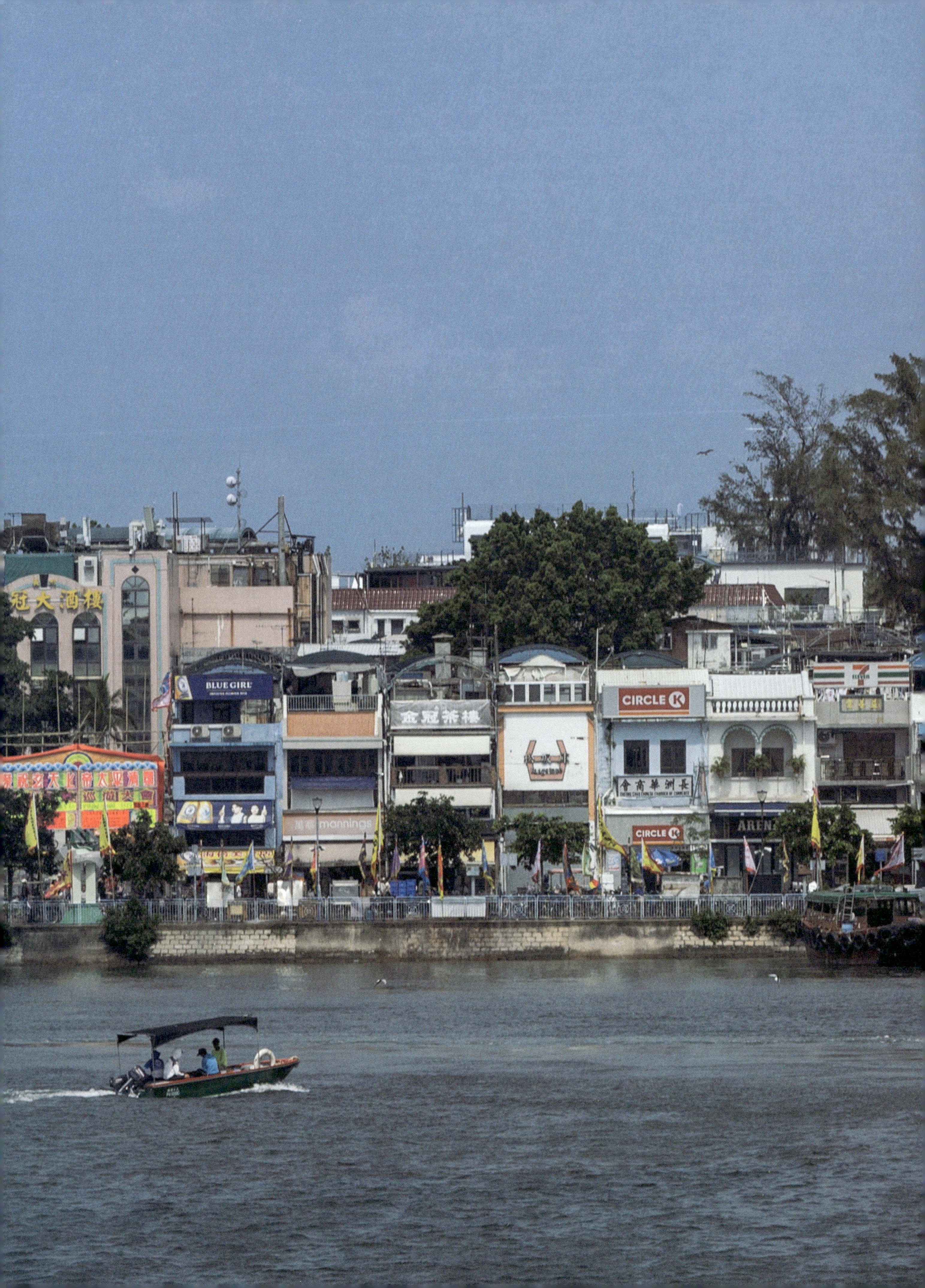
BLUE GIRL
金冠茶樓
CIRCLE K
mannings
CIRCLE K

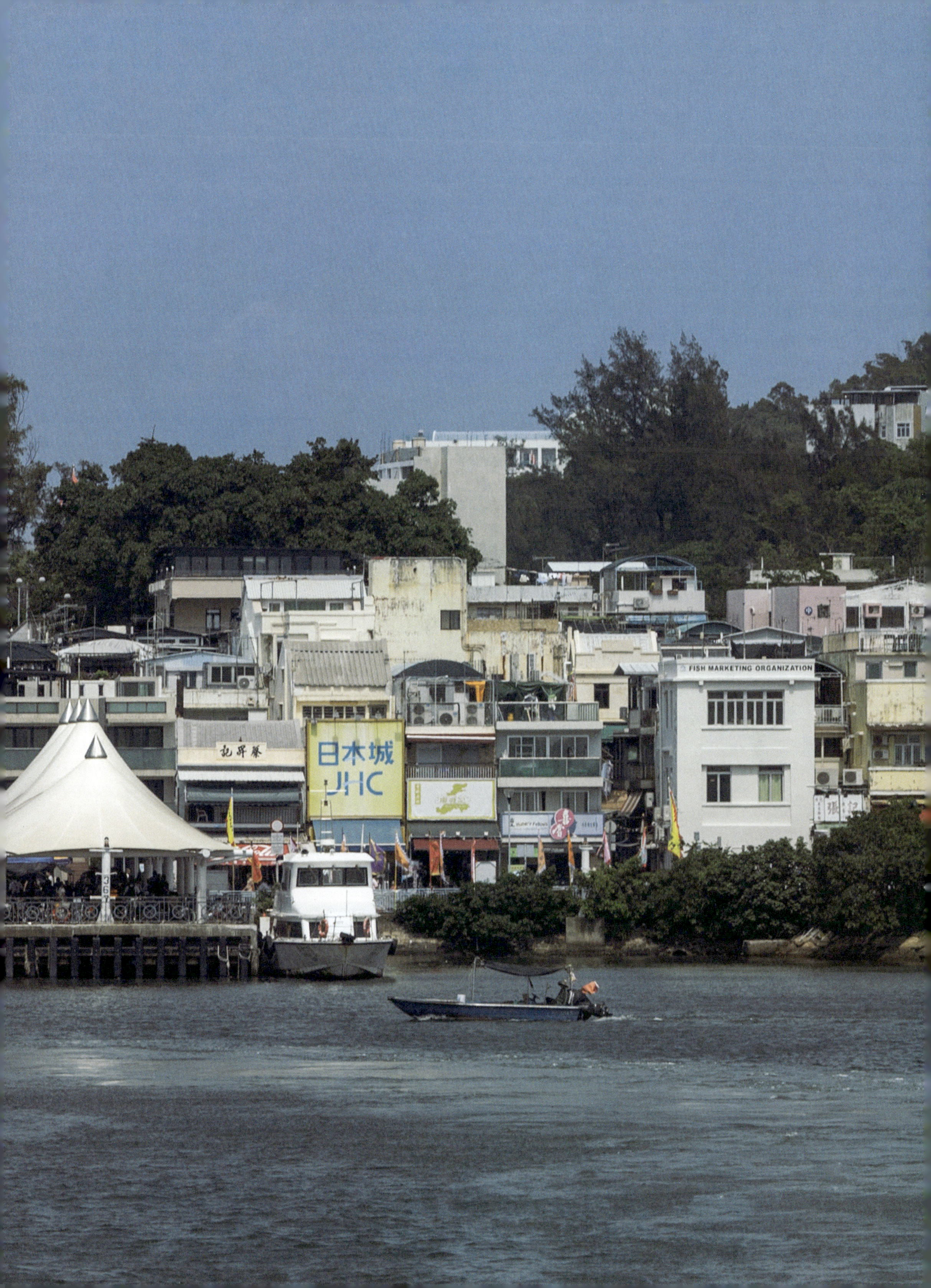
日木城
JHC
FISH MARKETING ORGANIZATION

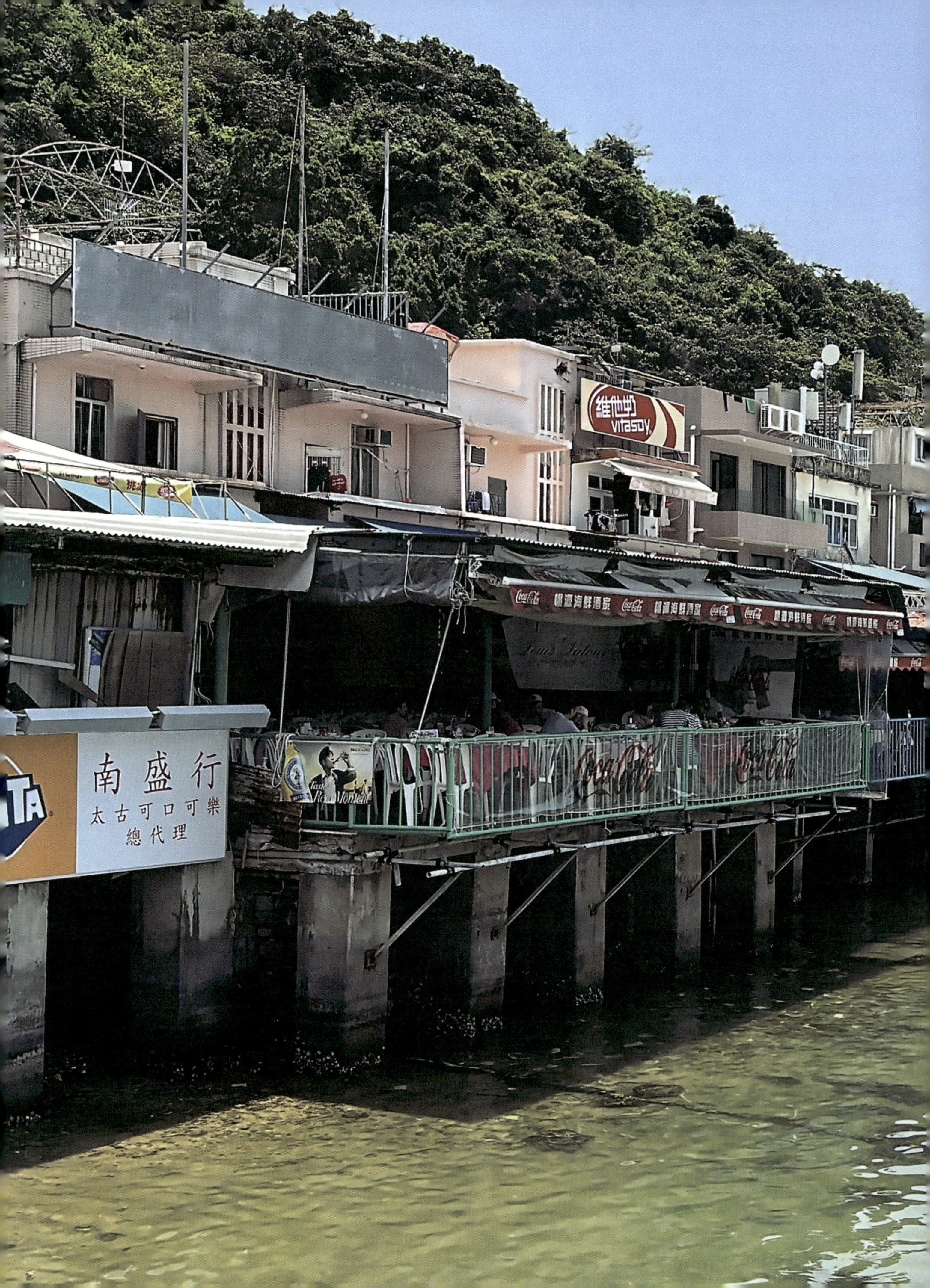
維他奶
vitasoy
Coca-Cola
南盛行
太古可口可樂
總代理

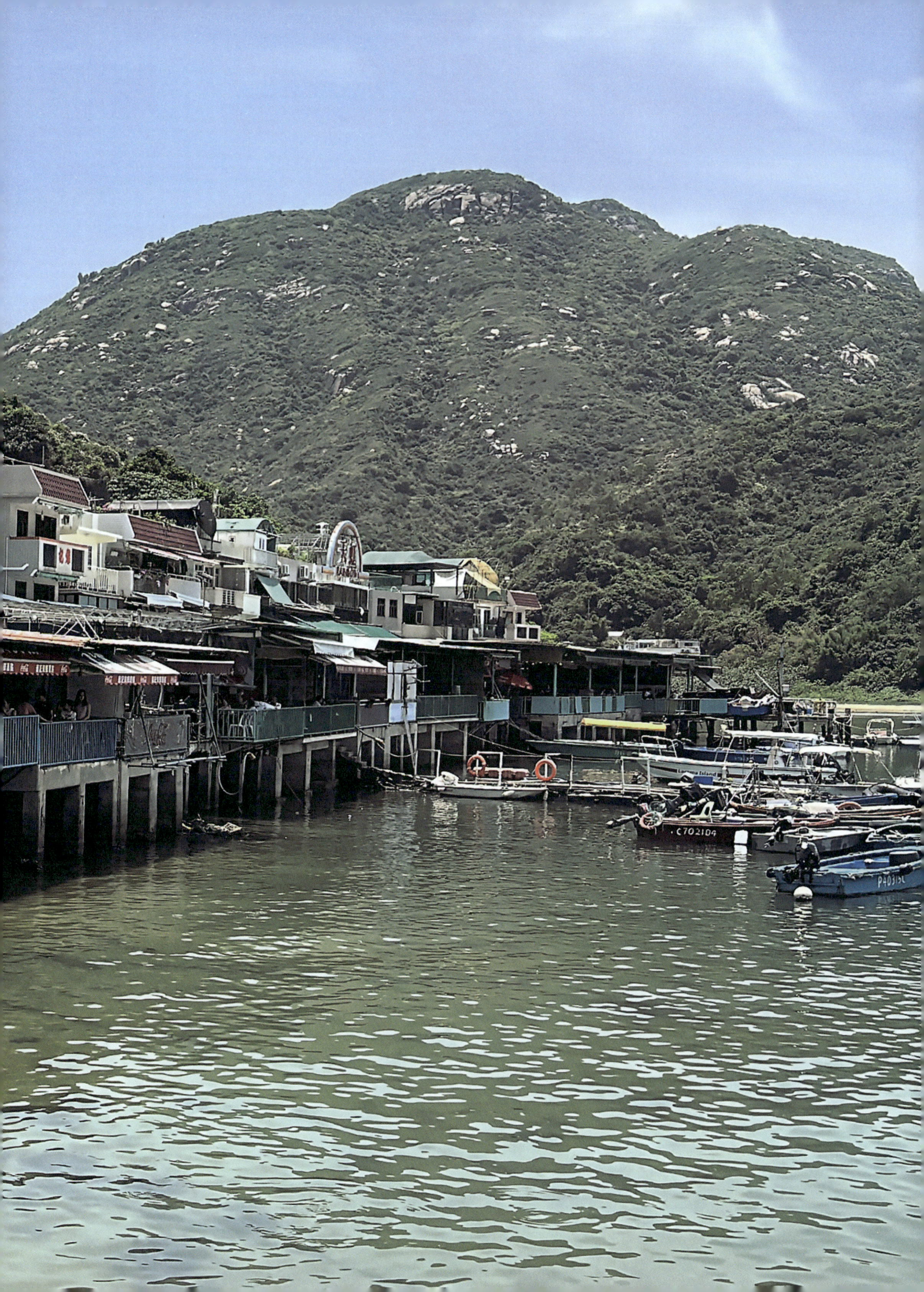
C70210A

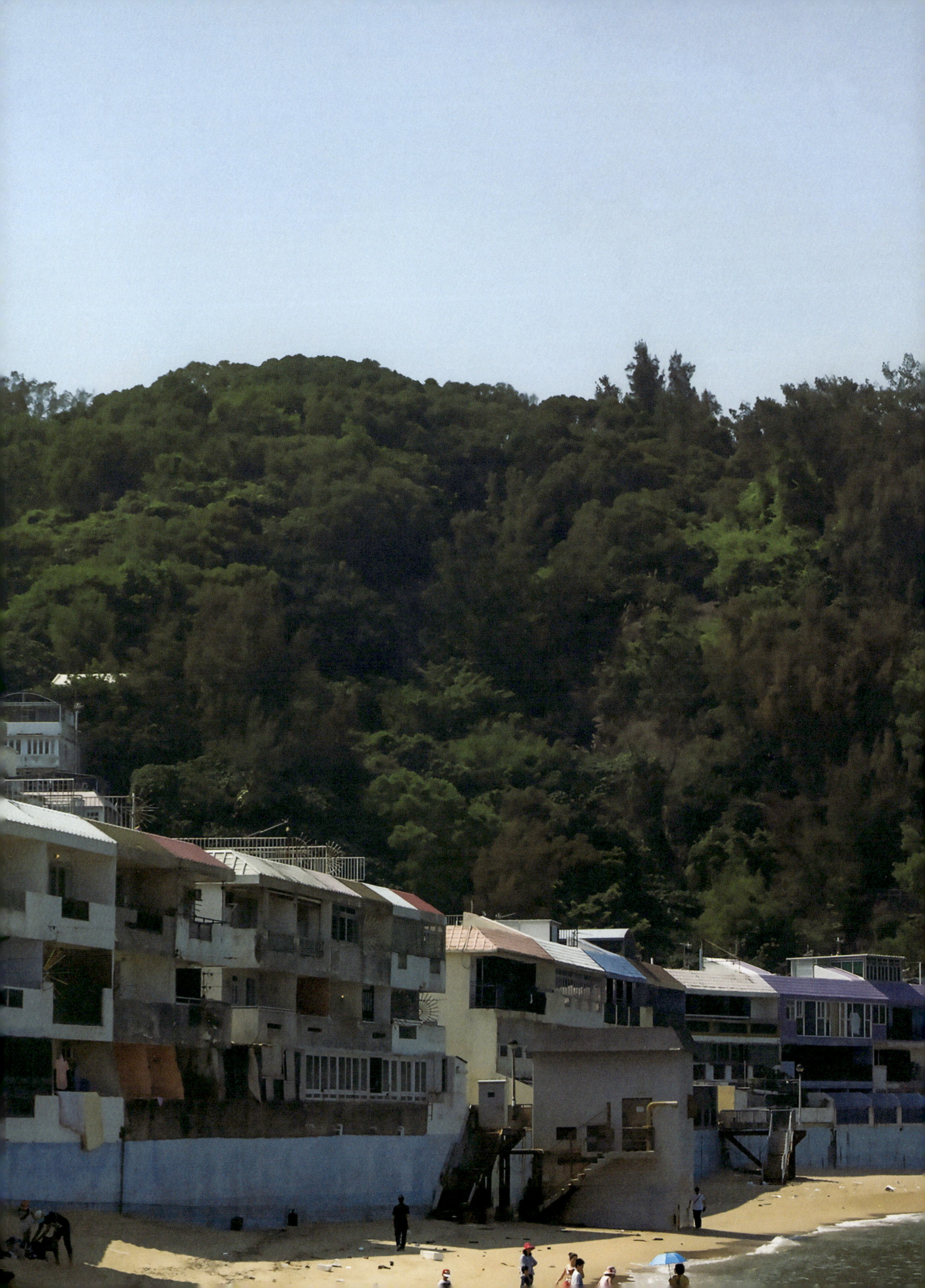

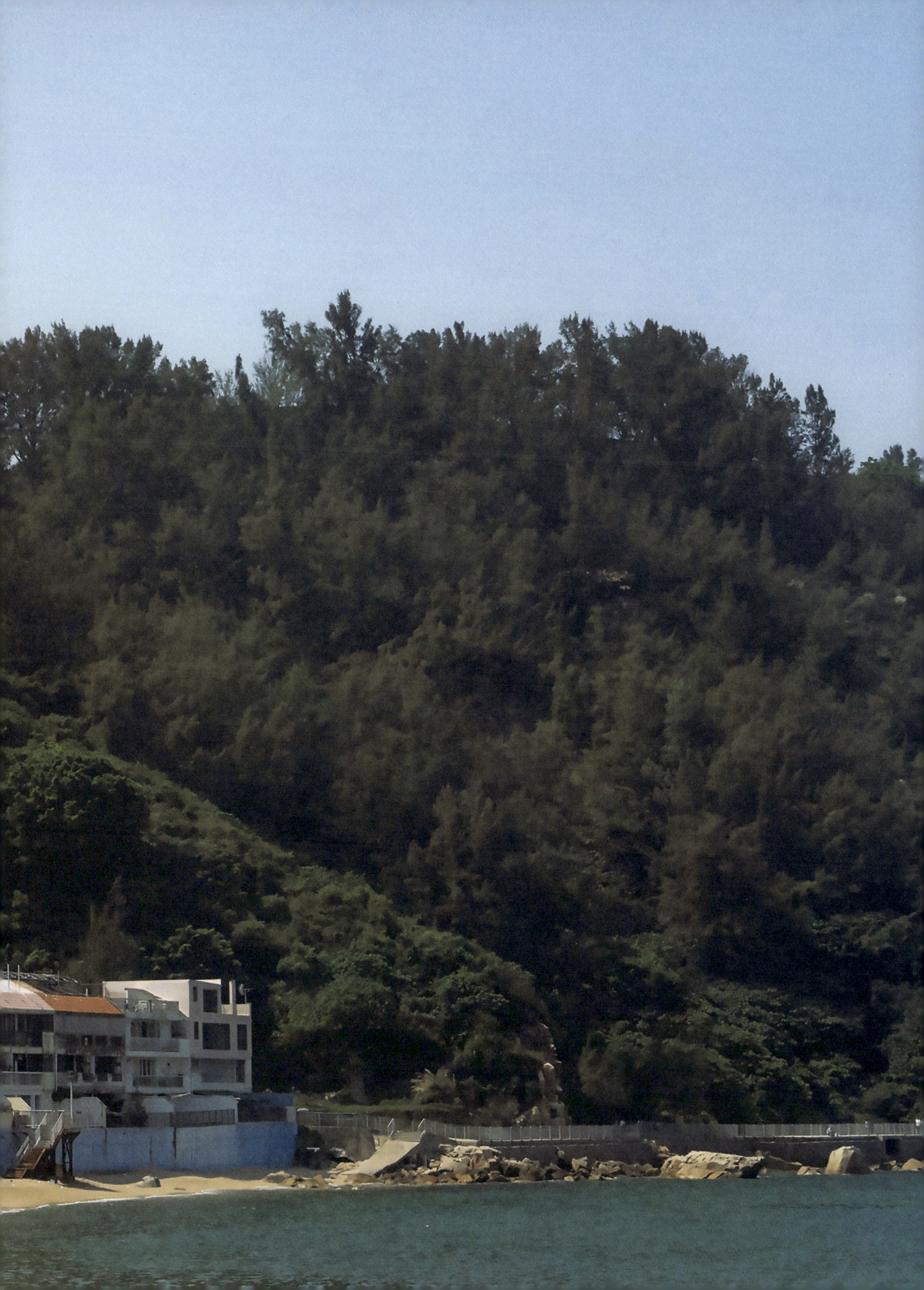

THE TRADITIONS

Hong Kong is a fully modern metropolis — yet one that is also rich in tradition and culture. You can see the combined Buddhist, Taoist, and Confucius influences in the many places of worship that dot the city.

It is customary for Hongkongers to pay respects at a temple during any Cantonese festival. I love going to the temples, as I remember going there often with my family.

The serene and calm Tsz Shan Monastery in Sha Tin, where the majestic Kwun Yum (Guan Yin) statue stands, is another favorite.

I also enjoy visiting the Big Buddha in Lantau, the Thousand Buddha Temple in Sha Tin, the Wong Tai Sin temple, and Man Mo Temple in Sheung Wan.

84. Incense coils and blessings at Man Mo Temple in Sheung Wan
85. Blessings and incense coils at Man Mo Temple in Sheung Wan
86. Deities passing through the streets during Cheung Chau Bun Festival
87. Outside a temple in Cheung Chau
88. The Nan Lian Garden Pavilion of Absolute Perfection in Diamond Hill
89. A banyan tree in a Cheung Chau courtyard
90. The Big Buddha statue on Lantau Island
91. The Guan Yin statue at the Tsz Shan Monastery in Tai Po

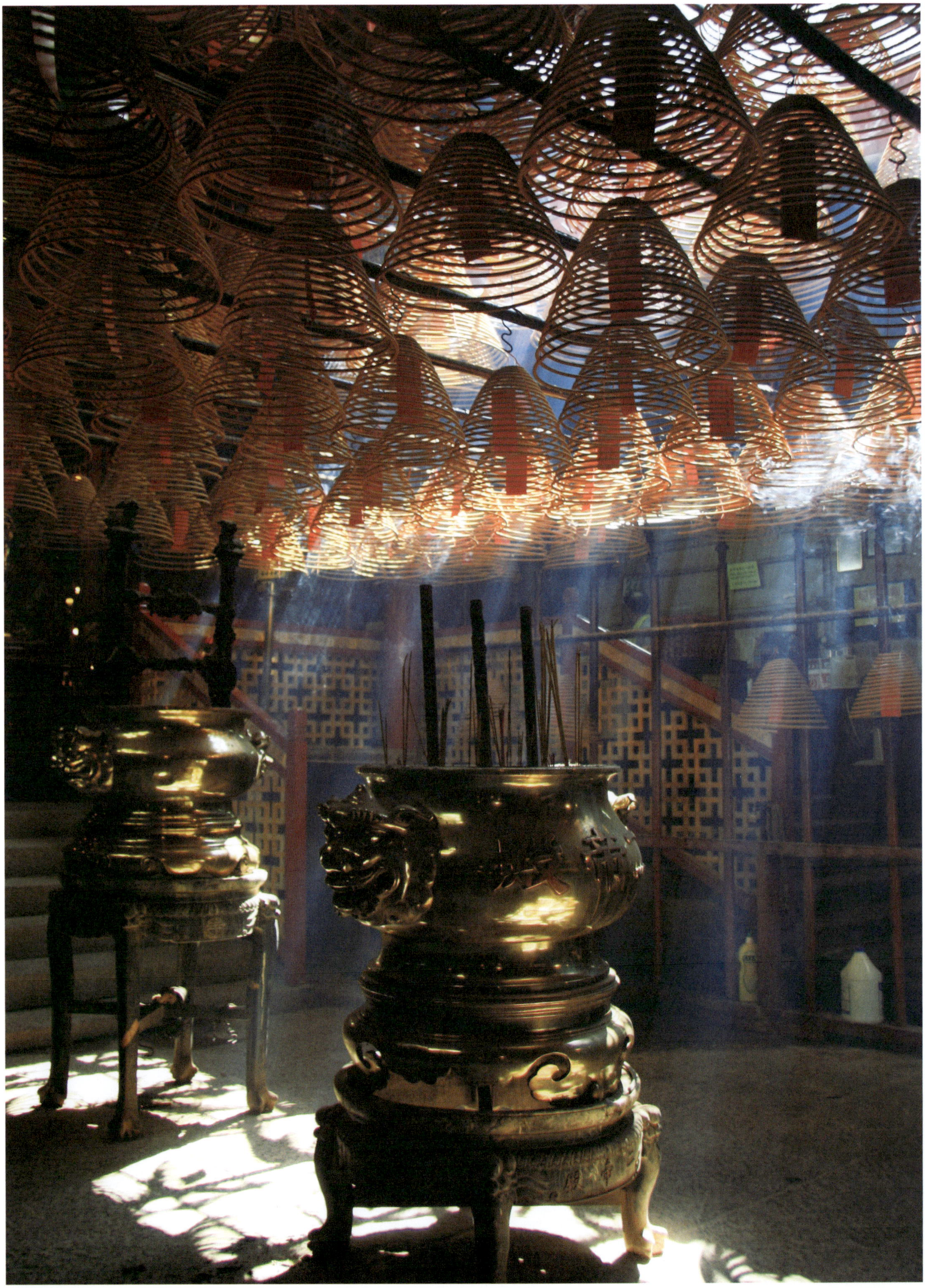

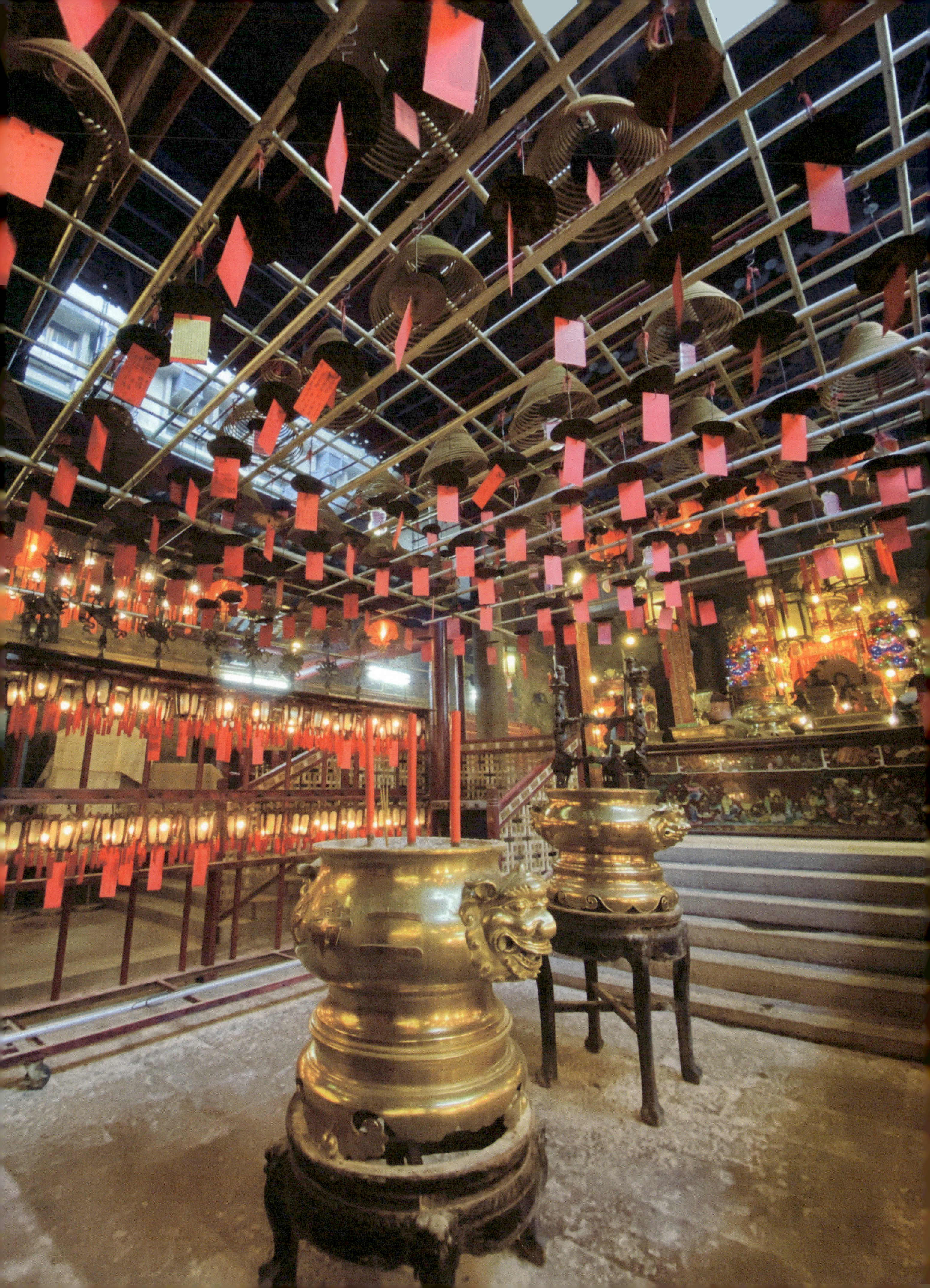

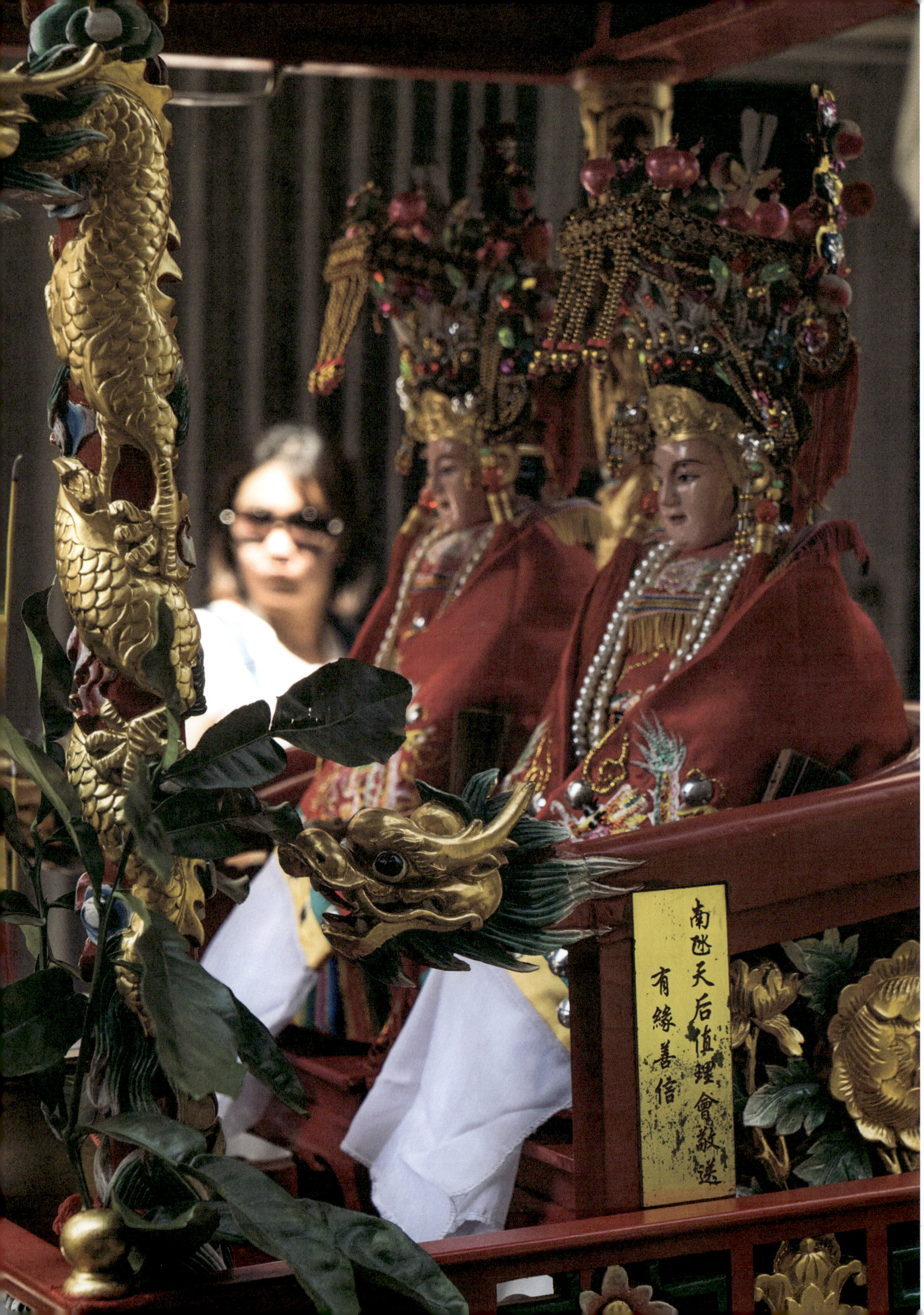
南凼天后值理會敬送
有緣善信

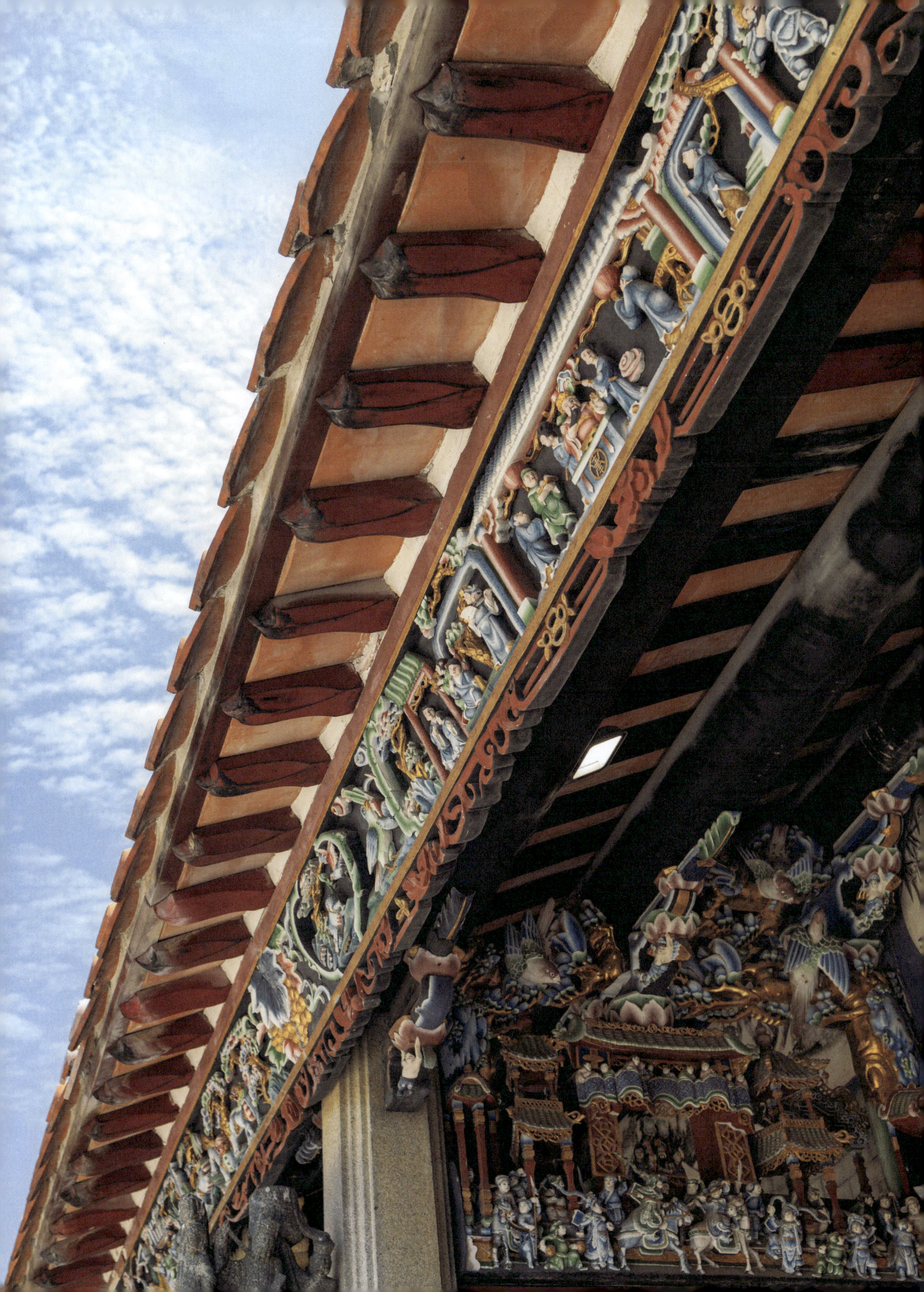

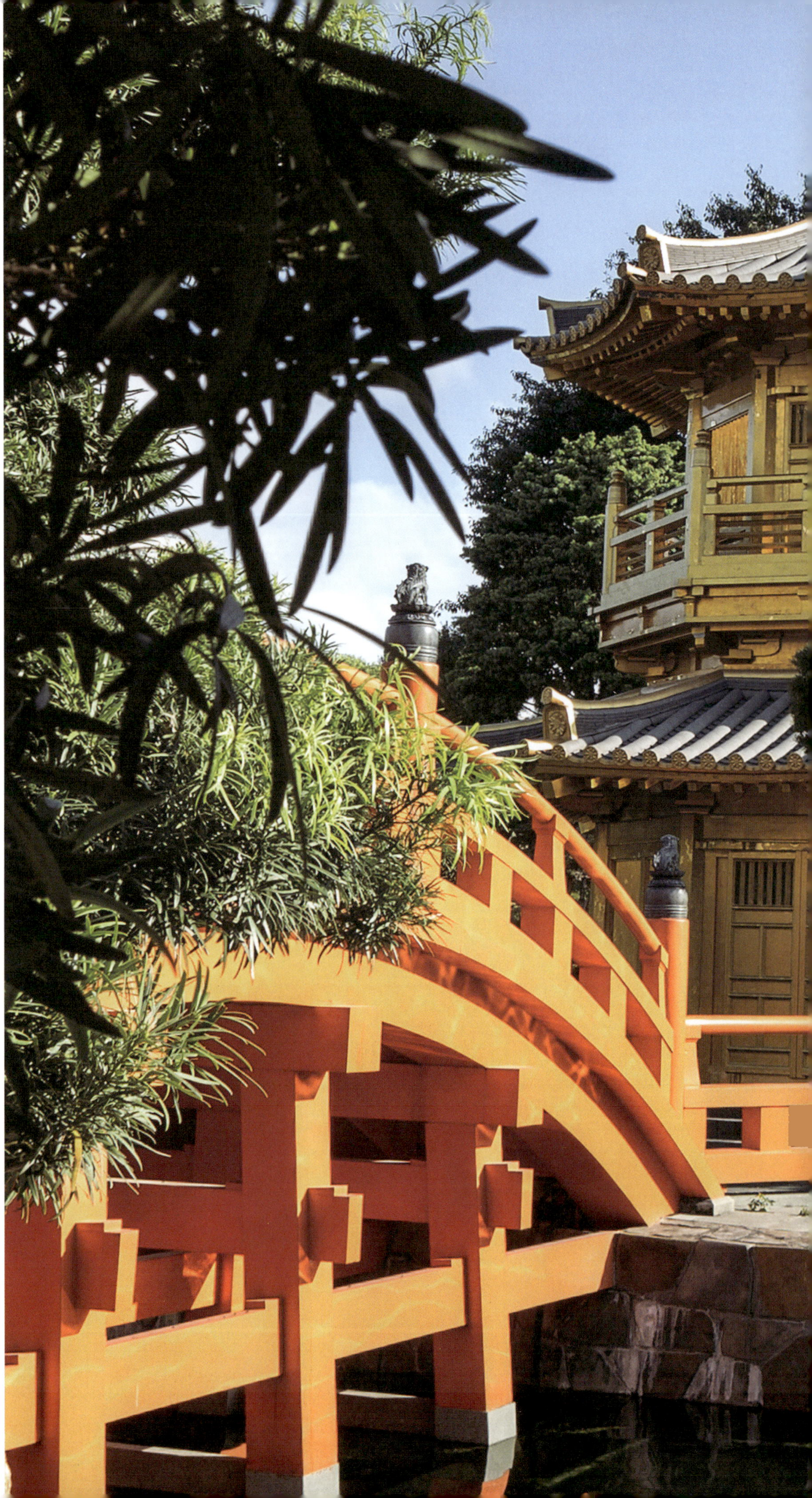

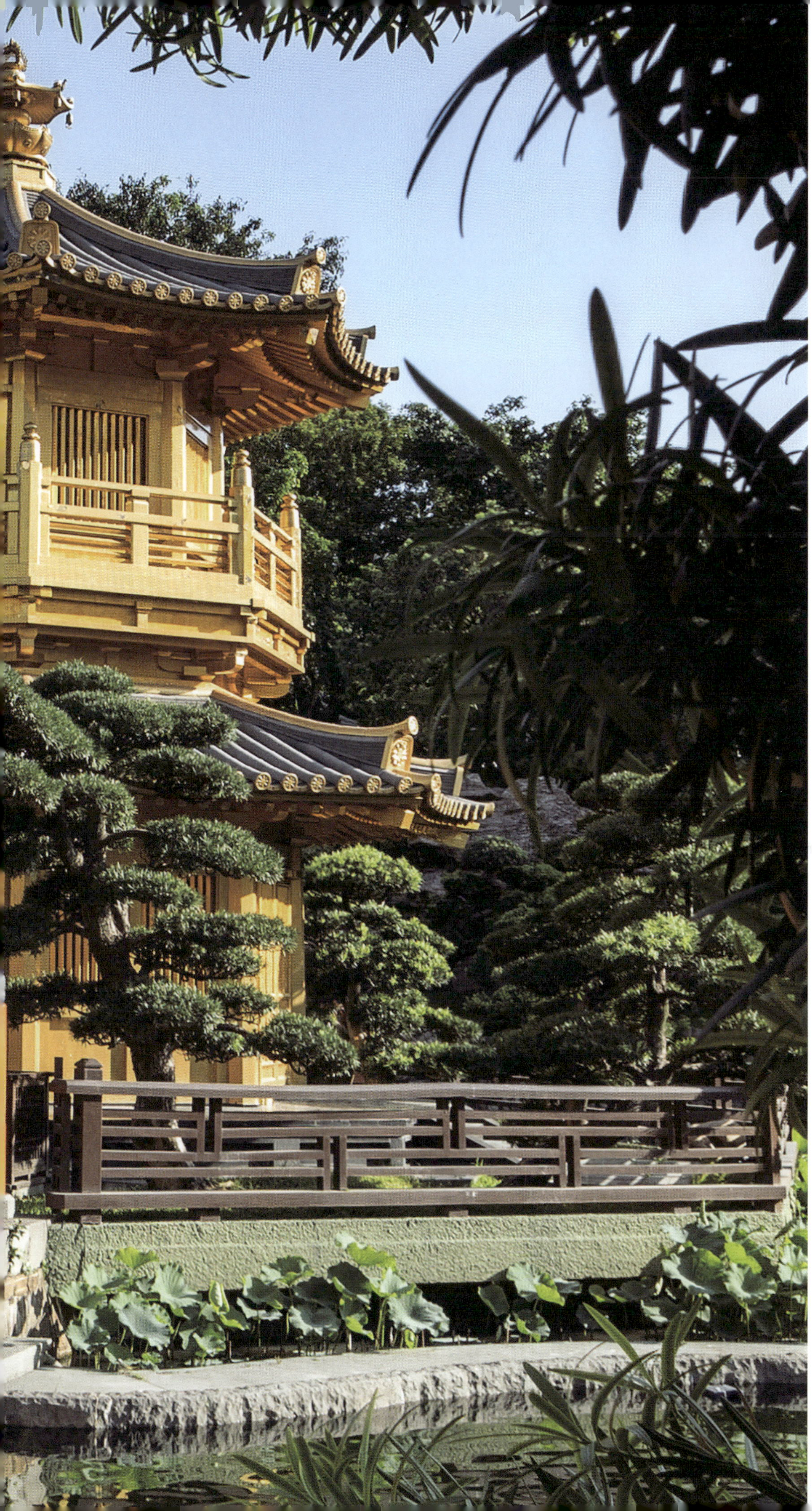

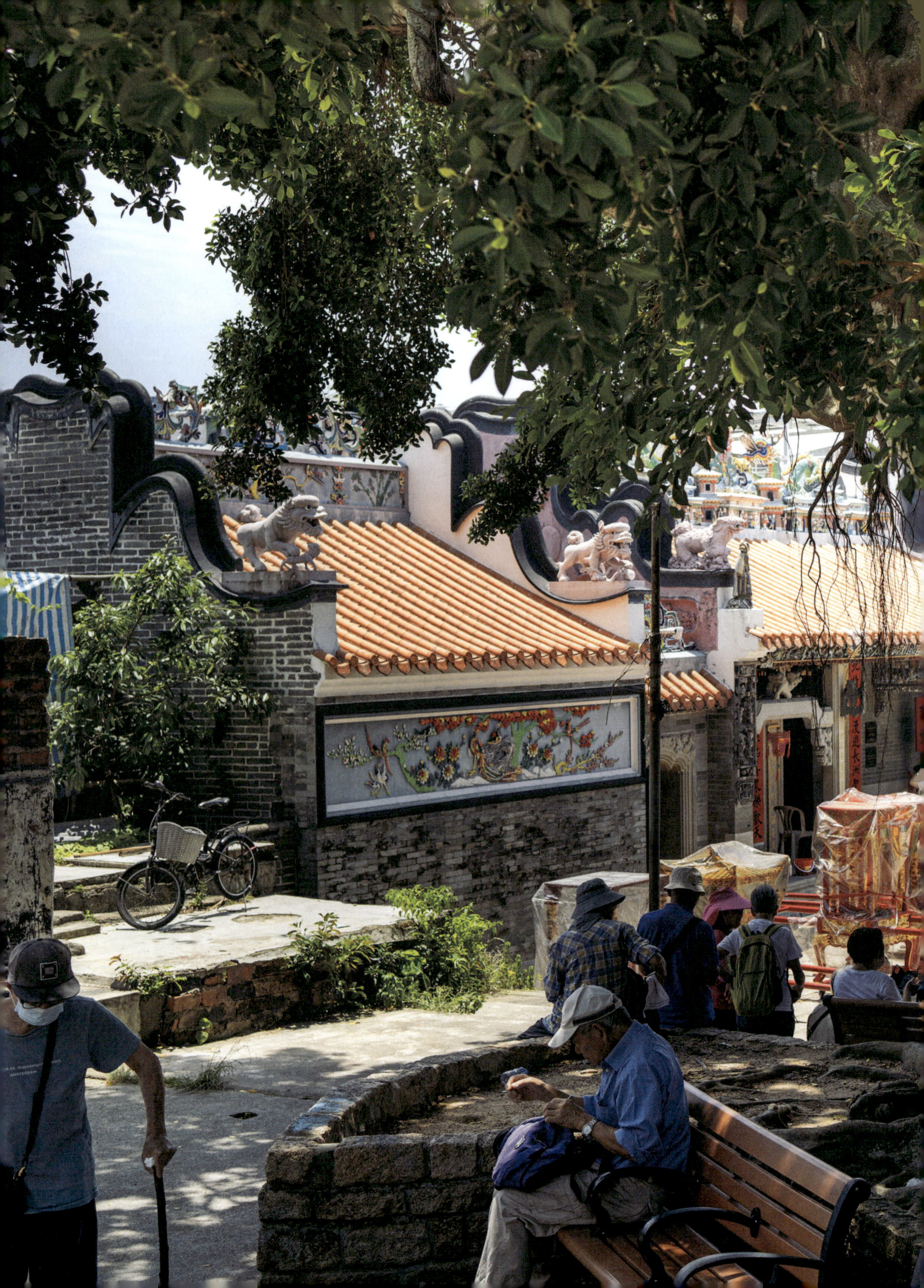

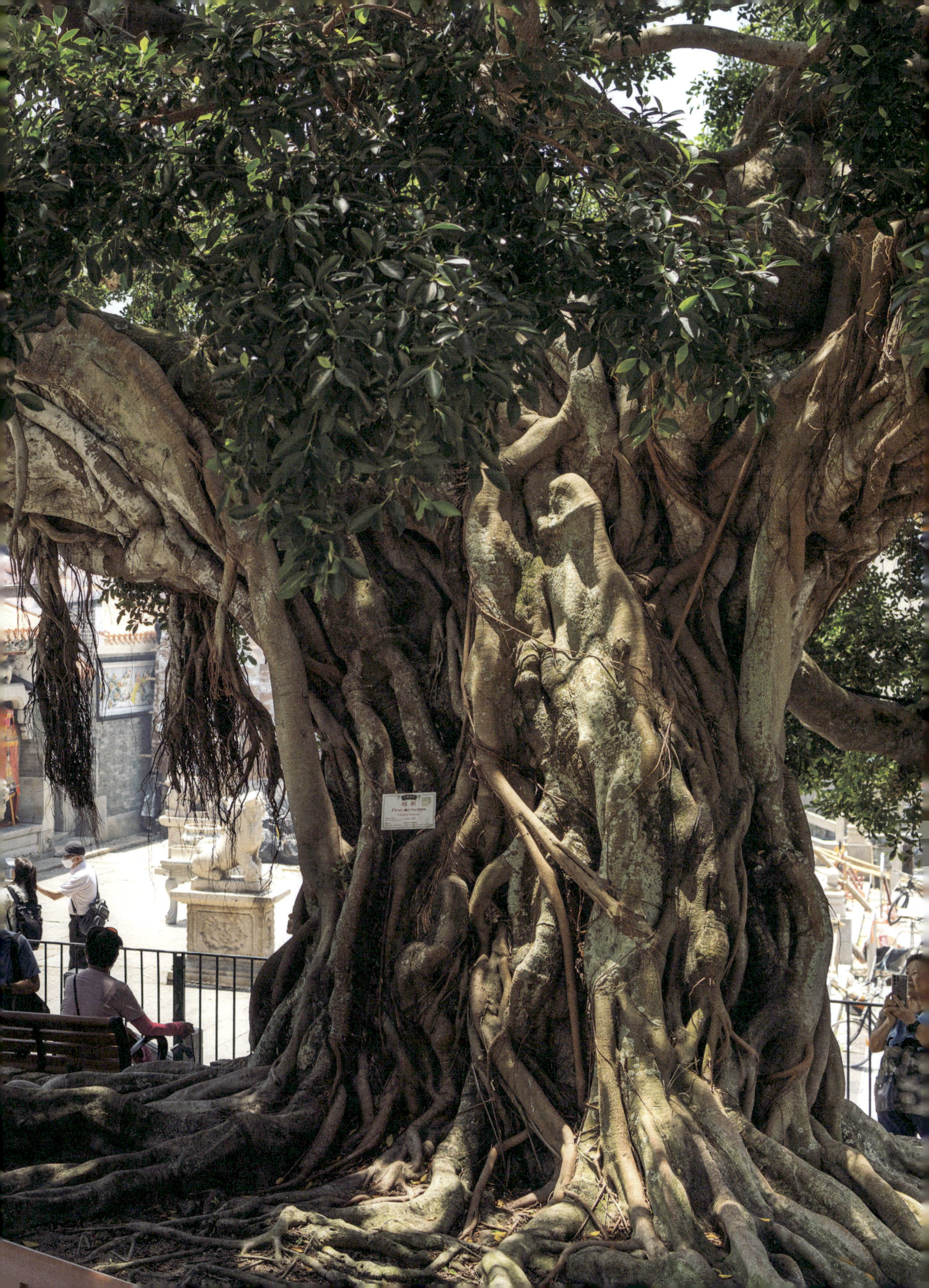

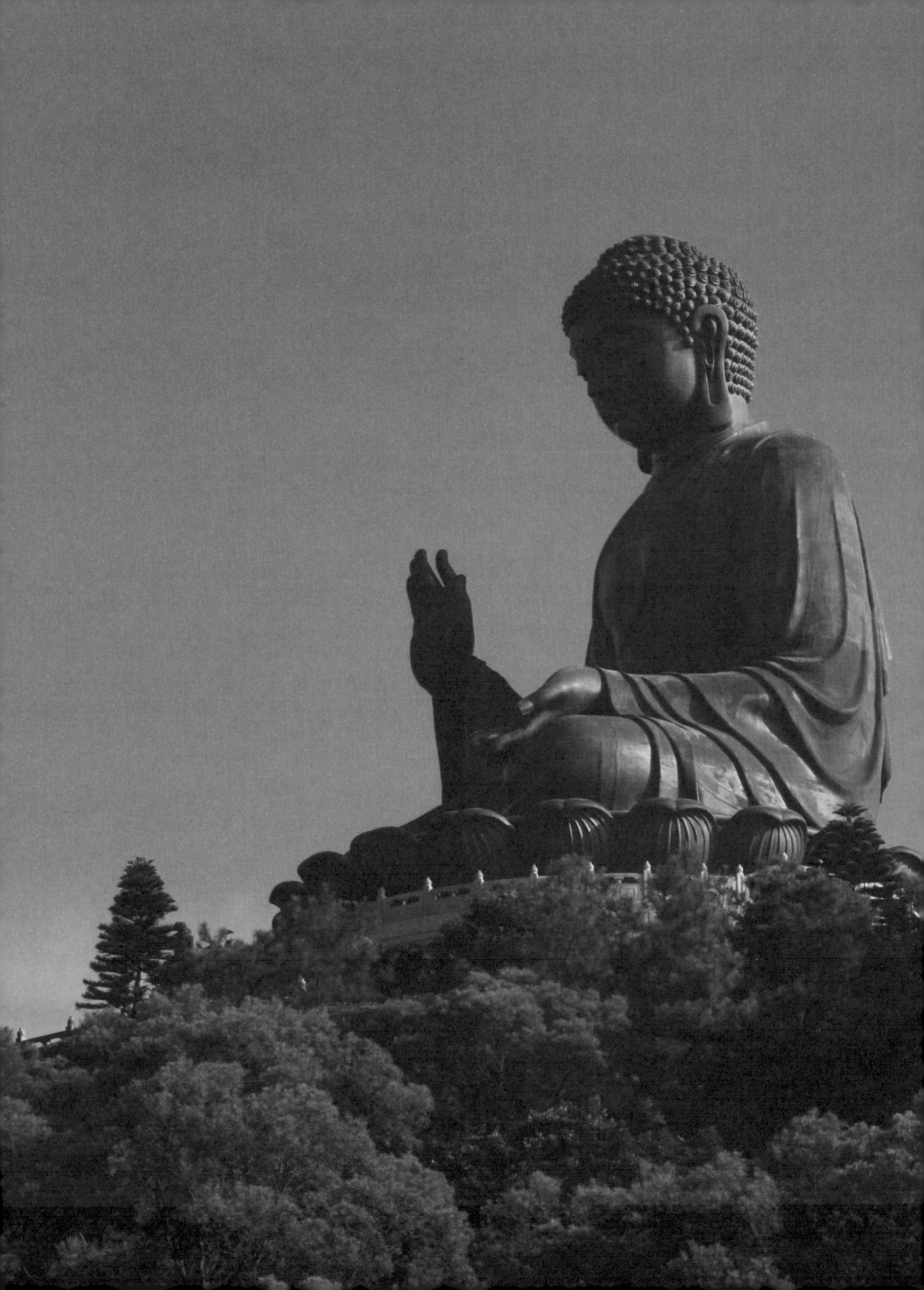

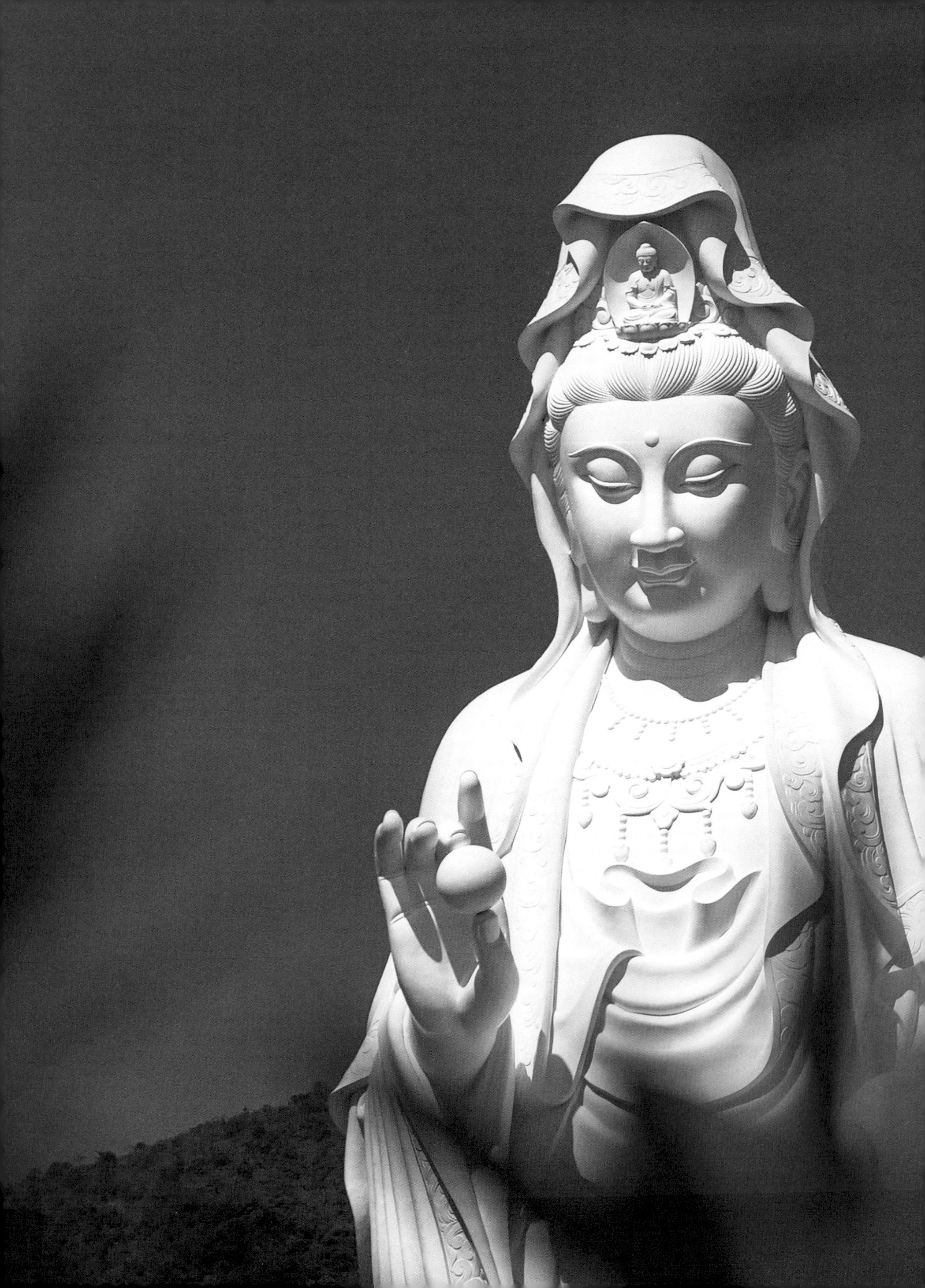

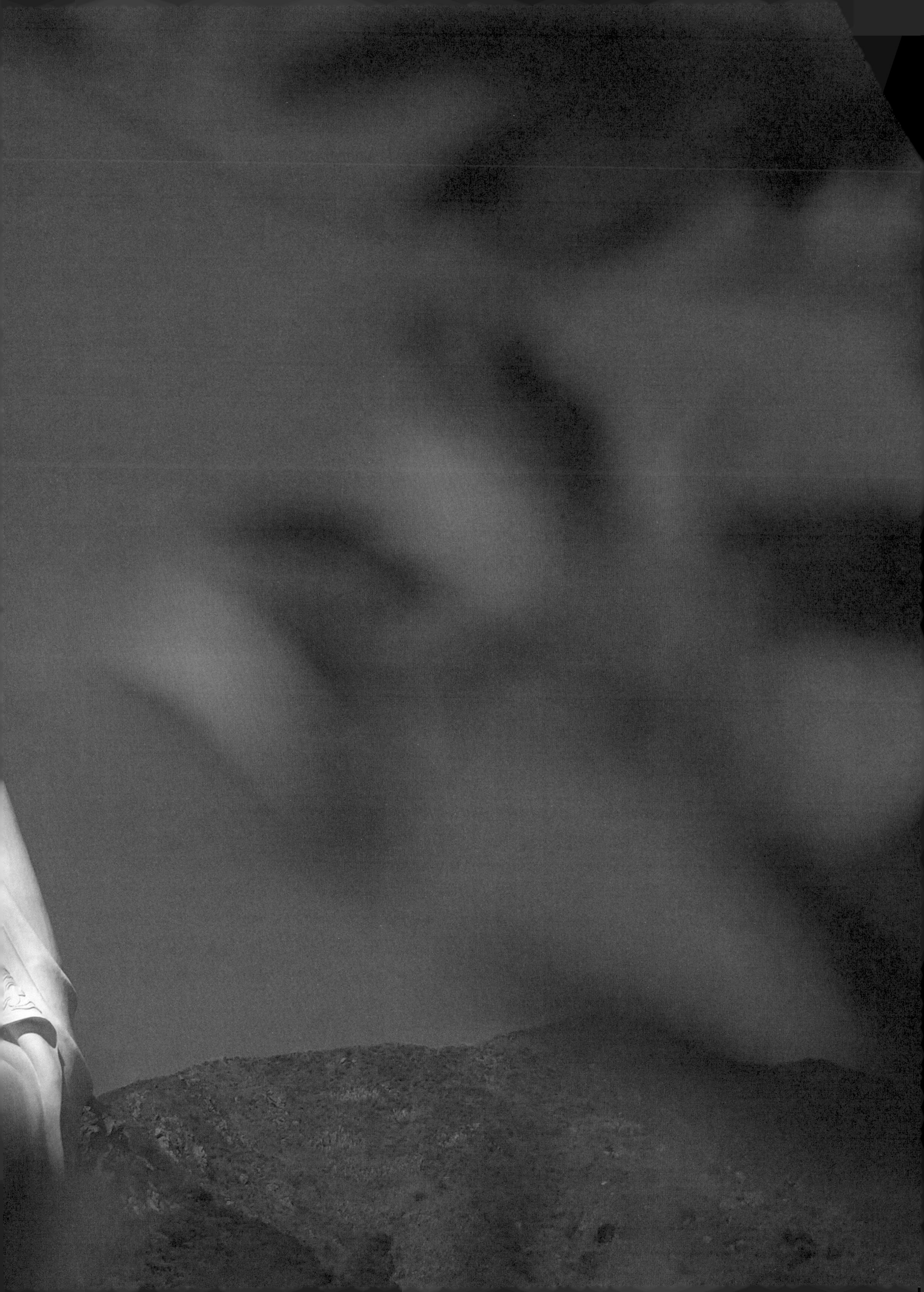

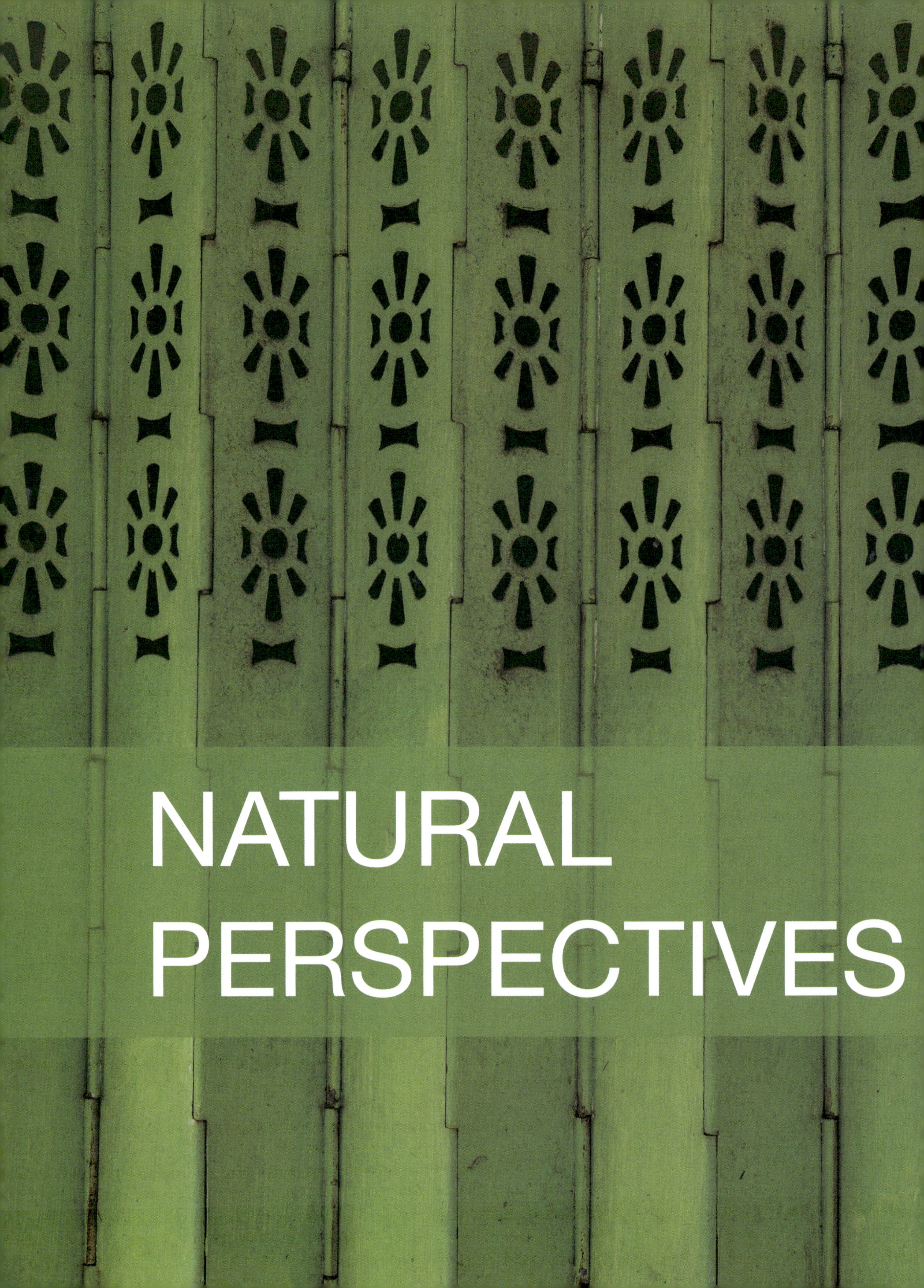

NATURAL PERSPECTIVES

The Skies
The Greenery

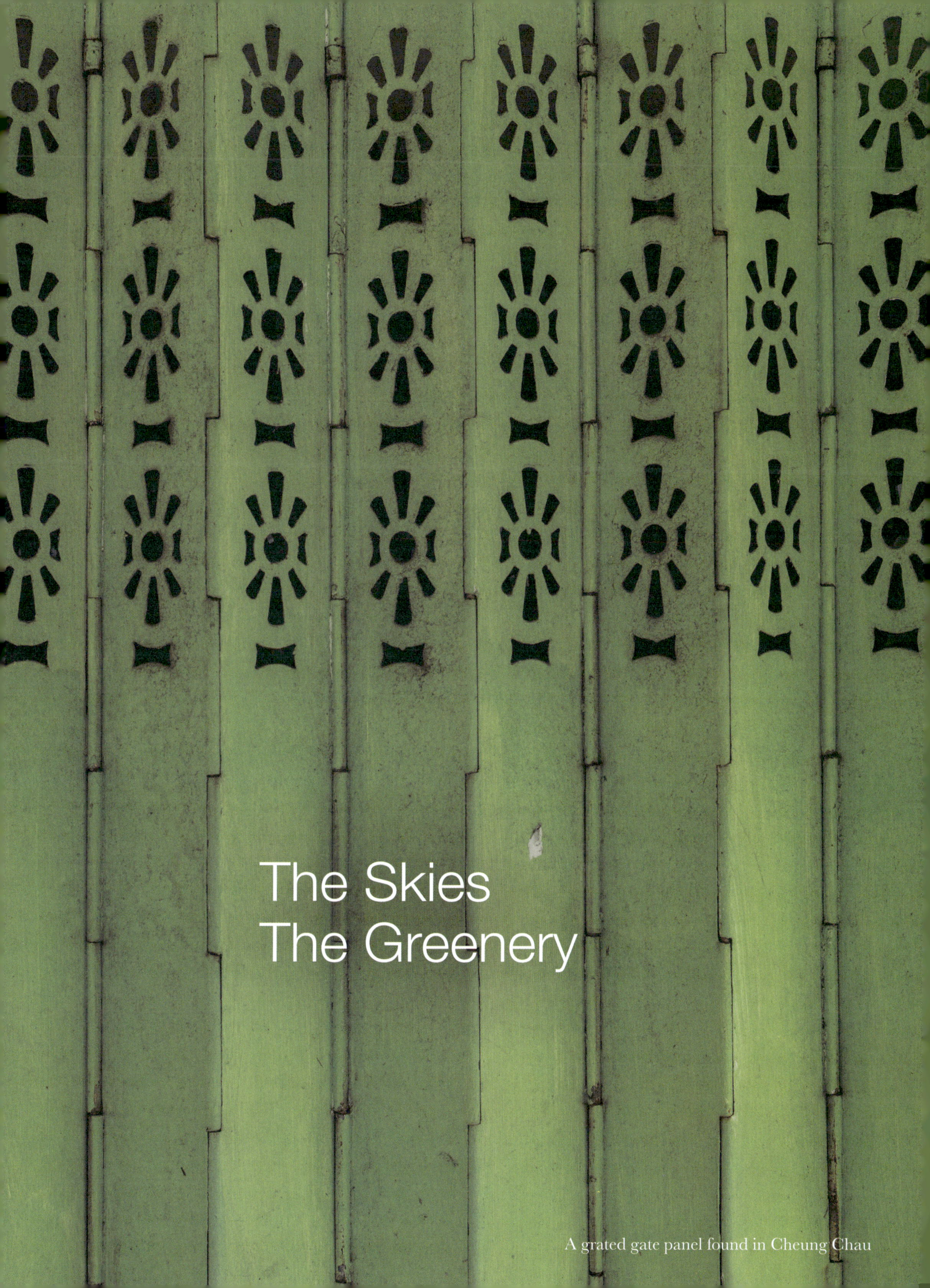

A grated gate panel found in Cheung Chau

NATURAL PERSPECTIVES

THE SKIES

Our city serves as such an amazing backdrop to a glorious sunrise or sunset. We have so many harborside and mountaintop points to catch them from. Not so much an early bird myself, I personally am more inclined to view and capture the later-in-the-day sunsets.

92. Moody skies, taken from Ap Lei Chau, looking toward Lamma Island

93. The sun tries to shine through in Ap Lei Chau

94. A fiery sunset above Lamma Island

95. A calm sky in Wu Kai Sha

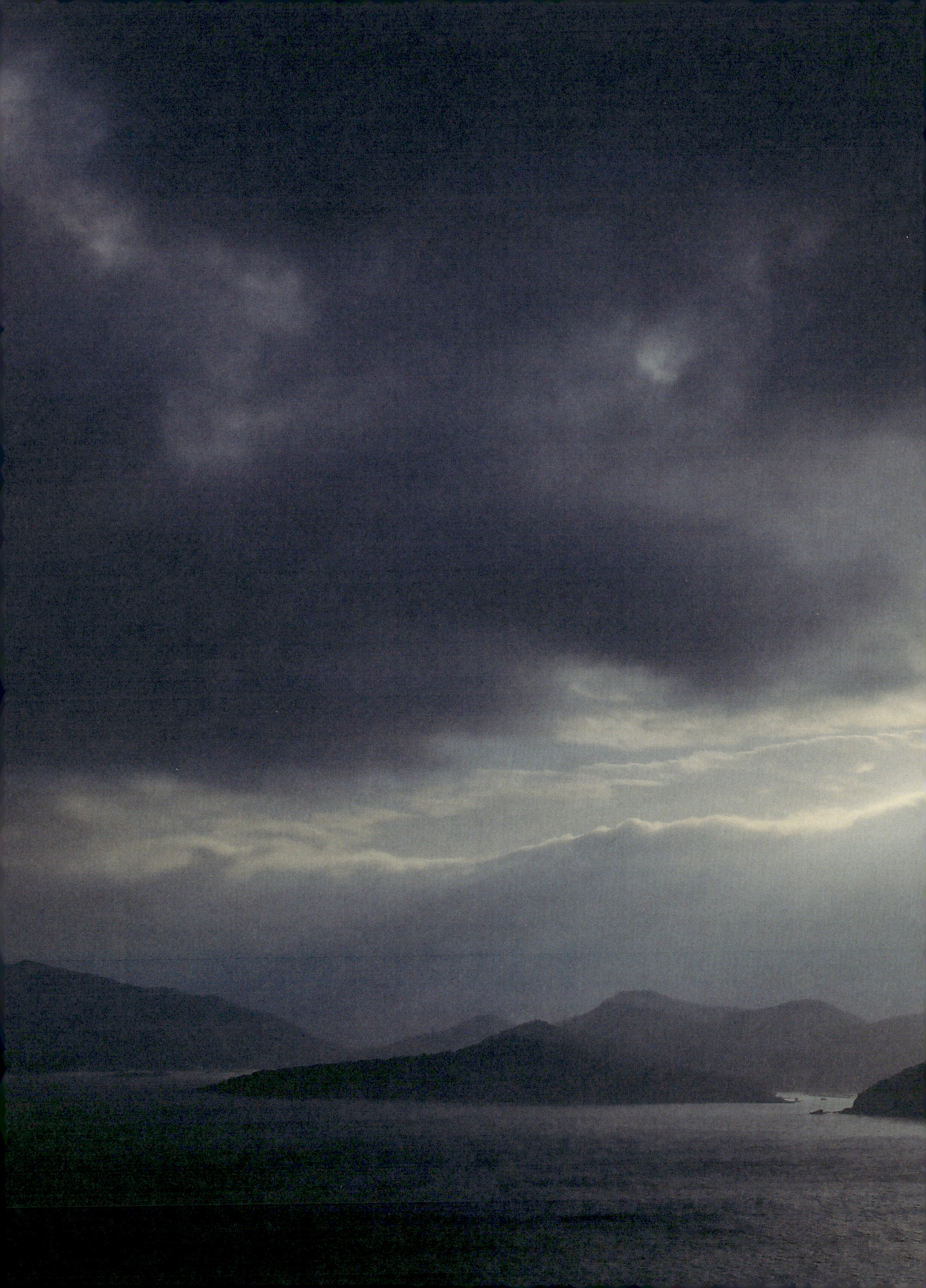

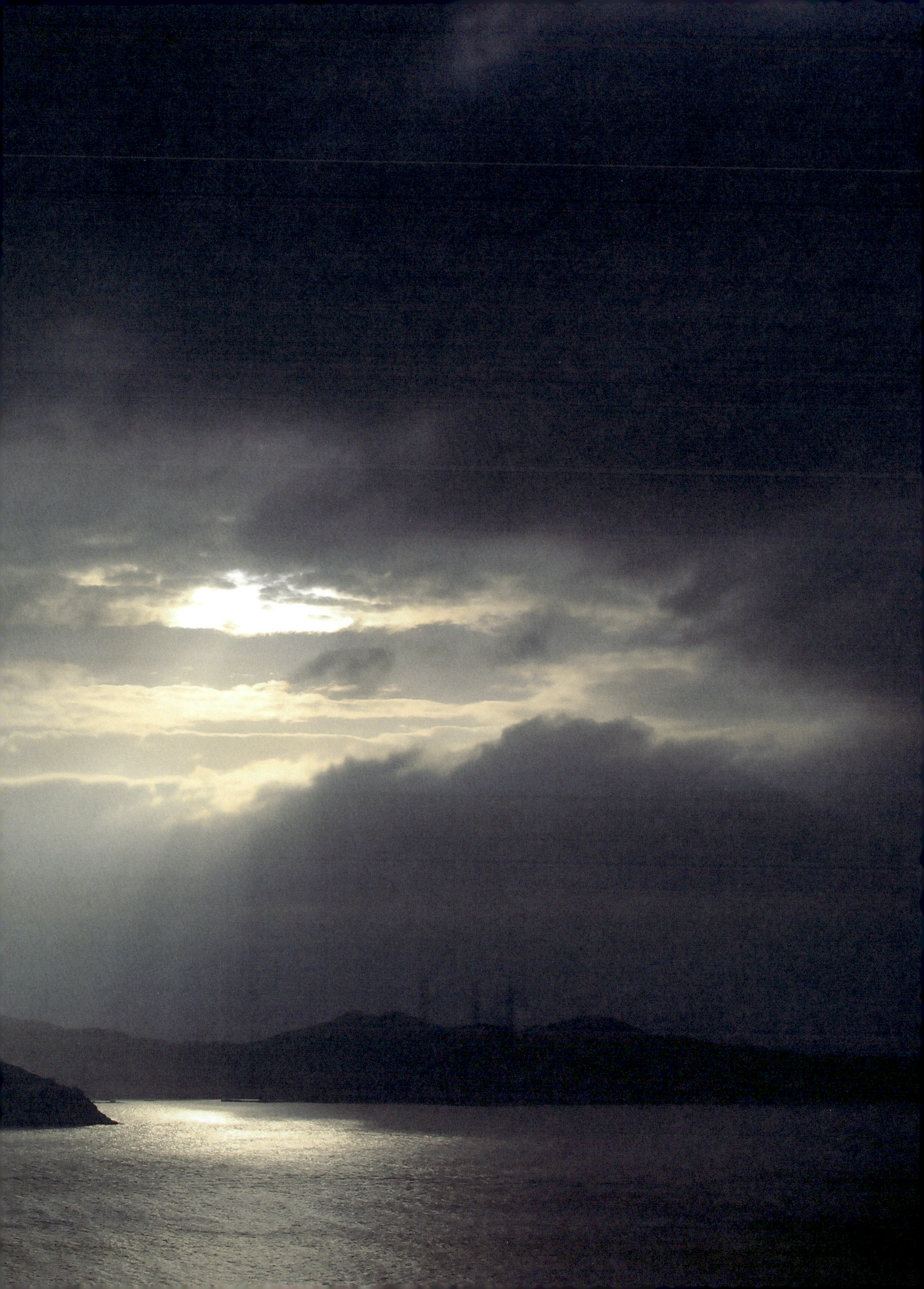

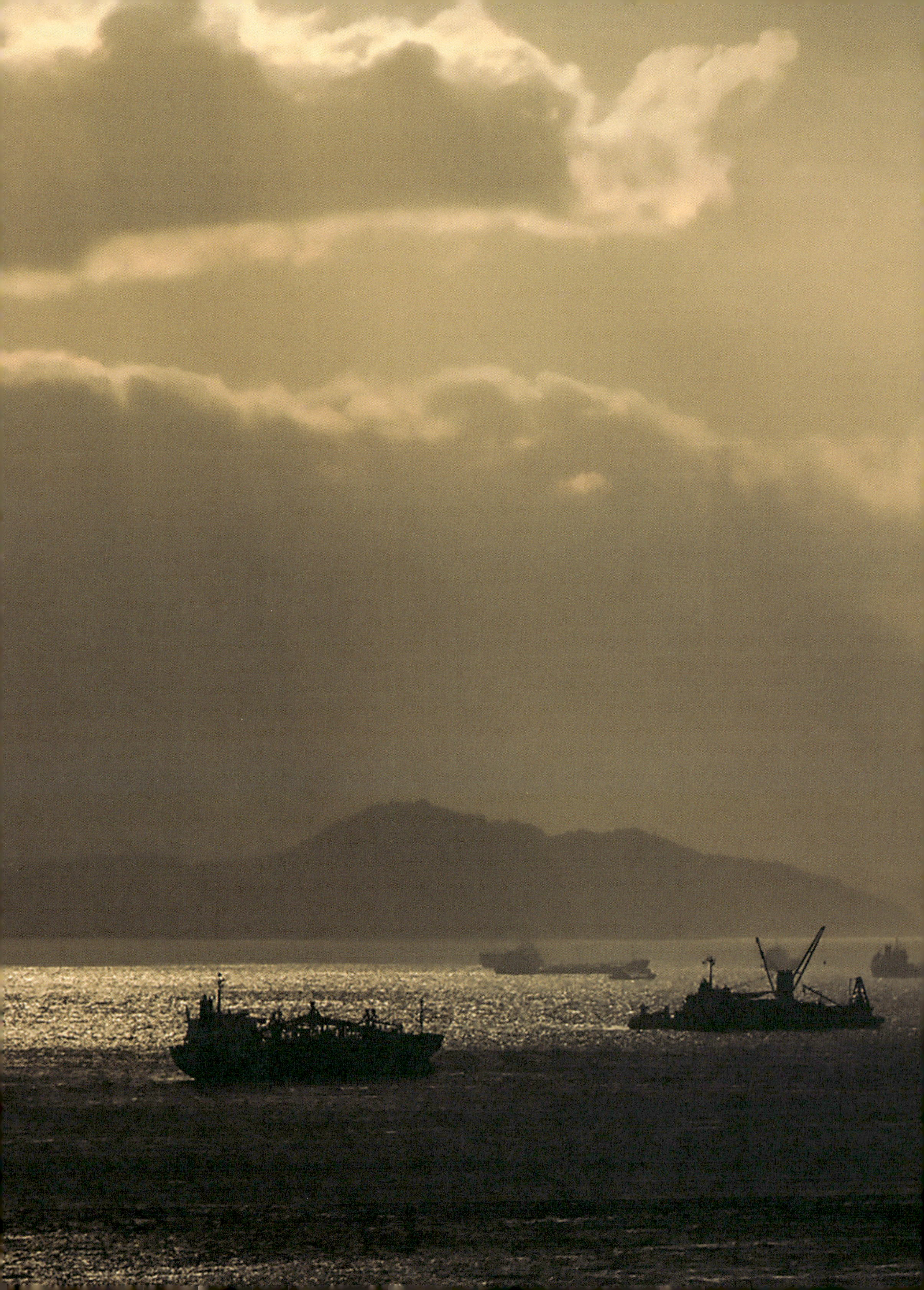

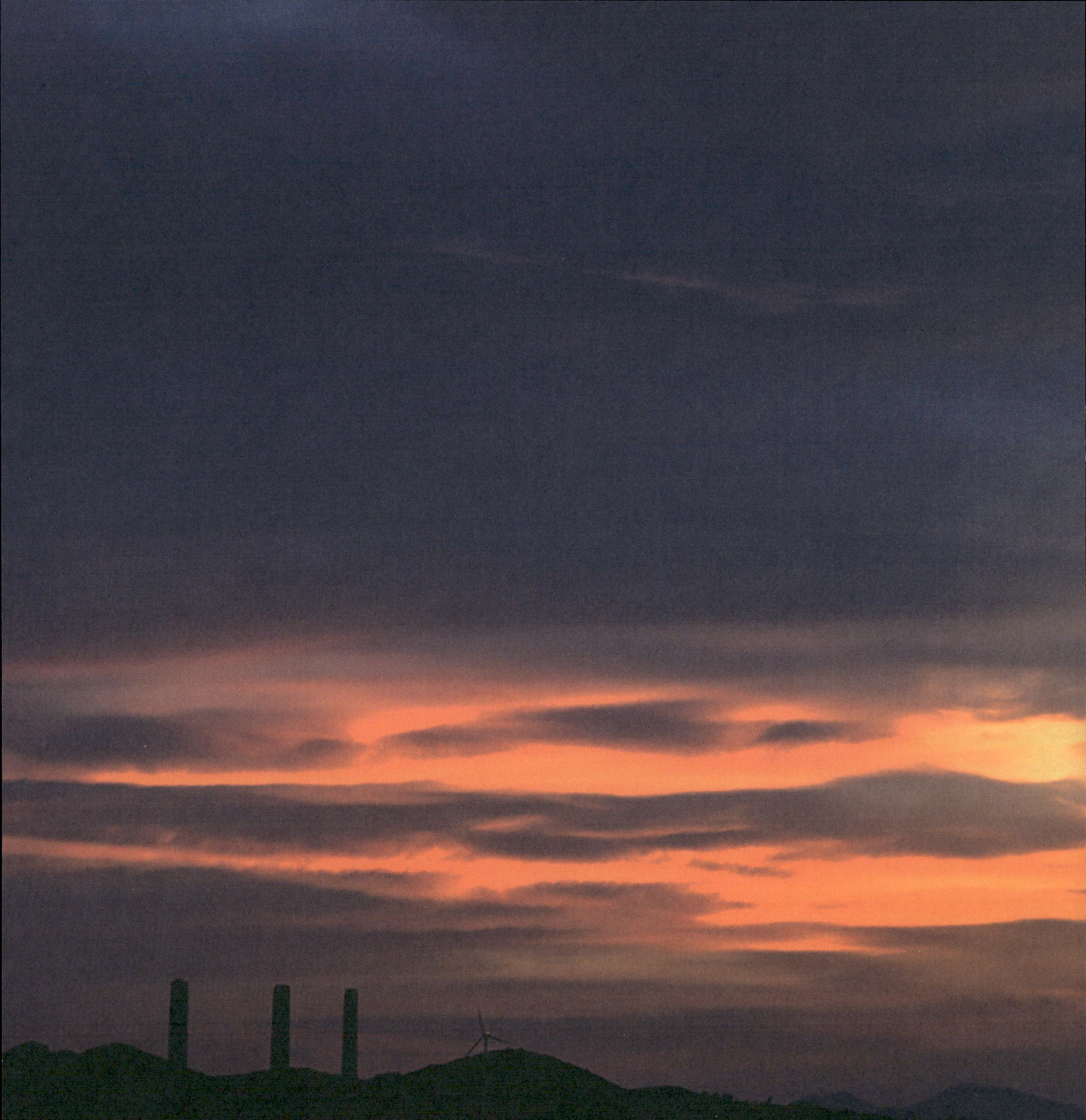

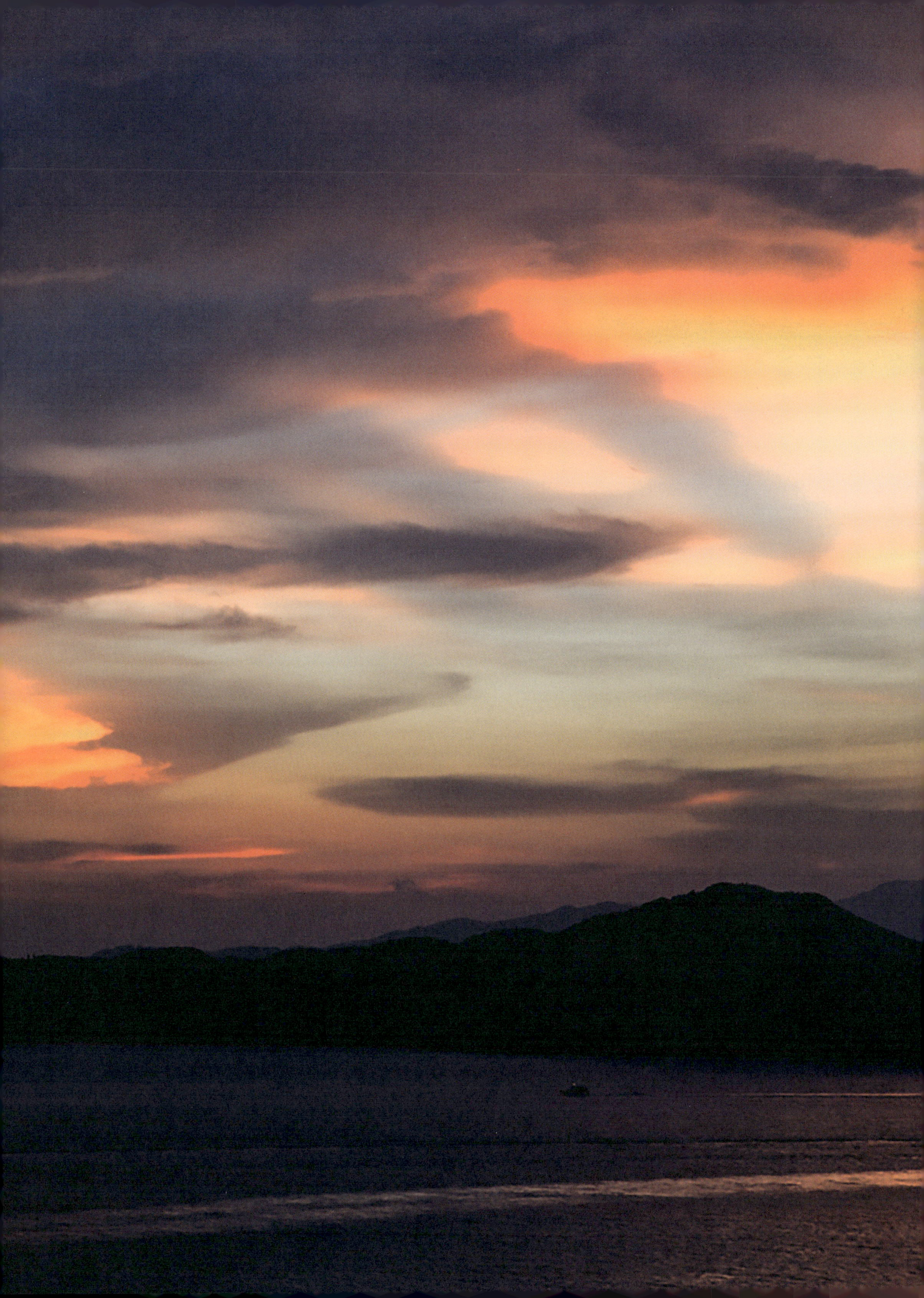

NATURAL PERSPECTIVES

THE GREENERY

About 40 percent of the land in Hong Kong is designated as country parks — and no developments can be built on them.

This means our city is actually incredibly blessed with greenery, although it might not always feel like it.

I myself live in the less densely populated New Territories and near a beach, so my family can easily escape to nature whenever we need to. I also love that we can kayak to the nearby beaches and islands.

But even for city dwellers, a beach, country park, or easy hiking trail is usually quite accessible. Hong Kong is very unique in this sense.

96. Aerial view of the southern region of Hong Kong

97. Aerial view of Tai Tam Reservoir

98. A lone building surrounded by greenery in Central

99. Views from Wu Kai Sha

100. Aerial view of Tai Tam

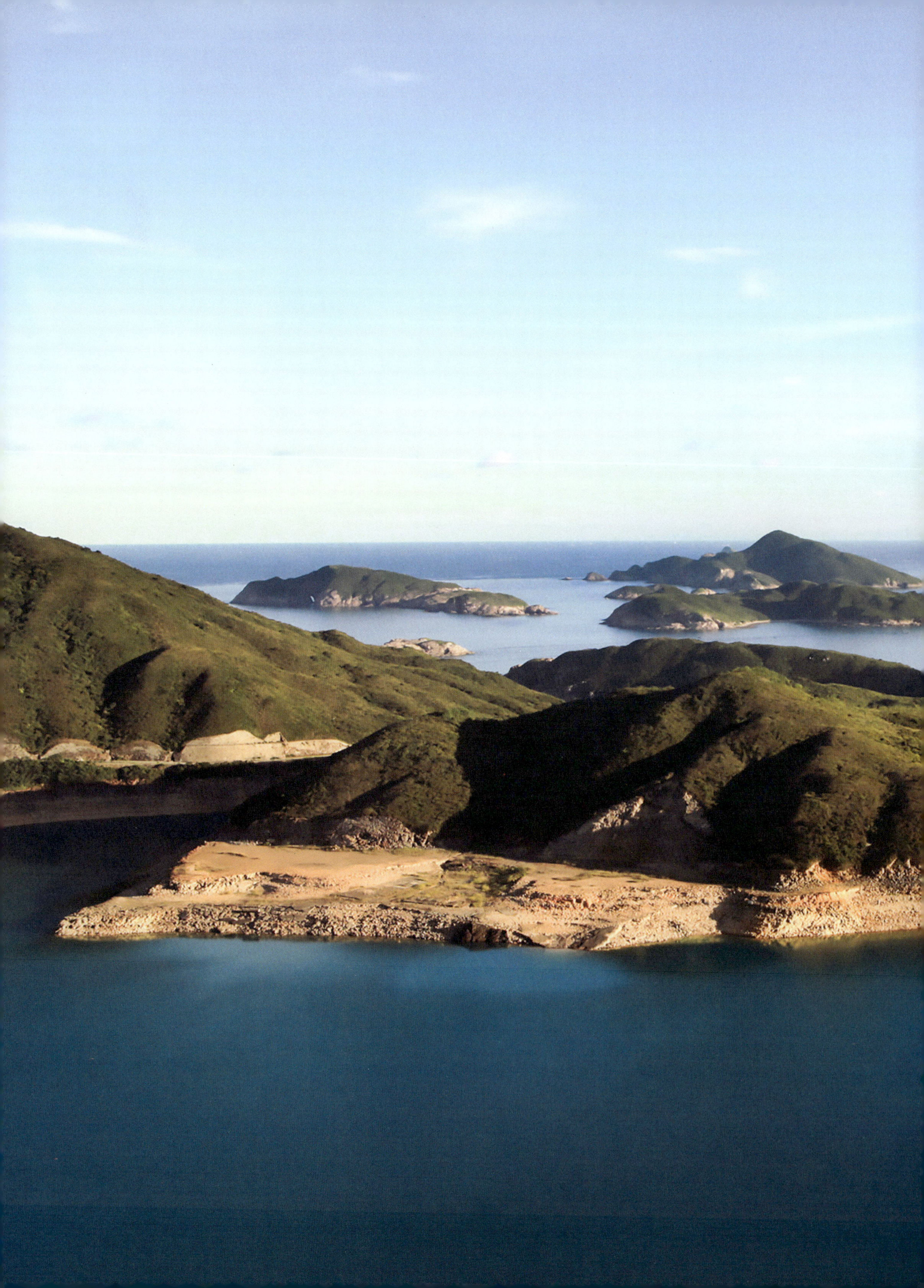

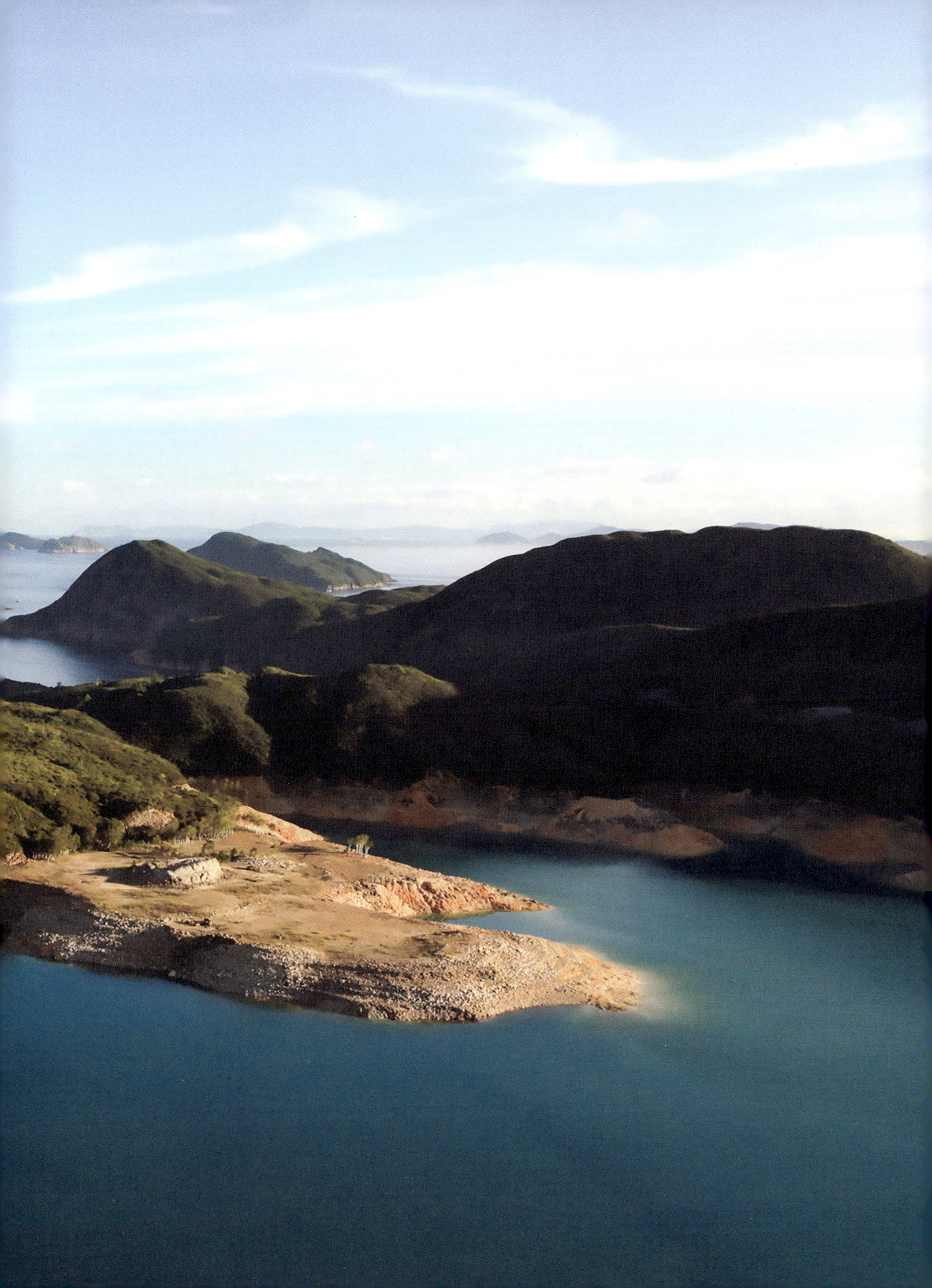

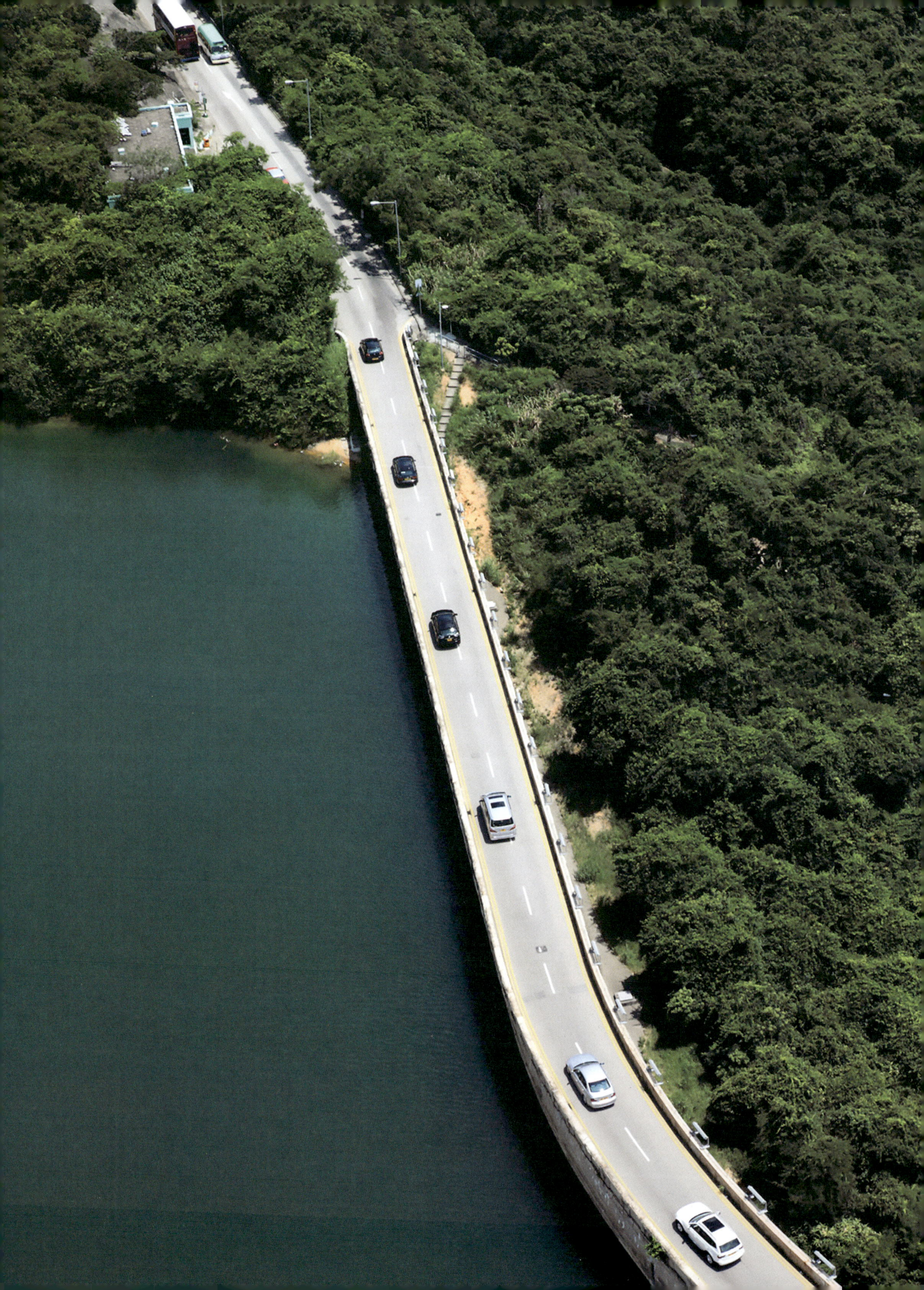

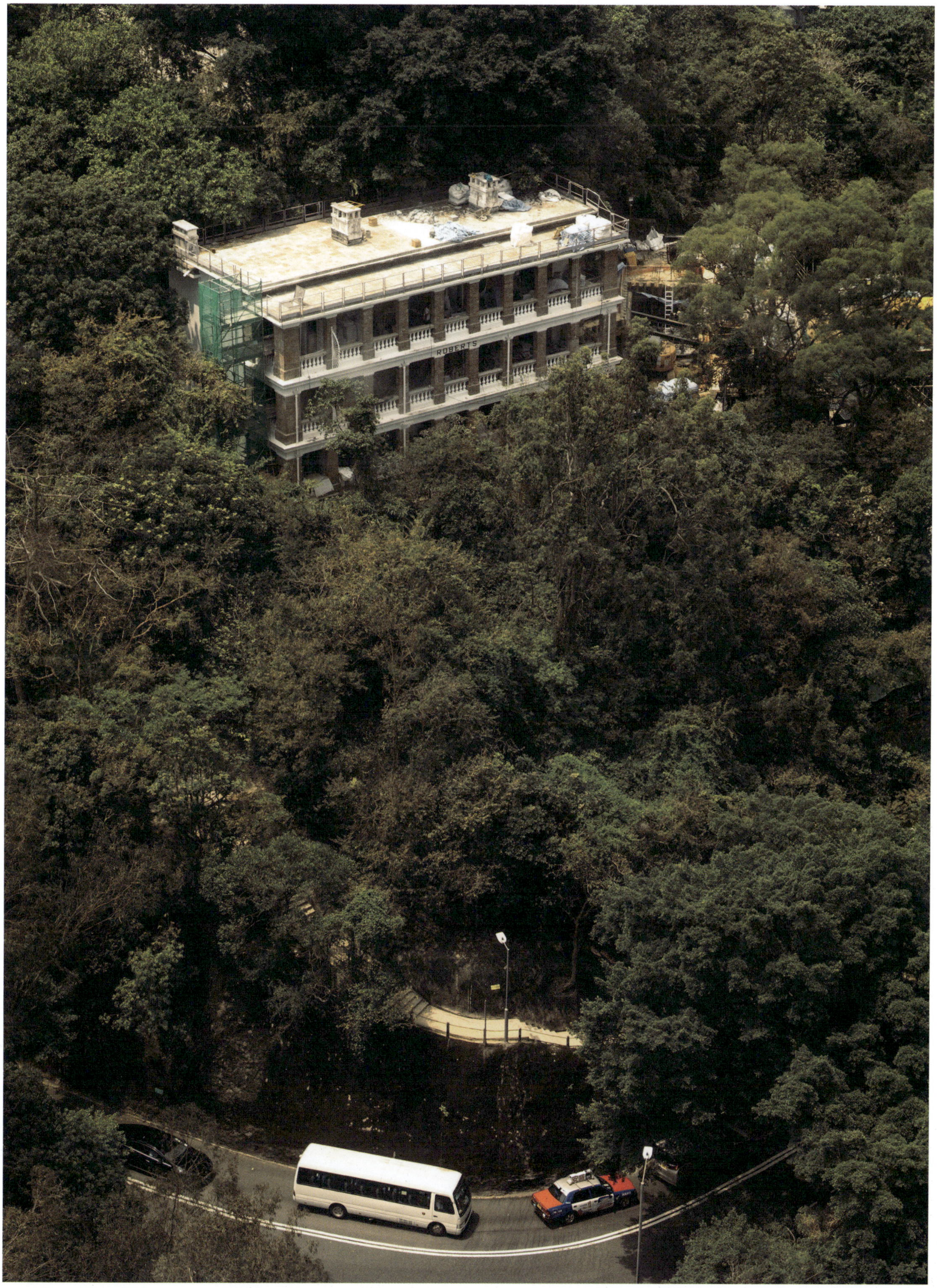
ROBERTS

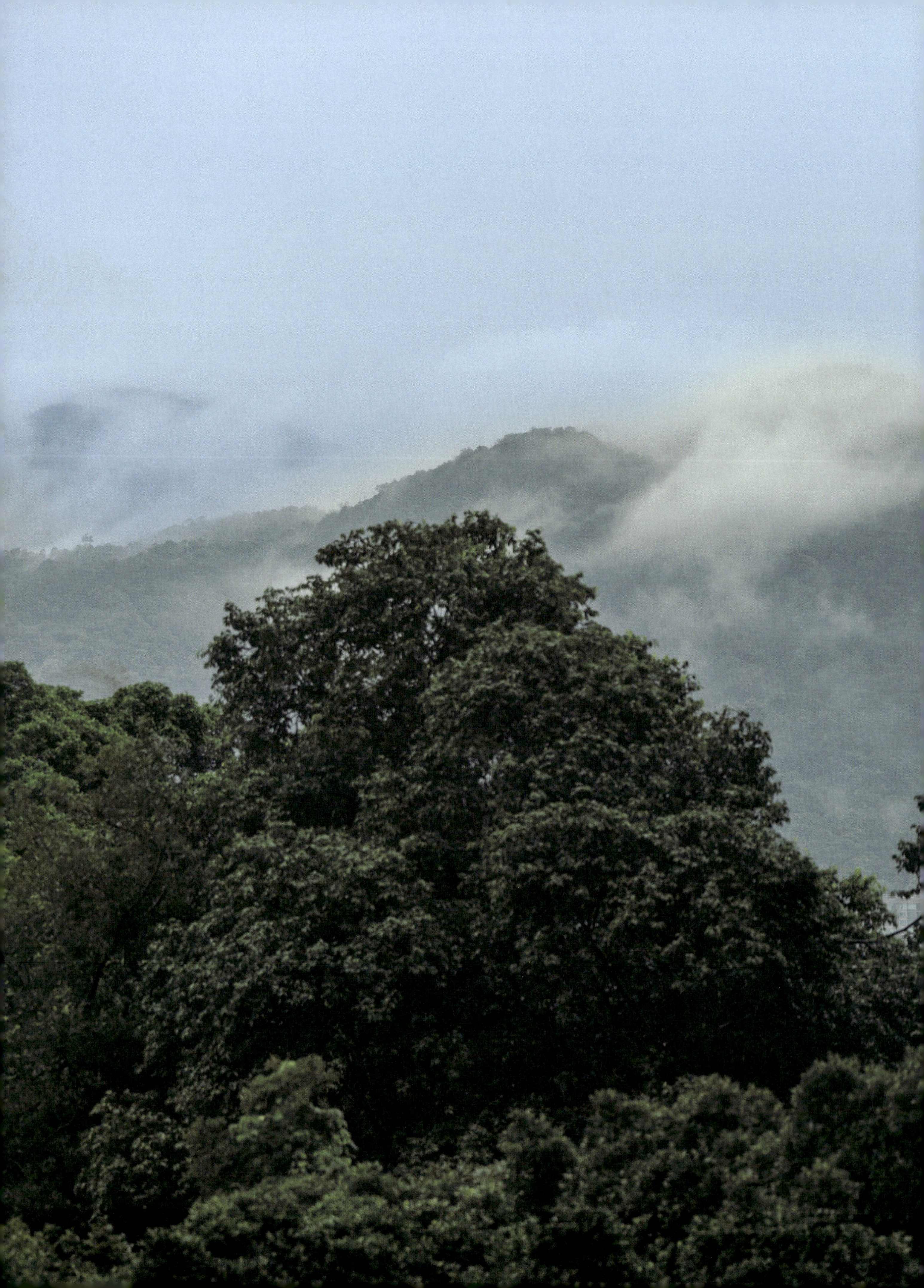

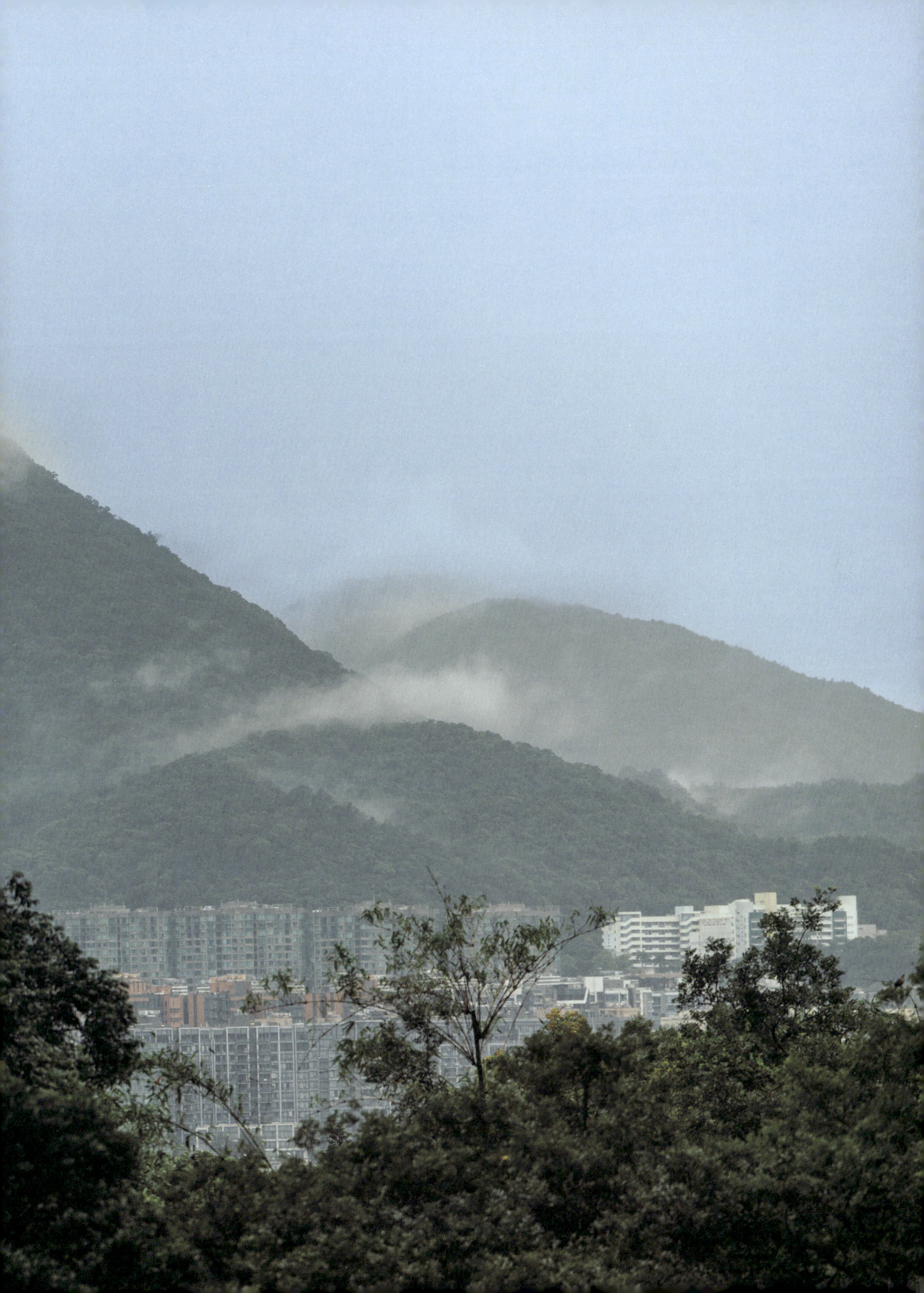

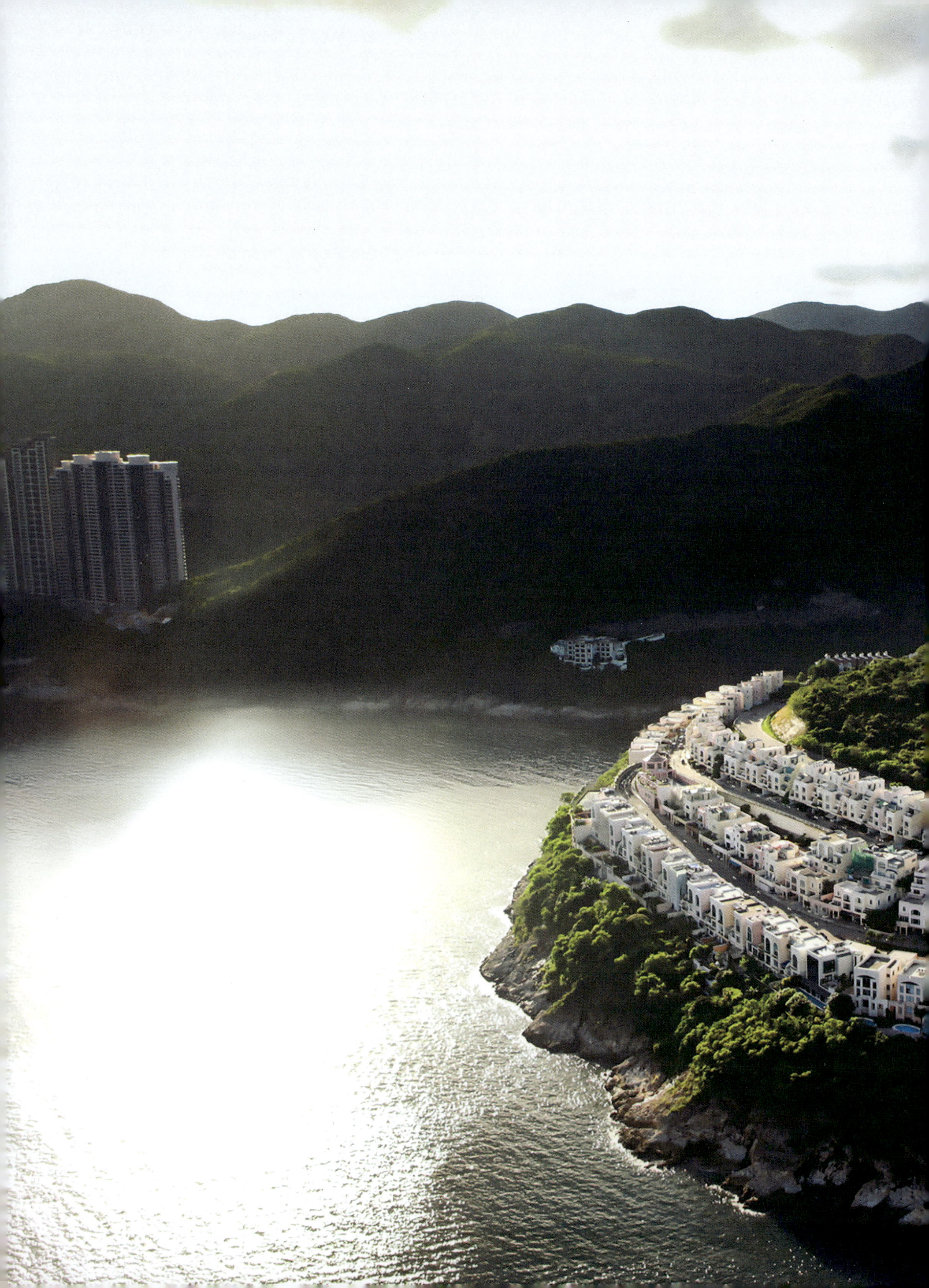

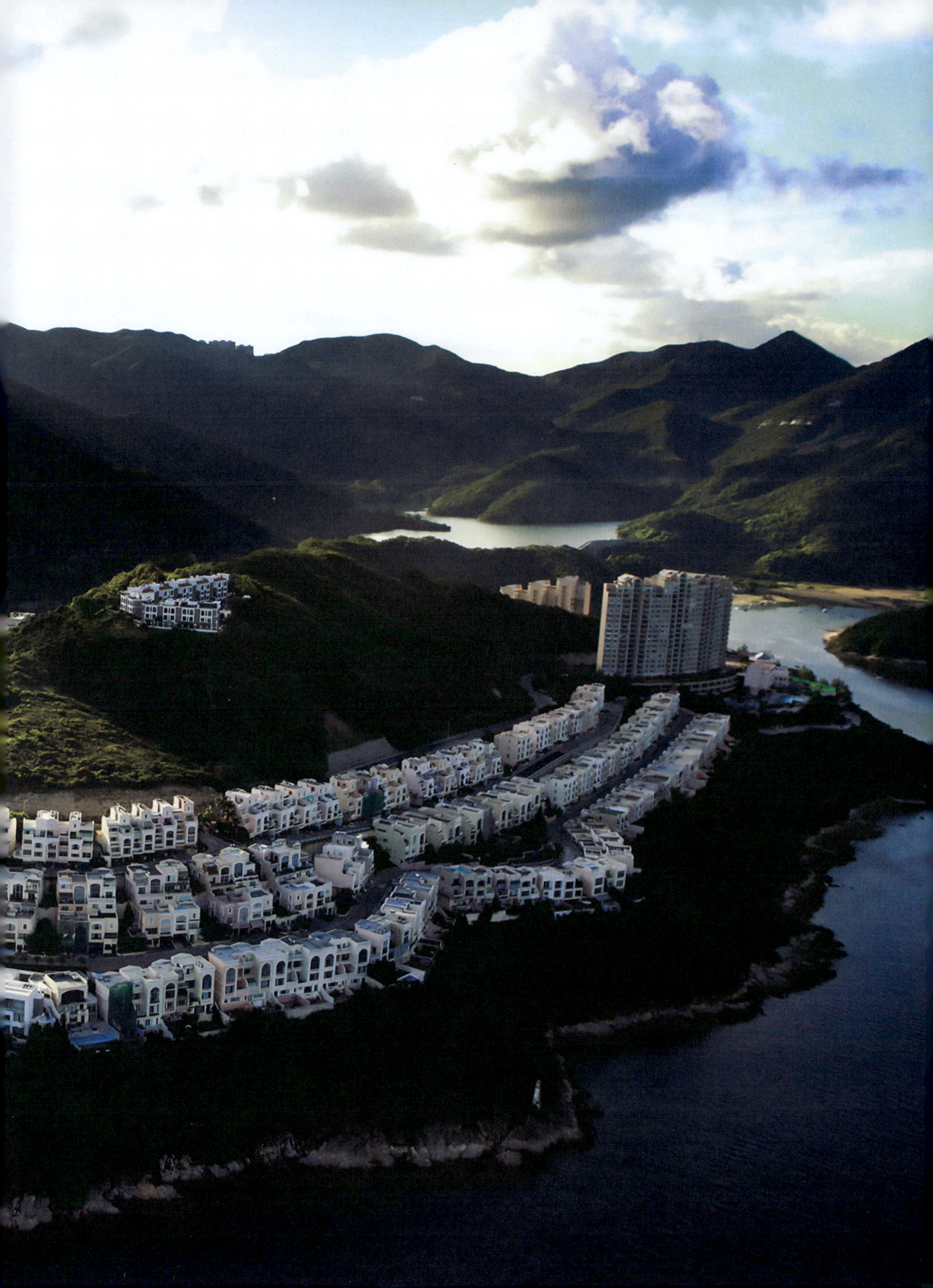

PHOTO INDEX

DAILY LIVING

URBAN RHYTHMS

59. A school bus in Ngau Tau Kok
60. Choi Hung Estate
61. A school near Shek Kip Mei Estate
62. Nam Shan Estate in Shek Kip Mei
63. Lok Wah Estate in Ngau Tau Kok
64. Yick Cheong Building, aka Monster Building, in Quarry Bay

CULTURE & HERITAGE

65. A streetside restaurant in Wan Chai
66. A street vendor in Mong Kok
67. A restaurant in Shek Kip Mei
68. Filling kettles at a traditional dim sum eatery in Sai Ying Pun
69. Ordering dishes at a traditional dim sum eatery in Sai Ying Pun
70. Dessert soups at a traditional dessert house in Mong Kok
71. A dessert display case in Wan Chai
72. Street food in Sham Shui Po
73. Condiments galore at a street food stall in Sham Shui Po
74. Red lantern decorations during Mid-Autumn Festival
75. Festive ornaments for the Lunar New Year, sold in Mong Kok
76. A bamboo theater for the Cheung Chau Bun Festival
77. "Tai Ping Ching Chiu" decor for the Cheung Chau Bun Festival
78. Cheung Chau Bun Festival street mural
79. Dragon Boat Festival races at Victoria Harbour
80. Small boats docked in Cheung Chau
81. Waterfront village houses in Cheung Chau
82. Shops by the water on Lamma Island
83. Houses by the beach in Cheung Chau
84. Incense coils and blessings at Man Mo Temple in Sheung Wan
85. Blessings and incense coils at Man Mo Temple in Sheung Wan
86. Deities passing through the streets during Cheung Chau Bun Festival
87. Outside a temple in Cheung Chau
88. The Nan Lian Garden Pavilion of Absolute Perfection in Diamond Hill
89. A banyan tree in a Cheung Chau courtyard
90. The Big Buddha statue on Lantau Island
91. The Guan Yin statue at the Tsz Shan Monastery in Tai Po

NATURAL PERSPECTIVES

92. Moody skies, taken from Ap Lei Chau, looking toward Lamma Island
93. The sun tries to shine through in Ap Lei Chau
94. A fiery sunset above Lamma Island
95. A calm sky in Wu Kai Sha
96. Aerial view of the southern region of Hong Kong
97. Aerial view of Tai Tam Reservoir
98. A lone building surrounded by greenery in Central
99. Views from Wu Kai Sha
100. Aerial view of Tai Tam

Published in Hong Kong
Printed in Shenzhen

ISBN 978-988-77560-8-8

ABOUT THE PHOTOGRAPHER

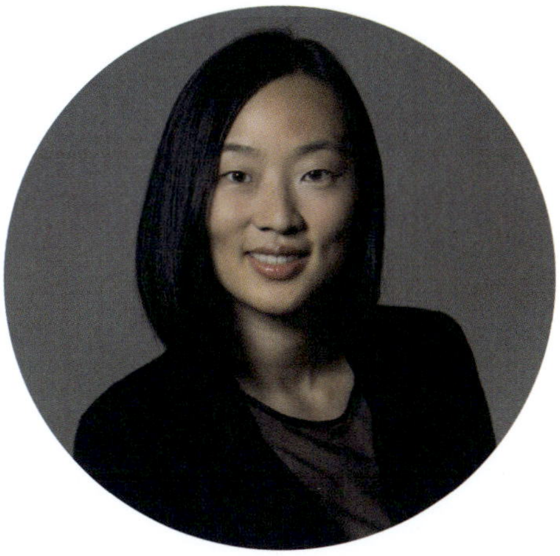

Joyce Yung is a professional photographer and producer based in Hong Kong. Her photography style is versatile and spontaneous. She specializes in portraiture and natural lifestyle photography — and she is always going places with her camera, ready to capture the moment. She was featured as one of the Top 100 Photographers From Around the World 2016, by Shutterstock. She graduated from Cornell University and worked in the financial industry before picking up her camera full time.

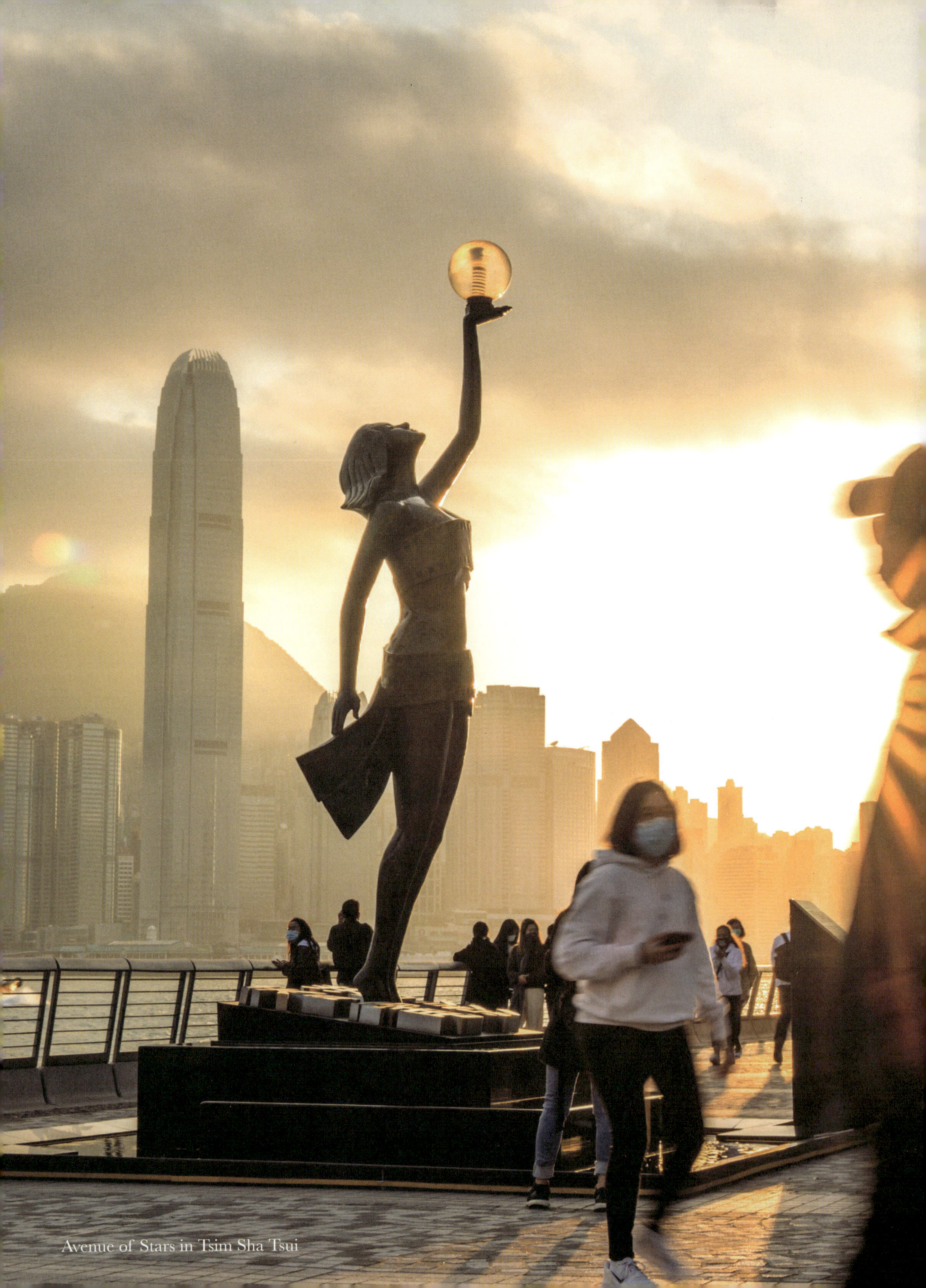

Avenue of Stars in Tsim Sha Tsui